D0081142

The World of the Office Worker

The World of

Studies of Urban Society

Michel Crozier

the Office Worker

Translated by David Landau

The University of Chicago Press Chicago / London

Originally published in 1965 as *Le monde des employés de bureau,*

International Standard Book Number: 0–226–12167–4
Library of Congress Catalog Card Number: 76–141150
The University of Chicago Press, Chicago 60637
The University of Chicago Press, Ltd., London

Contents

	Preface	vii
	Acknowledgments	xv
	Introduction	1
Part One	The Sociological Context	5
1	Evolution of the Group	7
2	Evolution of Ideas	21
3	Union Activity	41
Part Two	The World of Work and the Company	67
4	The Population Studied and Research Procedures	69
5	Adaptation to Work	77
6	Interpersonal Relations	107
7	Participation and Integration	135
Part Three	The Social and Cultural World	163
8	Social Status	165
9	The Cultural World	187
10	Class without Consciousness: Prefiguration of the Classless Society	207
	Name Index	215
	Subject Index	217

Preface

Intellectual and emotional fashions change so rapidly today that what were considered social problems twelve or fifteen years ago may now seem as remote as the problems that preoccupied our grandfathers. What justification is there, in 1971, for discussing awareness of class and status, cultural behavior and political orientation, among Parisian white-collar workers in 1957? Not only the subjects of such a study, but even the terms in which it is set forth, are unmistakably of the fifties.

The exotic appeal of this study is certainly not what recommends it today. Life-experiences that apparently are epitomes of dullness can have little attraction for the romantic. The discriminating, of course, may find some subtle French flavor in the interviews of my Parisian clerks. In writing a report on a piece of academic research, however, I was not trying to capture the romantic atmosphere of the Parisian petty-bourgeois, nor did I dare to dramatize my subject. My study, unfortunately, has nothing more than its own intrinsic value to commend it; more specifically, it must be judged for its scientific contribution and for whatever universal human traits it was able to extract from its narrow, and now dated, social and geographical context. The author, of course, cannot say how well his work meets such a test. He can only say what he himself now sees in his earlier effort.

When I began the survey that provided the bulk of the data for this study—a comparative survey of the attitudes of employees and supervisors in six insurance companies—white-collar workers, especially those "blocs" of them in insurance companies, were the best symbols of the men and women who inhabit the "little boxes" of our popular folklore. They were, indeed, at that time a kind of collective whipping-boy for the European intellectual vanguard. Orthodox Marxists asked why these persons could not learn the austere virtues of the authentic working class. Why could they not join the ranks of the grand army of the future? Other leftists pilloried these persons as willing victims of media manipulation and the poisons of a consumer society.

I, too, was deeply interested in such questions—the genuine as well as the misleading ones—which were a part of a general outlook at the time. But, naively enough, I wanted to know what it really felt like to live in one of those little boxes. That way of life was so distant from my own that it took time for me to readjust my feelings about it and to rethink my preconceived ideas on the subject. Such an effort was the price I had to pay for my commitment to this scientific endeavor. Today, when the working class of Marxist ideology has become little more than a figure of speech with no relationship at all, except accidentally, to typical blue-collar workers, this awakening to empirical truth may seem trivial and unimportant. In the process of our intellectual development we have all become men in boxes, however, and in the present neurotic concern over alienation this first attempt at describing the rules of the game for life in these boxes still helps me to maintain some degree of intellectual balance.

I instinctively chose for my study the most repressed, exploited persons, performing the most routine, meaningless jobs, in the only impersonal and metropolitan concentration we had in France at that time. These persons, nevertheless, were decent human beings whom I could and did like. Boxes need not be so dull and dehumanizing when one knows how to play with them. This note of optimism may be disconcerting to those who prefer to see doomsday as imminent; it does not, however, signify complacency or satisfaction with the established order. What I feel, rather, is a post-despair attitude.

For a Frenchman of my generation it was a strange experience to grow up during the disasters of 1940, the German occupation, and the Liberation (a time when masses of Frenchmen pretended to have won the war and made a revolution, all the while painfully adjusting to the grim realities made necessary by the effort to maintain the solvency of a second-rate capitalist economy). With the country morally helpless, the existentialist ethic, with its norms of absurdity, despair, and derision, became the new wave. We enjoyed hearing that nothing was worth a damn except those radiant revolutionary values that, in any case, were not to be realized in our time. Communism was oppressive and stupid, but it was a necessity, we were told, and we had to fight for it. Its time had come; it was our only hope. From our sacrifices—later—a new man would be born, but certainly not in time for our benefit.

This was a farcical philosophy, and as a way of life as unrealizable as many of today's dreams. Some people used this intellectual discourse as an excuse for indulging in their own idiosyncrasies and for settling down quietly without taking on any responsibility. But there were also honest, intent young idealists who felt the truth of this ideology in their very bones. For such persons, and I was certainly one of them, their experience was ultimately akin to a religious one and it helped them to achieve a new kind of tolerance.

Who could complain about a lack of meaning when everything was equally meaningless, or about alienation when everyone was equally alienated? Only a small step was needed to assert that everything and everyone had always been this way and always would be—and what difference did it make? We had the choice of becoming cynics or of attempting to escape from our insane logic and to differentiate between more or less meaningful situations and more or less alienated people. At this point, reform and responsibility were just around the corner.

Will the present generation follow this same path? I think so and I hope so. Young people will eventually have to discover, as some of us did in the late fifties, that organizational life has some advantages for us imperfect human beings. True enough, humanity will probably some day outgrow the dark ages of constraints and limits. This is a worthy goal to fight for, and one I share. But it is an unattainable goal now, and one we could not endure. When our successors achieve it, they will have, not a paradise, but a tense, puritanical world which will be just as harsh for them as ours is today for Mexican villagers.

In the meantime, organizational life—the life that puts us in our little boxes—remains a relatively cheap and efficient way of providing us with the limits we need in order to play the games we like: games of conflict and cooperation, in which we do not have to risk too much for ourselves or for our partners.

Another conclusion can be drawn from this study of French petty-bourgeois life in the late fifties, one which has nothing to do with circumstances of time, place, or intellectual climate. At first glance, my data did not confirm any of my own prejudices, but neither did the study invalidate those prejudices. Only through a more detailed analysis of the problem did I discover a contradiction in my own attitudes, one which resulted from the method I used.

Like too many social scientists, I had begun with a deterministic hypothesis and then arranged everything to support it. This was a false scientific posture as well as a social prejudice. I took it as self-evident that situations determined attitudes which, in turn, determined behavior; the only question was what attitudes and behavior could be predicted from a better understanding of the real situations. To do a good job, I was attempting, like most of my colleagues, to quantify key feelings in continuums that I assumed were unified and homogeneous. Fortunately, the correlations I found were shallow enough to force me to give more importance to the unforeseen contradictions than to the hoped-for regularities.

At this point, everything made much more sense if another mode of reasoning was adopted. Feelings are not the product of circumstances. The latter are, rather, the raw materials that the actors in this drama use for their own ends. People do not choose to be happy or unhappy, as if they were calculating machines tabulating the results of a series of converging operations. They complain about or enjoy things in an active way, depending on what may appear as profitable to themselves in their dealings with their environment. The future, not the past, shapes attitudes and behavior. And the future is uncertain. The simplified model I had adopted was, interestingly enough, the model of the consumer society I was attacking; I had caught myself projecting into reality the deterministic model I was complaining about.

In the real world, satisfactions never fit past or present circumstances, not simply because one never knows those circumstances well enough, but because people themselves do not want to fit those circumstances. People will always be able to defeat those scientific psychologists, idealistic reformers, and revolutionary nihilists whose belief in universal harmony or doom postulate a one-dimensional universe. Reality must be ambiguous and contradictory; if it were clear and one-dimensional, we would be trapped.

Feelings are escape routes. When persons exult or complain, they not only present a certain image of themselves, they also reveal, even though unconsciously, contradictory postures. This contradiction is necessary because only through it can come the freedom that is essential for the complex social games we play, games that require strategies of both defense and attack. Each actor uses a different mixture of these strategies; to rely on only one would be to incapacitate oneself as an actor. The Parisian clerks of our study, in their class and status affiliations, in their use of and participation in cultural activities, show the functioning of these strategic mechanisms.

Persons enjoy cultural products for their own sake, of course, and their positions in society do provide tangible rewards. They cannot help, however, being members of an ongoing system in which they must play certain parts if they are to rise in the system or even hold their own. They may become obsessed with the game, or alienated by it, but this is no worse a fate than to abandon it altogether, to withdraw from all participation. The pathological aspects of both kinds of behavior—participation or withdrawal—seem to prove only the strength of the game, a game which cannot be escaped except at an impossible cost.

Mass culture and mass society, it seems, cannot condition persons directly. They condition them only through the games persons play, in which they use the circumstances of their lives to differentiate themselves from those above and below them. One can, of course, become disgusted with the silliness of these games; but one must admit that they have always existed. What is new about them now is that they have become more open, more obvious, and—this is the great surprise revealed by the data of my study—less deterministic.

Why should this be the case? Barriers crumble when products and possibilities are offered, at least symbolically, on equal terms to all; persons can then develop incoherencies and inconsistencies that would have been inconceivable in earlier times. Parisian clerks show the most extraordinary range of behavior which is impossible to categorize in any stable, regular way. One finds everything from highbrow to soap-opera tastes, not only from person to person, but also within the same person, who may have tastes that by all usual standards are incompatible. This was a new phenomenon in Europe, where formerly great consistency could be found within social groups. And such a phenomenon arouses mixed feelings, since it is associated with a general breakdown of standards.

Yet in criticizing the philistinism of mass culture, one forgets the most fundamental consequence of this change in cultural standards—the tremendous opportunity for learning it affords, an opportunity which was very obvious from my study. If inconsistencies of the kind we have been discussing are easily accepted in a society, then persons can move up in that society without learning a whole new set of attitudes and behavioral characteristics. They can, instead, learn as they go, in ways that are easier for them.

Social situation, then, does not consistently determine attitudes either in the traditional class society, where persons were born into closed subcultures, or in the mass society, where persons are supposedly subject to constant manipulation in their tastes and fashions by those who control the society for their own ends. In a more active way, which is also a more chaotic way, persons use what is offered to them. There are trends and developments in this use, but not determinism.

The general emphasis throughout the study on the increase of individual freedom may surprise some readers. There is a different mood abroad now, but I would hypothesize that the same conclusions would be possible if the study were done today. I admit that there may have been special circumstances responsible for the clarity of my data. French clerks in the fifties were passing from the traditional paternalistic world of nineteenth-century business procedures to a new, more productive, but also more liberal, model of organizational society. By sheer contrast with the old model, the new one appeared to be more free. At the same time, the still very clear attachments to the old model made it possible to understand the motivation that to some degree still sustained that model. What persons feared in the change was the possibility of losing some of the traditional protections afforded by the old model. Old-style allegiance, which verged on subservience, was more useful than one might imagine; it could be a marvelous tool by which to control and manipulate management.

The situation examined by the study may seem extraordinarily remote by now in America, if not yet in Europe. Yet it is a situation which should not be dismissed lightly. It provides an opportunity for the sociological imagination to be confronted with what human beings really live through and experience. It provides this opportunity, moreover, within a historical context, which may be what is lacking in our attempts to judge the vagaries of our present social and cultural systems.

It is within such a perspective that I would like the general historical sketches of the first part of the book to be read. The story of French white-collar workers is puzzling in its complexity and fails to make much sense in a revolutionary perspective or one of unilinear progress. To understand the story, one must adopt a more open, flexible view. It is a story in which persons are constantly trying to make the best of shifting circumstances, always wanting to have their cake and eat it too—and, curiously enough, more often than not succeeding.

Acknowledgments

The present work was written on the basis of research projects I directed over the course of several years within the Institut des Sciences sociales du Travail. I would like to thank Yves Delamotte, secretary-general of the Institute, for the assistance he gave me during those years. Similarly, I would like to thank Francis Raison, Directeur des Services de Productivité du Commissariat général au Plan, whose administration—at that time the Commissariat général à la Productivité—agreed to finance the research program I had proposed; without his constant support, such projects would never have been carried out successfully.

The overall conception of these projects and the final analysis of their results are mine, but such an undertaking could not have developed, and did not actually develop, except as a collective work. May I therefore be allowed to thank all the researchers who, in various degrees, collaborated in it. Pierre Guetta analyzed together with me the results of our exploratory study, and collaborated actively in the elaboration of the definitive plan for the study; Hélène Dubost, Jean-José Marchand, Bernard Pradier, and Gérard Pautet carried out the interviews; Gérard Pautet and Bernard Pradier made the initial analysis of the results; finally, Bernard Pradier drafted, together with me, a first study-report on the problems of leadership.

A study in the end involves more than just the researchers. It involves a whole milieu whose collaboration is essential to its success. Obviously it is impossible for me to cite by name here the presidents and directors-general of the seven insurance companies who were willing to take the risk of allowing us to penetrate their establishments, or the names of the secretaries of the local unions and the joint worker-management committees who warmly assisted and cautioned us in our encounters with personnel. I thank them for their generosity and their understanding. In like manner, I thank M. Molin, then secretary-general of the Fédération des sociétés d'assurances; M. Fouchet, director of the Comité d'Action pour la Productivité dans l'Assurance; all the leaders of the employee and managerial unions, especially M. Bertola of the Confédération Française des Travailleurs Chrétiens (CFTC), M. Delon of the Confédération Générale du Travail (CGT), and M. Sidro of the Confédération Générale Travail-Force Ouvrière (CGT-FO), who offered me decisive support in my undertaking.

My gratitude, however, goes above all to the five hundred insurance company employees and executives who agreed with unfailing graciousness, honesty, and scrupulousness, to answer questions which may sometimes have seemed to them strange and indiscreet. This work necessarily had to be written with the perspective and detachment that are indispensable to any objective scientific analysis, but I hope that it has remained deeply marked by the warmth and the human quality of their testimony. It is with much gratitude that I dedicate it to them.

Introduction

The ever-increasing proportion of office jobs in the total spectrum of occupations surely constitutes one of the essential phenomena in the evolution of modern industrial societies. This development has been spectacular during the last fifty years and is becoming, it would appear, even more accentuated. In 1957, in the United States, for the first time in the history of human societies, the number of non-manual workers exceeded the number of manual workers in the employed population.[1] By the census of 1960, this gap had already become very wide. These changes, which occur in all industrial societies, have been slow and almost imperceptible, but their cumulative effects allow one to speak of a veritable administrative revolution comparable to the industrial revolution of the nineteenth century.

What are and what will be the consequences of a revolution of this sort for the social structure of Western societies, and for the social relations and the models of behavior which develop in those societies? Such are the profound questions which a

1. This evolution has been demonstrated by Everett Kassalow, director of research for the AFL-CIO. The validity of the results he obtains depends on the value one attaches to the naturally arbitrary classification he was obliged to use. Note, however, that his conclusions have not been contested. An account of his analysis may be found in "New Union Frontiers: White Collar Workers," *Harvard Business Review* (January 1962).

sociologist cannot fail to ask, and which have inspired the research whose results are presented in this work.

This field has until now been dominated by the Marxist approach to the problem. To summarize this approach crudely, one might say that the Marxists wanted to see in this phenomenon, above all, the disappearance of independent workers and of the old middle classes; they predicted, as Marx had proclaimed, that salaried workers would soon constitute the vast majority, if not the totality, of the employed population; they chose to ignore completely the feelings and peculiarities of the growing number of nonmanual salaried workers. But events have shown the weakness of this prophecy. The accuracy of the prediction concerning occupational evolution has by no means given rise to the consequences for the political order which were so imprudently derived from it. While salaried workers have certainly become the majority in all industrial countries, the working class, in the political sense of the term, has remained a minority.

This profound failure, which cannot be masked by analytical subtleties regarding cultural lag and survivals of bourgeois society, draws attention to the importance of subjective factors and of noneconomic determinants in social and political strategy. It suggests the development of a new approach to the problem whose three essential components might be the following.

To pose, first of all, the question of the allegiance of the new strata and, in particular, of white-collar employees. Do they consider themselves primarily as salaried workers subject to exploitation, or as nonmanual workers—that is, as nonworking-class members of the community? In which direction do they lean, and for what deep-rooted reasons?

To confront, in the second place, the question of the group's strategy itself. There is constant talk of an ineluctable choice, as though white-collar employees must in the end recognize the *truth* of their condition and their *true* interest. Might it not be in their interest, after all, to remain ambiguous in their allegiance? Might not their best strategy be to straddle both sides of the fence?

To raise, finally, the problem of the coherence and even of the existence of the group. Often the reasoning seems to be that adherence to the social group "white-collar employees" must be a matter of course for anyone who occupies a white-collar position. Is this necessarily so? What are the limits and the significance of this adherence? Might it not be less profound for the white-collar employee than for the laborer, and might it not be less profound for both today than it was in the past? This transformation of the relationship of the individual to the group is of decisive importance in understanding the evolution of class allegiance and the strategy of social struggle. If, indeed, one believes that the individual now has ever-greater freedom of choice in relation to his group and to his class, one might ask whether it would not be appropriate to analyze the attitudes and the behavior of white-collar employees, no longer merely as an example of a class without consciousness, but also as the prefiguration of a society much less marked by class differences.

In order to confront these new problems in a positive manner, and thus question current preconceptions regarding class relations, general statistics on occupational evolution are not sufficient; one must work in the area and study at close range how the situations at issue are actually experienced, so as to discover what influences are at work on individuals, how their situation is actually structured, and what is objectively, for them, the most rational strategy.

Only such empirical studies make it possible to shed new light on the problems which we have just raised. The research results which we will report here are certainly insufficient and do not allow any great advances to be made in a field which has, until now, been very little explored. The inquiries we conducted in seven Parisian insurance companies during the years 1956 to 1960 are in fact incomplete. The organizations studied are not at all representative of the whole white-collar milieu, since they are exclusively Parisian and bear on only a limited professional sector. This sector, however, is of considerable interest. It is, in point of fact, especially well-developed, both in the technical sphere and in the organization of work; at the same time, it is a sector whose individuals, working in the very heart of the capital, are subject to all the psychological stresses of modern life. While it cannot be considered representative, it seems on the other hand to be a particularly significant sector for anyone anxious to gain a better understanding of the manner in which situations are actually experienced.

Let no one, then, expect to find in this work a general picture of the attitudes and aspirations of the contemporary French white-collar world. What will be found, rather, is a thorough analytical essay dealing with a more narrowly circumscribed population. This permits a more concrete discussion of the diverse elements which exert pressure on the social strategy of a group like the white-collar group.

To place the discussion in its proper perspective, however, we will devote our first section to an overall analysis of the evolution of the white-collar group in society; to a discussion of the manner in which all the problems raised by this evolution have been studied by sociologists, political philosophers, and social theorists of different countries; and to a critical review of French white-collar union history.

Our research results bear, first of all, on the attitudes of white-collar employees toward the job, toward interpersonal relations and, in particular, authority relations in offices, and toward degree of involvement in the business. They bear, in the second place, on the more general social attitudes of white-collar employees, on the conception they have of their status and of their role in society, on their sensitivity to the messages of the mass media, and on their cultural attitudes.

We shall present these research results in a second and third sections, devoted respectively to the realm of work and to the social and political spheres.

PART ONE

The Sociological Context

1 Evolution of the Group

Definition of White-collar Employees

There exists no satisfactory definition of the term "white-collar employee."[1] A number of authors, in particular Fritz Croner, past councillor of the Organization internationale de Travail for problems of nonmanual workers, have done their utmost to elaborate a logical and rational definition. Their efforts, though interesting from a theoretical point of view, since they have served to give added importance to the character and the causes of differences between white-collar and blue-collar employees, remained too formal and hardly seemed to yield results that would be applicable in practice.[2]

It is not the type of relationship to an employer or any such juridical notion which determines current usage of the term "white-collar employee," but rather association with those professions where the task executed and the place and conditions in which it is accomplished are close to those of several char-

1. Throughout this work, the contrast between the French occupational categories *employé* and *ouvrier* plays a crucial role. While exactly parallel categories exist, for example, in German—*Angestellter* and *Arbeiter*—no single English work adequately renders *employé* and *ouvrier* also presents difficulties in certain contexts. It has therefore been necessary to use the rather cumbersome term "white-collar employee" to render *employé,* while *ouvrier* has been alternately translated as "blue-collar employee" and "manual worker," and occasionally as "working-class man."—TRANS.

2. Fritz Croner, "Les employés dans la société moderne," *Revue internationale du Travail* 69, no. 2 (Geneva, 1954).

acteristic groups such as office employees. Roger Girod shows quite clearly, for example, how subjects who are asked to arrive at a classification rank a streetcar conductor among "white-collar employees" when this profession is presented to them in association with that of a ticket-collector, and rank it as a "working-class profession" when it is presented in association with truck drivers.[3]

According to current usage, two large groups of occupations comprise the nucleus around which the notion of white-collar employee has crystallized: the occupations of office employee and sales worker.[4] These are lines of work which have in the end been retained by most of the statistical censuses which are carried out in the world today. American unionists, working with data provided by the U.S. Census, have proposed a distinction which seems convenient and quite clear. They contrast nonmanual activities with manual activities, service activities and agricultural activities; and they distinguish, under nonmanual activities, between professional, technical, and related occupations (doctors, engineers, teachers, technicians, and the like), managerial and related occupations (managers, officials, and proprietors), office jobs and the like (clerks), and sales workers.[5] Like all classifications, this one has its problems. In particular, it is quite difficult in certain industries to distinguish between office workers and "professional" men. Let us keep in mind in any case that, in those industries, supervisors of white-collar jobs are considered "white-collar employees" while designers fall within the category of technicians.

French censuses cannot be regrouped into these categories because they draw the lines differently. In effect, they give far greater importance to the placement of authority, and make of executive personnel (*cadres*) a separate category, thus reducing to some extent the size of the two categories of office work-

3. Roger Girod, *Études sociologiques sur les couches salariées* (Paris: Rivière, 1961), p. 120.

4. The terms "office employee" and "office worker" will be used interchangeably to render the French term *employé de bureau.* While the former is a more literal translation, the latter is, at least in America, the more commonly accepted term.—TRANS.

5. Kassalow, "New Union Frontiers." *Harvard Business Review* (January 1962).

ers and sales workers. Moveover, they separate civil servants from white-collar employees, distinguish inadequately between civil service executives and the mass of public employees, and in no way mark out laborers in the public sector.[6] The figures available for different countries must therefore be used with care, since they are not exactly comparable.

We do not intend to propose, as did Fritz Croner, a rational model of classification. Our research has been devoted to occupations which in any case, in all countries, are placed in the same category, namely, office jobs and the like. Only a study of the characteristics of these populations, which no one has any difficulty in classifying, can provide the elements we need in order to evaluate other sectors.

In this first overall analysis, which will necessarily outline the framework for our study, we will stick essentially to the category of office workers and to the closely related categories of commercial employees and civil servants, and contrast these to the category "liberal professions, executives [*cadres*], and technicians" and to the categories comprising manual laborers.

General Patterns of Evolution

Four broad patterns seem to us to characterize the evolution of the categories of "white-collar employees" in the various industrial societies during the last hundred years: their enormous increase in size, the reduction of their economic advantage compared to the blue-collar group, the progressive feminization of the group, and the profound transformation of the tasks that are assigned to it.

The Increase in Size

The first and most striking characteristic of this evolution is, naturally, the increase—quite spectacular when viewed in perspective—in the number of white-collar employees and in

6. In any case, the distinction between executive personnel and white-collar employees dates only from 1954; earlier censuses grouped subordinate office and commercial employees in the same category as junior and senior executives. Since the size of these executive categories cannot be determined with any degree of accuracy for this earlier period, we will have to be satisfied, for long-range comparisons, with the wider definition of the term "white-collar employee" (*employé*).

their proportion in the total population. André Siegfried spoke quite justifiably of the entrance of humanity into *the administrative age.* What we have been witnessing for the last fifty years is, in fact, a veritable administrative revolution, comparable to the industrial revolutions of the nineteenth century. It has resulted from the acceleration in technical progress, the ever-increasing importance, whatever the political regime, of state intervention, and the general development of methods of planning and control. Like its precursors, the industrial revolutions, this revolution has its primary effect on the organization of work; but it entails, at the same time, a considerable change in the distribution of occupations. The great upheavals of the nineteenth century assured the transition of a large portion of the populations of Western countries from agricultural activities to wage-earning industrial occupations. The slower and perhaps more regular—but no less extensive—transition from manual to nonmanual activities, will very likely complete and correct the traditional portrait of industrial society.[7] Most telling are the results of the latest American censuses. Office and commercial employees, who constituted 7.5 percent of the active population in 1900, constituted 21.2 percent in 1961. The various categories of laborers (skilled, specialized, manual), on the other hand, together made up no more than 37 percent of the employed population—practically the same percentage as in 1900 (35.8 percent).[8] This period of rapid growth in office jobs seems, however, to be at an end. These occupations had more than doubled in number from 1940 to 1957, increasing from 4,371,000 to 9,264,000, while during the same period the percentage of the active population they

7. The problem has naturally attracted the attention of numerous authors. Among others: Colin Clark, *The Conditions of Economic Progress* (London, 1940); Jean Fourastié, *Le grand espoir du XXe siècle* (Paris: Presses Universitaires, 1950). Together with Georges Friedmann we have ourselves dealt with it in our Introduction to a special issue of the *Bulletin International des Sciences Sociales* concerning the social consequences of automation (vol. 10, no. 1 [1958]), and in a personal communication entitled "Le rôle des employés et des petits fonctionnaires dans la structure sociale française contemporaine," in *Actes du Troisième Congrès mondial de Sociologie*, vol. 3 (1956), p. 311.

8. The current percentage is on the decline compared to the mean of the years 1920–50 which consistently stayed near 40 percent.

represented increased by more than half, changing from 9.6 percent in 1940 to 14.6 percent in 1957. But this increase seems to have stopped since the recession of 1957–58. Instead, it is another group of nonmanual workers—the group consisting of "liberal professions, managers and technicians," which grew from 8.6 percent in 1950 to 11.1 percent in 1961—that has accounted in large measure for the increase of nonmanual workers at the expense of manual workers.[9]

The French situation, like the European situation in general (Sweden excepted), is totally different. In this respect we are still in the situation of the United States before 1940. The white-collar group has, of course, increased greatly during the last hundred years. One can estimate that it grew from 5 percent or 6 percent of the employed population in 1900 to 12.5 percent at present.[10] But we have not yet experienced the acceleration of the American postwar era. To be more precise, certain industries have known changes comparable to those which occurred in the United States. For example, during five years, the number of white-collar employees has increased from 7.5 percent to 12.5 percent of the total work force in the metals industry.[11] But these transformations, while very important qualitatively, have been masked by the general development of the industrial sector due to the efforts of the French economy to make up for lost time, by the still preponderant weight of the less developed sectors, and by the earlier hypertrophy of the traditional public sector and of the sector comprising activities not directly related to production (*secteur tertiaire*). Substantial modernization was possible without many transfers into office jobs, to the extent that the percentage of nonmanual workers had until now been excessive in relation to the real development of the economy. We have, for example, witnessed a noticeable contraction in the volume of

9. See *U.S. Statistical Abstracts* (Washington, 1959), p. 218, and Everett Kassalow, "White-Collar Unionism in the U.S.," in *White-Collar Trade Unions: Contemporary Developments in Industrialized Societies,* ed. Adolf Sturmthal (Urbana, Ill., 1967).

10. Calculated on the basis of the results of the general censuses of the population of 1911 and 1962, published by the Institut national de la Statistique et des Études économiques.

11. *Les Employés dans les industries des métaux,* research conducted by the Union des Industries métallurgiques et minières, pamphlet (Paris, 1960).

employment in public administration between 1948 and 1954, while this is the domain that experienced the greatest expansion in the United States during the same period.

There is reason to think, in any case, that if the expansion continues, we will witness a rapid new acceleration which will be, at most, slowed down by the development of automation. Modern nonproduction activities (*activités tertiaires*) must indeed assume greater and greater importance as a consequence of the new level of prosperity which we have achieved. Despite the substantial technical investments which have been effected in the banking and insurance sectors, the number employed in these areas has risen from 244,000 in 1954 to 320,000 in 1962, which represents an increase of 31 percent.[12] The public sector, especially on the local level, must experience an even greater expansion if the population is to be assured services equivalent in number and quality to those available in the most highly developed countries.

Note, however, that the group consisting of engineers, technicians, and the like, have a tendency, as in America, to develop even more quickly than the white-collar group. It is that group which will henceforth, in France, incarnate the administrative revolution much more than the white-collar group.[13] Finally let us add that, for the moment, France and America are not as different as one might suppose when it comes to the number of nonmanual workers in the employed population. The main difference does not, in fact, lie in the magnitude of the overall percentages, but in the composition of the nonmanual categories which, in France, still encompass a considerable percentage of small businessmen, artisans, and independent workers who could just as well be ranked among manual workers.

Reduction of Differences in Remuneration

The increase in size of the white-collar group has been accompanied by a notable reduction of the differences in remunera-

12. Compared to a mean increase of 13 percent for all industrial occupations. General census of the population of March 1962, *Bulletin hebdomadaire de statistique,* no. 781.

13. Technicians in the private sector, for example, have increased in eight years from 193,000 to 289,000—an increase of 45 percent.

tion between white-collar and blue-collar employees. As the white-collar group became more important numerically, it came ever closer economically to the blue-collar group. It is this general pattern of evolution, anticipated by Marxist theoreticians, which constitutes the principal argument in favor of the thesis of proletarization of white-collar employees.

Let us look at the figures a little more closely. Our best data comes from England. In his book on English white-collar workers David Lockwood devoted himself to a very precise analysis of existing statistics and, above all, of the interpretations of these statistics by social researchers during the last eighty years.[14] What emerges from this analysis is that the considerable differences which once existed between white-collar and blue-collar workers were greatly reduced during the social crisis provoked by the First World War. These differences, at least in part, were reestablished quickly from the 1920s onward and settled at a stable level during the interwar period with a certain tendency toward intensification during crisis. The deterioration in the status of white-collar employees dates from the recovery which followed the Great Depression. The Second World War induced a relative subsidence, since the salaries of white-collar employees increased much less quickly than those of blue-collar employees who had the advantage of overtime pay. Since the war, the remuneration of white-collar employees has remained very nearly comparable to that of skilled laborers.

The statistics presented by Robert K. Burns concerning the salaries of American office workers are less extensive but perhaps more precise.[15] In relation to blue-collar salaries, the salaries of American white-collar employees have followed a curve analogous to the one established by Lockwood for England. From 1890 until the First World War, the disparity between white-collar and blue-collar salaries increases gradually in favor of white-collar employees. During the years of war and inflation, the gap diminishes substantially, returning

14. David Lockwood, *The Blackcoated Worker* (London: Allen and Unwin, 1958).

15. Robert K. Burns, "The Comparative Economic Position of Manual and White Collar Employees," *Journal of Business* 27, no. 4 (October 1954).

during the deflation of 1920–22 to its original level. In 1929, the difference, on the average, is 30 percent. It rises to 60 percent at the climactic point of the depression (1933) and returns to 30 percent in 1937. The difference disappears only with the war economy and full employment. In 1943–44, blue-collar employees outearn white-collar employees for the first time. During the initial postwar years, the two curves practically overlap. Burns' analysis stops in 1952, but recent statistics appear to weaken his thesis, according to which the traditional disparity would have disappeared once and for all. It has in fact returned to 13 percent in 1960. These figures do not relate to the difference between white-collar employees and skilled laborers, as in England, but to the white-collar/blue-collar difference.

The French statistics analyzed by Henri Mercillon are far less precise than the American ones.[16] But their general import is exactly the same. Indeed, this author shows that the increase in pay of blue-collar employees is a function of the decrease in pay of white-collar employees and supervisors. Actually, according to the latest evaluations of the INSEE, concerning only the private and semipublic sectors, the average difference has decreased from 12 percent in 1955 to 11 percent in 1960.[17] Broadly speaking then, taking into account the fact that Lockwood makes his comparison to skilled workers, it seems that there is not that much of a difference between the principal Western countries on this point.

The global differences, however, provide too summary a picture of reality. Lockwood shows, as a matter of fact, that the structure of compensation for white-collar employees has changed completely. While before 1914 there was a virtual chasm between well-paid white-collar employees and their colleagues (in that era, 45 percent of white-collar employees in banks and in insurance companies earned more than 160 pounds a year, while the average paycheck for the rest of their colleagues was only 85–90 pounds), the differences today are

16. Henri Mercillon, *La rémunération des employés* (Paris: Colin, 1954).

17. Supplement to *Bulletin hebdomadaire de statistique,* no. 721 (7 April 1962), published by INSEE.

in the order of no more than 40 percent.[18] The experience we have gained concerning the hierarchical organization of French private and public administration leads us to think that this highly pertinent fact raises another problem. The well-paid white-collar employees of yesteryear have not disappeared, but rather now have the status of executives and, at least in France, fall outside the white-collar category; in practice, then, the differences have been reduced less than at first is apparent.

Another fact emphasized by Lockwood is of even greater importance, namely, the distortion introduced into overall comparisons between blue-collar and white-collar employees by the different ratio of males to females in the two categories. If one compares blue-and white-collar salaries separately for the two sexes, far more substantial disparities emerge. For example, in France in 1961, while the overall difference was 11 percent, the specific differences were 17 percent among wage-earning males and 39 percent among wage-earning females.[19] Taking these qualifications into account, one must agree that evolution has not been as unfavorable to white-collar employees as would appear at first glance. The loss of economic privilege of white-collar employees can be examined in large measure by the progressive invasion of white-collar occupations by women, whose level of compensation is distinctly lower across the board in all industries.

Progressive Feminization of the White-Collar Category

The feminization of office jobs is certainly one of the fundamental phenomena in the evolution of the occupational structure. This is too often forgotten in discussions of the problem of social classes. The proletarization of white-collar employees does not have the same meaning at all if it is women, and not heads of family, who comprise the majority of the group. Yet that is precisely what is now going on in the various Western countries.

18. Lockwood, *The Blackcoated Worker,* pp. 40–60.

19. The mean salary of male white-collar employees was 17 percent greater than that of male blue-collar workers, while among females the difference was 39 percent. The global or combined difference is less pronounced because of the different composition of the two groups.

Lockwood calculates that in England the percentage of women in offices has changed from 0.8 percent in 1851 to 59.6 percent in 1951. In France, the figure we arrived at in 1956 was 54 percent; it is now 58.2 percent.[20] If we take American evolution as our example, feminization should become more and more accelerated. In the United States, the percentage of women in offices has risen from 54 percent in 1940 to 61 percent in 1950, and to 67 percent in 1960. Eighty percent of the fantastic increase in the number of American white-collar employees during the last twenty years is due to the massive recruitment of females. In France, we have so far experienced this evolution only partially. But if, among us, the number of office employees increases as spectacularly, it will very probably also be due to recruitment of females. Even now, recent recruitment in the civil service and in banks and insurance companies shows the way of the future.[21] At least three women are hired for every man. A new equilibrium is in the process of being established. For this type of occupation and for the compensation offered, only women can be recruited.

This transformation has profound consequences, since the arrival of women, coinciding as it did with very great expansion, was superimposed on a process of mechanization and automation, whose effects upon males were therefore diminished.[22] The latter were pushed toward more skilled occupations and toward executive positions, so that the general proletarization of the white-collar group—which seems quite clear if one analyzes its composition, its remunerations, and its tasks in the abstract—was not experienced as such by those directly involved. To the old white-collar group which had pretty much retained its social status—when it had not improved it by technical and hierarchical promotions—was added a new group consisting in part of females with a distinctly inferior social status. To be sure, many white-collar employees

20. General census of the population of March, 1962, preliminary documents distributed by the INSEE, n.d.

21. Between 1954 and 1962, compared to an increase of 21 percent in the number of males in banks and insurance companies, we note a rise of 43 percent in the number of females. See *Bulletin hebdomadaire de statistique,* no. 781.

22. Lockwood was the first to draw attention to this phenomenon, *The Blackcoated Worker,* p. 67.

were personally victims of these transformations, but many among them were, on the other hand, beneficiaries.

Transformation of Tasks

The transformation of tasks can be considered the last fundamental element in the evolution of the white-collar group. This transformation is of great importance, but here again careful interpretation is required.

Mechanization and scientific organization have, it is true, completely transformed office work and even sales work. The introduction of accounting machines and then statistical machines has resulted in a series of small industrial revolutions, whose effects are now accelerated with the advent of automation. Since the introduction of these innovations, a split has taken place between highly qualified employees charged with handling matters demanding judgment, experience, and responsibility, and a mass of unskilled employees assigned a series of simple unchanging operations. In the administrative services of banks, insurance companies, or large accounting firms, there have for some time been numerous cases of assembly-line work, sometimes even using conveyor belts.

As in the factory, automation will very likely reduce the number of these new "specialized workers" in the long run but, for the moment, they still constitute the majority in the profession. Accompanying the transformation of tasks, we have seen a transformation in discipline and training. The paternalism of former times, with all its humiliating by-products, has vanished, but at the same time control has become more severe and the rhythm of work more arduous. We have moved from the discipline of respect to the discipline of efficiency and, for the same reason, from apprentice-type "on-the-job training" which corresponds to a slow acculturation to the professional milieu and its bourgeois traditions, to stratified recruitment based on education—the latter more egalitarian to be sure, but less conducive to direct mobility in the company.

But these changes themselves must be interpreted in the same perspective of promotion and renewal of the group. From this viewpoint, there are gains to be noted. On the one hand the development of rationalization has tended to decrease the proportion of nonmanual workers who are direct victims of mechanization, in comparison to all those in intermediate positions whose task consists essentially of dealing with human relations, that is, with facilitating or organizing them. It is true of course, on the other hand, that the 900,000 French office workers of 1920 certainly had a more bourgeois status than the 1,920,000 white-collar employees of 1962. But to the 600,000 male employees of 1920 there now correspond probably 350,-000 supervisors and 250,000 highly-qualified employees whose status is at least equivalent to that of their predecessors of 1920.[23] As for the 650,000 females newly entered into the profession, thirty years ago they were laborers, seamstresses, or maids.[24] As deadening and as alienating as their assembly-line work may be, for them it may constitute a promotion.[25]

Finally, as far as the future is concerned, as has been noted by Hans-Paul Bahrdt, a contemporary German author who analyzed with great perspicacity the evolution of work in the office sector, the most difficult moment in the technical evolution—characterized by the phenomenon of the large mechanized office subject to the oppressive discipline of supervisors preoccupied exclusively with efficiency and productivity—appears now to have passed.[26] Automation tends to force the creation of smaller groups disposed to cooperation. Even key-punchers, whose occupation symbolizes efficiency and mechanization in their most brutal aspect, rarely form important

23. Figures calculated on the basis of the general census of the population of March 1962, INSEE, provisional documents.

24. While two-thirds of the office workers in the private sector are females, two-thirds of the middle and upper management positions are occupied by males. On the other hand, the movement of females from manual work to white-collar work is underscored by the decrease in the number of female blue-collar workers, which changes in forty years from 33 percent to 21 percent of the industrial work force, while their proportion in the employed population decreases by only 5 percent during the same period.

25. See the testimony of a woman employed at the hard job of operating an accounting machine: "I am content. The atmosphere here is different, one moves upward. My dream in life was to be a school teacher or an office worker. . . . My temperament is somewhat authoritarian. Being a maid was not at all my cup of tea."

26. Hans-Paul Bahrdt, *Industriebürokratie, Versuch einer Soziologie des Industrialisierten Bürobetriebes und seiner Angestellten* (Stuttgart: Enke, 1958).

groups, and one does not rediscover among them the atmosphere of a large manufacturing office.

What are the consequences of these transformations? Commentators habitually concentrate on only one or another of their aspects. Partisans of the conflict thesis wish to see only the proletarization manifested by the degradation of tasks and compensations. The opponents of Marxism highlight the proliferation of intermediate occupations which fall outside the class struggle.

Observation of reality leads to more subtly nuanced interpretations. To be sure, the professions of white-collar employees and minor functionaries are, on the whole, considerably devalued compared to their status only fifty years ago. But this devaluation of the great mass of jobs has been accompanied, we have seen, by a much greater differentiation and a change in recruitment. The majority of white-collar tasks are less interesting, less prestigious, and bring lower remuneration, but they are carried out by women with reduced aspirations, and (if one views families rather than individuals) proletarization is much weaker than it appears at first glance.

Finally, within the general perspective of social hierarchy, the elements which we have retained—loss of economic privilege and devaluation of tasks—cannot be considered without taking into account, at the same time, the general increase in size of the group. It is because the number of nonmanual tasks has increased to the point of becoming a majority in the most advanced countries that these occupations have ended by losing their prestige. They remain attractive only to the extent that they involve a degree of specialization and training which places their incumbents in the middle categories of the social hierarchy. The position of the white-collar employee without training can no longer be as desirable, since he finds himself in the second, rather than the first, half of this hierarchy. From the point of view of rank, his place is henceforth taken by the group consisting of executives and technicians. But if we consider the whole system, the intermediate social strata whose orientation one attempted to predict have not become proletarized. Quite the contrary.

2 Evolution of Ideas

At the end of the nineteenth century the evolution of the social structure toward differentiation and greater complexity of groups and of social relations, placing directly into question the initial Marxist schema, began to become the focus of attention. The debate opened in Germany, in that era the country of "scientific socialism." There the case of white-collar employees played only a limited role at first, since theory was the primary issue at hand. But beginning in 1910, that issue became the central point in the controversy and studies on the problem multiplied. Curiously, discussion as well as research remained limited to the German milieu, and disappeared moreover, evidently due to the advent of nazism. And it is only since the end of the Second World War that Englishmen, Americans, and Frenchmen have begun to take an interest in this issue.

German Marxists and Anti-Marxists

Marx himself did not devote much attention to the intermediate categories of clerks, functionaries, and the like. To be sure, he analyzed the role of state bureaucracy, but in the political sense. Considering it as a social group, he distinguished between the senior officers of capitalism (engineers, managers, management representatives) and its junior officers (foremen, supervisors, superintendents). He emphasized the ambiguity in the role of the latter, themselves exploited and at the same time charged with guaranteeing exploitation; but the existence of this group remained for him a minor point compared to the main one—the disappearance of proletarization of the traditional middle strata as a result of capitalist concentration. In any case, the intensification of exploitation due to the rationalization of methods, which simplifies and devaluates tasks, and the diffusion of training, which tends to increase availability, must, he thought, radically reduce the number of white-collar employees to the vital minimum.

The schema was simple and coherent. But from 1890 onward it was quite clear that reality did not correspond to these expectations. The traditional middle classes endured better than one might have expected, and the members of the rapidly growing white-collar group, rather than rejoin labor organizations, created separate organizations or unions hostile to labor unions. A debate sprang up around the celebrated Bernstein-Kautsky polemic. Confronting each other were three intellectual positions, which are worth delineating precisely, since they reappear in all the discussions which preceded nazism. They are: the anti-Marxist position, represented then by Gustav Schmoller; the evolutionary position, defended by Eduard Bernstein; and the revolutionary or orthodox position, whose uncontested champion was Karl Kautsky.

Gustav Schmoller, the father of academic socialism (*Kathedersozialismus*) at the beginning of the age of Bismarck, began to become interested in the middle classes and in white-collar employees during the 1890s.[1] He emphasized, in a sort of inverted Marxism, the attrition of the old ruling classes (the aristocracy and monied bourgeoisie) and saw intellectuals and higher civil servants as the rising class and the only one capable of incarnating the general interest. The natural support for these new leaders lay in the new middle classes, composed of white-collar employees and lower civil servants, since both

1. Gustav Schmoller, *Was verstehen wir unter dem Mittelstand* (Göttingen: Vandenhock and Ruprecht, 1897), pamphlet. A more detailed analysis of Schmoller's arguments may be found in Girod, *Études sociologiques*, pp. 27–30.

groups were free of the mercantile and egoistic interests of the old middle-classes and of the suffocating pressure of penury and ignorance which overwhelmed the laboring classes. They must naturally contribute to the reinforcement of social monarchy.[2]

Neither in his polemical articles in the *Neue Zeit*, nor in his famous book *Die Voraussetzungen des Sozialismus und die Aufgaben der Sozialdemokratie*,[3] did Eduard Bernstein accord white-collar employees an important position. They are only one of those elements in the general picture of the new society whose development seems to contradict Marx's arguments. Bernstein is just as puzzled, if not more so, about the subsistence of small entrepreneurs and about the extraordinary diffusion of the capitalist phenomenon which brings with it the proliferation of small stockholders. Anyway, in all three cases, the problem is the same. The growth of intermediate activities contradicts polarization around two classes. The social differentiation this growth engenders once again brings into question the very foundation of the Marxist theory of action. If capitalism multiplies specialties, hierarchies, styles of life, and points of view, evolution toward socialism—or, if you will, progress—cannot take place except through discussion and compromise. The idea of a rupture or of a necessary choice between antagonistic classes does not correspond to a natural pattern of development. Thus, as far as white-collar employees are concerned, Bernstein sees them neither as a group destined to disappear nor as a group apart, but as a group which the socialist movement can integrate, on condition that it opens itself to compromise and to discussion.

As for Kautsky, he reaffirms orthodoxy.[4] He adopts Marx's image of officers and subofficers of capitalism and attempts to find, in the facts available, a confirmation of the thesis of proletarization. Thus he devotes himself more to a study of the

2. Max Weber did not express himself directly on this subject. As we know, he was interested more in bureaucracy than in bureaucrats, but he was inclined toward this sort of argument. On the subject, see J.P. Mayer, *Max Weber and German Politics* (London: Faber and Faber, 1943).

3. (Stuttgart: Dietz, 1899).

4. Karl Kautsky, *Bernstein und das Sozialdemokratische program* (Stuttgart: Dietz, 1899).

laws of the marketplace, minimizing the sociological aspects of the problem in favor of economic factors. To be sure, he recognizes that, for the moment, the majority of white-collar employees are hostile to blue-collar employees. But, because the white-collar employees' situation naturally deteriorates as a result of the inexorable laws of the capitalist economic system, this antagonism is only temporary. Already, some of them have rejoined the proletariat; moreover, intellectuals must, in general, constitute the natural guides of the socialist revolution.

In Kautsky one already finds the germ of the following important idea, which Lenin would develop and which would, in the end, become one of the key principles of the Communist revolutionary struggle: The proletariat is incapable of arriving at a true consciousness of its interests and can move forward only under the impulse of the intelligentsia. So far as white-collar employees are concerned, this idea represents a curious and ambivalent attitude: on the one hand, real contempt and sometimes even hatred for the petit-bourgeois whose collapse is hailed, and for whom the role of servant to the working class is predicted for the future; and on the other hand, an extraordinary exaltation of the role of the intellectual as the advance guard of progress. The white-collar employee, the executive and the engineer are at one and the same time this bugbear and this figure of hope.

The Controversy of the 1920s

The rapid increase in numbers of white-collar employees during the years 1900–1920 and the crisis in the social system brought about by defeat and inflation prompted the translation of the theoretical positions of the 1900s into empirical analyses and practical decisions. Large numbers of articles and books were then devoted to the problem. These works, however, do not add much to the arguments already at hand. They constitute illustration and application. But they do not bring into question the principles of the discussion, since they are devoted exclusively to a description of the external conditions of white-collar employees in order to speculate on their possible reactions, but do not really attempt to understand how these employees experience their own situation.

In 1912, the most important specialist in this problem, Emile Lederer, had written the great social-democratic book on white-collar employees.[5] His serious and well-documented analysis led him to a moderate position, close to that of Bernstein. He clearly showed the heterogeneity of the group, whose upper strata leaned toward the bourgeoisie, while the "proletarians in false collars" might one day rejoin the blue-collar class. But, at the same time, he discovered among both parts of this group an incompatibility between a bourgeois style of life and bourgeois attitudes on the one hand, and salary conditions on the other.[6] And he concluded that this group was too divided to have an autonomous politics, as Schmoller maintained, or to accept the dictatorship of the proletariat proposed to it by revolutionary laborers. White-collar influence was always exercised in the direction of social progress and compromise. This reasonable and idealistic outlook did not stand up to the shock of the defeat and social crisis of the 1920s. In his later works, Lederer clearly adopted Kautsky's line. The war, he believed, had obliged lower white-collar employees and lower civil servants to choose, and they had chosen the proletariat. He considered them, from then on if not already, as conscious proletarians, or at least as "proletaroids."[7]

But Lederer is not the only author to take an interest in white-collar employees. His argument was supported and opposed by numerous other writers on society. We will not get involved here in presenting their ideas, but will simply call attention to the arguments used by two of them, Simon Kracauer and Carl Dreyfuss, who, with less subtlety than Lederer, present this portrait of the white-collar employee, victim of bourgeois society, who finally discovers that he too is a proletarian.[8] In effect, both of them bring out a new theme, that of spiritual alienation. Until then, what had been placed in the balance

5. Emile Lederer, *Die Privatangestellten in der Modernen Wirtschaftsentwicklung* (Tübingen: Mohr, 1912).

6. His method consisted essentially of analyzing family budgets.

7. This position corresponds very well with one of the more powerful literary myths of Germany of the 1920s, which expresses itself especially in the works of writers like Heinrich Mann and Hans Fallada.

8. Simon Kracauer, *Die Angestellten aus dem neuen Deutschland* (Frankfurt, 1930). Carl Dreyfuss, *Beruf und Ideologie der Angestellten* (Munich and Leipzig, 1933).

were arguments of an economic order in favor of proletarization, such as loss of independence and reduction in remunerations, and arguments of a sociological order in favor of the bourgeois influence, such as style of life. Kracauer, and above all Dreyfuss, were the first to advance arguments of a psychological and sociological order in favor of the proletarization thesis. According to them, white-collar employees suffer not only economic alienation, but also—and much more so than members of the working class—spiritual alienation, since it is their person itself and not only their capacity for work which is treated as a thing by the capitalist system.[9]

Events would rapidly give the lie to these prophecies and hopes. Nazism stirred many echoes among proletarians in false collars, and Daniel Guérin, mouthpiece in 1937 of the intransigent Marxists, was obliged to recognize that it was among the lower levels of the middle classes, and especially among white-collar employees, that Hitler found his best troops.[10]

White-collar Workers in Contemporary Literature

Compared to the intellectual effervescence of this debate in Weimar Germany, the discussion concerning the social and political evolution of white-collar employees during the years following the Second World War seems quite dull. Strangely enough, interest in the problem seems to have waned just at the point when the renowned proletarians in false collars, to use the Marxist imagery, multiplied most rapidly in number. A few works are worth examining. Three authors in particular

9. Nevertheless, the moderate point of view still has its defenders during the same period. The excellent work by Theodor Geiger must be cited: *Die Soziale Schichtung des Deutschen Volkes* (Stuttgart: Enke, 1932). Geiger very forcefully criticizes the idea of *Mittelstand,* dear to conservatives, but recognizes no better than them the increasing dichotomy of German society. His analysis of divergences between mentality and ideology allows him to renew the traditional polemic. In particular he applies himself, with much success, to a study of civil servants who identify with the state in a society permeated through and through by bureaucracy.

10. This did not prevent Guérin from maintaining his original position. It was only because the working class was not firm enough and revolutionary enough that white-collar employees, at loose ends and threatened by proletarization, did not rejoin it. Daniel Guérin, *Fascisme et Grand Capital,* new edition (Paris: Gallimard, 1945), pp. 51–58.

emerge from a much less abundant literature: the American C. Wright Mills, the Englishman David Lockwood, and the German Hans-Paul Bahrdt.

The most orthodox by far is C. Wright Mills. It is no small irony in this international comparison to discover that the only person truly faithful to the German and revolutionary spirit of the 1920s was an American.[11]

In his book *White Collar*,[12] C. Wright Mills adopts as his own all the German arguments concerning the proletarization of the middle classes and the natural rapprochement between manual and nonmanual workers, both equally victims of capitalism. He utilizes in particular, with all the vigor and literary talent of which he is capable, the arguments of Kracauer and Dreyfuss concerning the spiritual alienation of the new middle classes.[13] But the paradox is explained if one takes into account C. Wright Mill's isolation, the marginal character of his work in American social literature, and also the very original position he took in this dispute. His argument, if one examines it at closer range, can no longer really be seen as an application of the general Marxist schema to an important, or even a strategic, group. The situation of white-collar workers becomes the very symbol of *neocapitalist* oppression, and the critique of spiritual alienation becomes the foundation of a *neo-Marxism*. The analysis of the frustrations of white-collar employees is only a means for Mills to give vent to an overall critique of American society. In the world that he denounces, exploitation is no longer tied to surplus value but to the fact that the "intellectual worker" *has had expropriated from him the means without which one cannot communicate.*

Unfortunately Mills's work, no more than those of his predecessors, is not a true research study. In effect, it is not the feelings of alienation which may actually be suffered by the salesgirl or by the intellectual at an advertising agency that interest

11. He had, however, an extremely interesting predecessor, Lewis Corey, who presented in 1947, in a book entitled *The Crisis of the Middle Class,* a brilliant analysis of the decline of the old middle classes.

12. (New York and London: Macmillan, 1951).

13. *White Collar* is, from this point of view, Mills's best book. A generous spirit infuses even his most indignant outburst. Attorney-like, he pleads for an image of man which might be considered romantic, but at the same time reveals Mills's ultimate humanity.

Mills, but rather objective alienation of these persons as it might be reconstructed by analyzing the forces which exert pressure on them. This attitude pretends to be more scientific than a poll of opinions, but it is so only in appearance. If we were to adopt Mills's own definition, in which constraint and alienation are easily confused, social life without alienation would in effect be impossible. The individual is always necessarily limited by his place in the social structure; the commercial smile of the small independent shopkeeper is at least as alienated as that of the salesgirl. To understand the real import of that smile, there is no way of escaping the study of subjectivity.

As for David Lockwood and Hans-Paul Bahrdt, they are not marginal; on the contrary, they are extremely representative of the young intellectual generation in Germany and in England. But their national roles are reversed. Lockwood seems determined to introduce into British social science the discussion of distribution of categories and classes in society as a whole, as well as the speculation on social outcomes, which until then had characterized the German tradition.[14] Bahrdt, in turn, seems to have broken almost completely with the Marxist and German tradition of the years before nazism. He cites none of the abundant German literature of the years before nazism. His very suggestive book is, despite some obscurities, marked above all by the influence of modern American sociology. He does not cite directly, but his argument consistently makes use of, organizational and social-systems terminology dear to Americans; his aim is, in essence, to integrate the traditional European analysis of social movements into the general stream of American functionalist sociology.

These two approaches nevertheless deserve to be analyzed more closely. Lockwood reasons exclusively in terms of the market. Bypassing completely a discussion of alienation, he examines, on the one hand, the characteristics of the situation and evolution of white-collar employees and, on the other

14. In Great Britain before 1940, literature on white-collar employees is practically nonexistent. We note only one title in the area of social research: Klingender, *The Condition of Clerical Labour in Britain* (London, 1934).

hand, their collective reactions, that is, the development of their unions. This approach was a coherent one, and a realistic analysis of the market allowed him to draw attention to essential points which had eluded his predecessors, such as the consequences of feminization which we have emphasized above, or the evolution of the salary structure and the promotion system. Nonetheless, the end product falls short of the author's deeper intentions, and even of his manifest objectives. He would like to be able to assess the importance of white-collar employees' union activity and to predict the likelihood of their political evolution toward the Labor Party. Even if one restricts oneself to the area of unions, such an enterprise is hazardous. One is always obliged to explain differences in terms of cultural lag which, from the point of view of a sociologist, is quite insufficient. In our opinion, Lockwood is too readily satisfied with a simplified model of rational economic process in the labor market. Several models are possible, depending on whether the individual reasons in terms of personal or collective facts, in terms of the present facts or of his personal future or the future of his children. Even if it is the collective strategy that motivates him, it is not easy to maintain this single point of reference exclusively, nor is the choice between solidarity and antagonism in relation to other points of reference so easily made. All these choices depend on sociological or cultural factors which cannot be ignored, as they too often are in Lockwood.[15]

As for Bahrdt, his interest is not in the market but in large enterprise, in the social system it constitutes, and in the position white-collar employees occupy in such an enterprise. From a sociological point of view, his reflections are far richer. He perceives clearly the relationships between organizational structure, the definition of tasks, the system of domination, and the possibilities for alienation which this system engenders. Nevertheless, his analysis remains rigid. He idealizes the co-

15. In addition, one often encounters affirmations which become extremely fragile when viewed in a broad perspective. Indeed, once one is aware of the vigor and the importance of civil service unions in France, it is not too clear how the timidity of British national and local civil servants with respect to unionization can be explained in terms of the "respectable" character of their occupation.

operative system which will, according to him, be imposed by the introduction of automation. But even if the decentralization of tasks and the softening of hierarchical relations often accompany new technical progress, this consequence is never automatic. It would be more correct to hold that, in the ever more complex collectivity which a large production unit constitutes, the margin of freedom allowed by technical imperatives is not radically restricted, and that centralization of any type of activity depends as much on economic and historical facts and on cultural models as on the degree of technical progress. Finally, Bahrdt would like to effect a conciliation between his very optimistic functionalist outlook and a "laborist" political orientation, and here he runs into a curious contradiction. The introduction of the cooperative system in offices must, he thinks, give white-collar employees the same sense of camaraderie, of professional pride, and of independence enjoyed by blue-collar workers. But if pride and independence are associated with a system of cooperative organization, how is it that the majority of blue-collar employees, subject so long to the oppressive discipline of mass production, have not long ago lost these feelings?

Before concluding this general survey of theories concerning white-collar employees and their evolution, we should discuss the works of two authors whose socio-political ideas are less widely held and who devote themselves more to describing and defining the role of white-collar employees in society than to speculating on the direction of their evolution. The one who is chronologically first, Maurice Halbwachs, remains the more convincing.[16] He proposes that the function of a white-collar employee and a lower civil servant be distinguished from that of a blue-collar employee by the extent to which the former function does not consist of working with inert matter, but of applying rules concerning the relations between persons and intellectual operations. These rules are supplied by the leaders, and involve a greater or lesser degree of understanding; the

16. Halbwachs's study first appeared in 1938 under the title "Analyse des mobiles dominants qui orientent l'activité des individus dans la vie sociale" in the *Enquêtes sociologiques* of the Institut Solvay (Brussels). It was reissued after the war in a small work published in Paris: *Esquisse d'une psychologie des classes sociales* (Paris: Marcel Rivière, 1955).

degree of autonomy they leave to the white-collar employee determines his place in the social hierarchy.

The second of these authors, one of Lederer's students, is Fritz Croner, who settled in Sweden where he directs the research bureau of the union of white-collar employees' central office. In a book originally published in 1951, and recently reissued, Croner supports a theory which he calls a theory of delegation.[17] This theory is not so different from that of Halbwachs, but it is less suggestive, since it makes use of a more juridical notion whose influence on behavior is less clear. According to Croner, the function of the white-collar employee corresponds essentially to a dismemberment of the activity of the leader, and is distinguished from the function of the blue-collar worker to the extent that it necessarily entails "delegation." Strangely enough, Croner elsewhere adopts a violently anti-Marxist attitude, and refuses to accept any idea of superiority or hierarchy within social categories, despite the fact that the criterion he uses has no meaning unless it implies a notion of power.[18]

17. Fritz Croner, *Die Angestellten inder modernen Wirtschaft* (Frankfurt-Vienna, 1951; Cologne, 1962).

18. We could cite several other authors, like Michel Collinet, who treated the problem rather cursorily in *Essai Sur la Condition Ouvrière (1900–1950)* (Paris: Editions ouvrières, 1951), and above all Roger Girod, whose work, *Etudes Sociologiques sur les couches salariées,* we have already cited several times. This work contains a very interesting critical analysis of earlier theories, a curious study of the categories utilized by American statistics, and several monographs on the working environment, the values, and the ecological distribution of Genevan workers. Girod holds in general that the difference between white-collar and blue-collar employees is arbitrary and is becoming obliterated but he clearly shows the insufficiency of the traditional criteria for making this distinction; he gives no account of how the differences which, according to him, still subsist are experienced.

The most lively interest in this area continues to be found in Germany. Five new works, for example, have appeared during the last three years, besides the republication we have already mentioned of the book by F. Croner: A. Nikisch, *Zur Neuabgrenzung der Begriffe Angestellter und Arbeiter. Ein Ausschussbericht,* Gesellschaft für Sozialen Fortschritt (Berlin, 1959); L. Neundoerfer, *Die Angestellten, Neuer Versuch einer Standortbestimmung* (Stuttgart, 1961); G. Hartfiel, *Angestellte und Angestelltengewerkschaft in Deutschland* (Berlin, 1961); R. Bayer, ed., *Der Angestellte zwischen Arbeiterschaft und Management,* collection (Berlin, 1961); Th. Pirker, *Büro und Machine* (Tübingen, 1962).

The Direction of Evolution

As we have seen, practically all authors agree in emphasizing the ambiguity of the situation of the white-collar employee.[19] This determination cannot, however, serve as a conclusion; the problems raised for sociological theory concerning the peculiarities of the white-collar group have to do with the origin, the consequences, and above all the possible future of this ambiguity. In our opinion, most authors made rather short work of this subject, because they believed, after inadequate consideration, that contradictions such as those presented by the situation of white-collar employees could be no more than provisional. Evolution, they thought, would soon force this hybrid group to make a choice. Some envisioned its development into a separate class or into one of the essential elements of a new *Mittelstand;* others—the largest number—expected that it would discover itself to be proletarian. Even those who looked forward to a slow evolution seemed willing only to refuse to commit themselves.

Marxist logic wanted the place of each individual in the great class struggle to be determined by the weight of various interdependent socio-economic factors. The uncertainty of white-collar employees was analyzed as a legacy of the past, which the action of the socialist movement would dispel to the extent that, in revealing the contradictions within which the petit-bourgeois struggles, it would help him attain a consciousness of the mystification of which he is victim. The opponents of Marxism denied this conclusion but accepted this approach to the problem.

19. Fritz Croner is practically the only one who, at least theoretically, holds a contrary position. In the 1962 edition of his *Die Angestellten in der modernen Wirtschaft,* pp. 106–8, he reproaches us for accepting this legacy of Marxist romanticism. For him, there is no class difference between blue-collar and white-collar employees, but only functional differences. To insist on differences is to introduce categories of power and hierarchy which do not correspond to reality. Such an outlook is conceivable as an argument for the classless society of tomorrow, but as an analysis of the present it is contradicted by the facts. The question arises, however, why Croner himself attached so much importance to this problem if white-collar employees never constituted more than a professional category, tailor-made for statistics.

Now one might ask whether, after all, this ambiguity, which one writer after another has inevitably discovered in the course of a long evolution, is not on the contrary destined to subsist and even—why not?—to become more widespread. It has by no means been demonstrated that coherence is a necessity in the attitudes and in the behavior of social groups, or that the maintenance of contradictions is not rational.

In fact, if the behavior of white-collar employees and minor civil servants is ambivalent, if they generally feel themselves to be both exploited workers demanding their rights from a boss or from the state, and collaborators who have a part in directorial power in relation to laborers, this is not so much the result of a lack of intellectual coherence—which rational disclosure might dissipate—but rather the sign of a profound contradiction which they experience in their situation itself.

The situation of a white-collar employee is very much the situation of a manual worker, carrying with it most of the limitations endured by that worker so far as salary, lack of autonomy, and subordination are concerned. But it is at the same time a situation which facilitates identification with the world of the ruling classes and which offers substantial compensations to those who manage to move into that world.

The world of the ruling classes exercises its influence on individuals in a dynamic perspective. It brings into play the amalgam of the individual's career and the careers of his children. Labor's influence, on the other hand, represents a collective and static pressure. But the pessimistic outlook that accompanies the latter does not correspond to reality any more than the optimistic outlook implied by the marshal's baton in the soldier's knapsack.

The white-collar employee does actually have a better chance to attain or to see his children attain higher posts. If he models himself on the upper class, it is not simply because he finds himself subject to the influence of rulers by virtue of his physical proximity to them—because of his place of work, his clothing, the abstract nature of his functions and the type of human contact which they involve[20]—it is also, and above all, because he is well aware that they have a tendency to choose

20. This factor is well-emphasized by Girod, *Etudes sociologiques*, pp. 138–39.

for eventual promotions those persons whose behavior comes closest to their own standards. To be sure, the white-collar employee is at the bottom of the ladder, but at least he is already on the ladder. However great his timidity may be, he is nevertheless somewhat acquainted with the leaders and those who advise them. He is aware of what stands a chance of pleasing these leaders and what one must do to advance, or at least to help one's children advance.

This hypothesis of anticipatory socialization is, in our opinion, the only one which allows a satisfactory interpretation of the reactions peculiar to white-collar employees and to civil servants in public opinion surveys. At work, both these groups are more preoccupied with the future, better informed, and more sensitive to company morale than the laborer. In their nonworking lives, they are better informed, both with regard to commercial products and to political and social facts. Their interest in politics is different from that manifested by manual workers and by peasants, and approaches the more abstract type of interest manifest among the middle classes. Finally, their cultural level is far higher than that of manual workers.[21]

On a different level, the study of Dr. Heuyer of school-age children showed that in France children of white-collar employees are clearly ahead of children of manual workers and peasants at every age-level studied, even if one eliminates the influence of place of residence.[22] The milieu within which the children develop does seem to favor a raising of their intellectual level. Thus parents' anticipatory socialization has an immediate and tangible effect on their children's chances for social advancement, and the attitudes of the parents, even when they fail completely on the personal level, nonetheless retain a large measure of rationality if one takes the family group into account.[23]

21. Through the courtesy of the IFOP, we have been able to do a detailed analysis in this respect of public opinion surveys taken in the years 1947–53. See Crozier, "Le rôle des employés et des petits fonctionnaires" p. 311.

22. Dr. Heuyer, *Le niveau intellectuel des enfants d'âge scolaire* (Paris: Cahiers de la collection Travaux et documents [INED], no. 13, 1950, and no. 22, 1954).

23. It would be interesting to utilize and to develop the observations of Kinsey, who shows that anticipatory socialization comes into play even with regard to sexual behavior, since persons who have raised

The objection might perhaps be raised that the world of white-collar workers is composed not only of persons who are in the process of rising on the social ladder, but also of those who are descending. This is quite true, but the two movements, even if they are symmetrical when it comes to the distribution of occupations, are not symmetrical as far as attitudes and behavior are concerned. Not only have those persons who have descended the social ladder not generally adopted in advance the behavioral characteristics of the group to which they will find themselves consigned; but, once consigned there, they will naturally persist in identifying themselves, just as before, with the ruling classes.[24]

The influence of the ruling classes is exercised not only in motivating upward aspiration, but also in producing resistance to descent. In this perspective, the white-collar group constitutes one of the most important groups for the maintenance of a certain type of social cohesion. For it is through this group that a great part of the upward and downward movement, most significant for class allegiance, operates. By providing them with a respectable façade, this group keeps within the bourgeois orbit all those who were in the process of descending, and pulls into this orbit all those who were able to make it to the first rung. At the same time, the white-collar group has a tendency to gnaw away at the blue-collar group, insofar as white-collar employees who have been forced to accept manual work generally persist in retaining their middle class behavior patterns.

The pressure from below, that is, the influence of the blue-collar group, is not of the same kind. It consists not of a separate attraction, based on reasonable chances for success in the

---

themselves in the social hierarchy have manifested, since their adolescence—that is before this rise had taken place—sexual behavior altogether similar to that prevalent in the category which they had attained, and very different from the category in which they originated. This would allow an interpretation of certain personality traits widely encountered among white-collar employees.

24. Harold Wilensky and Hugh Edwards have shown this very clearly in a most interesting study of the problem of descent on the social scale: "The Skidder: Ideological Adjustment of Downward Mobile Workers," *American Sociological Review* 24 (April 1959). See also Seymour Liebermann, "The Effects of Changes in Roles on the Attitudes of Role Occupants," *Human Relations* 9, no. 4 (1958).

long run; rather it is a kind of collective means of defense for the maintenance and improvement of the present condition. There is no need to conceive of this defense as an act of solidarity with the blue-collar group. While imitation of blue-collar action may be the result, this does not yet imply any tendency toward alliance. The white-collar union movement still remains ambivalent, even when it is associated with the labor movement in a limited way.

The situation which we have just summarized, while at the same time trying to bring out its logical mechanism, seems perfectly explainable in the framework of French society today or, more generally, in the framework of Western societies. But is not this situation transitory? Have not the consequences of an ever-accelerating technical and economic evolution already made it obsolete?

This would certainly be the case if evolution were governed only by the classical laws of the marketplace. If one could reason in those terms, the privilege enjoyed by nonmanual workers should have vanished long ago. In a less developed society, where only a small percentage of the population has even a minimum level of school training, nonmanual workers naturally have a privileged position, even if their standard of living is very low compared to that of their Western counterparts. When literacy becomes widespread the advantage of these workers disappears.[25]

But if theoretical reasoning in terms of the market allows us to account for the relative situation of nonmanual workers in terms of the level of development of societies,[26] a study of the facts does not allow us to be so positive. The various advantages which a sociological analysis of the situation of white-

25. Nevertheless, one might say that, even in such a comparison, human relations are just as important as the economic factor. In underdeveloped societies, the fringe that has sufficiently assimilated the modes of thought of the ruling classes has, by that fact—regardless of its situation in the labor market—an enormous advantage over the great illiterate mass.

26. Provided we admit that the need for nonmanual work always exceeds the supply; yet this is not always the case, since numerous underdeveloped countries have known periods of surplus supply. The considerable differences between manual and nonmanual workers which continue to exist, even during those periods, cannot then be explained without appealing to sociological criteria.

collar employees in modern society discloses do not depend directly on the laws of the market in the narrow economic sense. There is even reason to believe that subjective factors have a direct and often decisive influence on the market itself. The chances for social mobility, the opportunity for participation, anything that permits the individual to attach more value to his social position, constitute equally important differentiating factors; these factors do not depend directly on the law of supply and demand, and tend to belie it.

To be sure, these factors are not autonomous or immutable; they depend on the general system of domination, hierarchy, and prestige which prevails in a given society, and we have certainly noted a profound transformation of this system. But this transformation is not directly and narrowly connected with the economic process. The apparent strength and the great weakness of the Marxist theory of class struggle was that it confused the two analyses by claiming at one and the same time that the laws of the market consecrated the relations of domination and at the same time undermined them from within. Actually, the interdependence of the two systems of human relations is not that close; what seems contradictory when one postulates their coherence becomes altogether tolerable when one restores the autonomy of each.

It is thus conceivable that, from the point of view of the market, the white-collar employee could become more and more assimilated with other workers, so far as salary and the processes of bargaining are concerned, but that at the same time could retain a degree of social privilege, as a result of his readier contacts with leaders and because of his cultural advantages, as long as the general system of domination might make difficult hierarchical relations and communication between social categories. If we accept this analysis, which the facts seem to verify in the short and in the intermediate run, we must, on the other hand, foresee that participatory behavior in the social process—which we have sought to characterize by saying that the employee is at the bottom of the ladder but already on the ladder—will tend more and more to erode the well-known traditional classes. Far from disappearing, the ambiguity in the situation of white-collar employees will very likely become even more extensive. The very real rapprochement which we have noted between white-collar and blue-collar employees signifies embourgeoisement of the blue-collar employee rather than proletarization of the white-collar employee.

The Cultural Dimension

All the problems which we have just examined—social climbing and the manner in which it is experienced, choice of a strategy for the individual (individual or collective, short term or familial), frame of references, the question of the very existence of coherent social categories, and the question of communication between these categories—extend well beyond the case of white-collar employees alone. They bring into question the overall organization of society, in particular its hierarchical system and the type of relationship of domination which it accepts.

This somewhat narrow relationship between the attitudes and behavioral patterns of white-collar employees on the one hand, and the models of social hierarchy prevalent within a society on the other, has until now hardly attracted the attention of researchers. Studies of white-collar employees have so far stayed away from the problem of the relationships between social categories. The idea of white-collar employees as an intermediate group is, for example, almost completely ignored in contemporary empirical sociology.[27]

27. In an article entitled "Trends in occupational sociology in the U.S." (*American Sociological Review* 19, no. 4 [August 1954]), Erwin O. Smigel presents some extremely significant documents. Of all the research on occupational sociology, only 2.2 percent was devoted to office workers, while articles in specialized journals came to 3 percent, compared to 33 percent devoted to the medical professions. This statistic is all the more surprising given that a large number of the studies of the leadership and functioning of organizations have dealt with office workers, and that the mass of data collected concerning this professional category appears indirectly to be quite considerable. But in each case the subjects interviewed were studied as members of an organization and not as representatives of a particular socio-professional category. See, for example: Nancy Morse, *Satisfaction in the White-Collar Job* (University of Michigan, 1953); James Worthy, "Organizational Structure and Employee Morale," *American Sociological Review* 15:169–70; George Homans, "Status among clerical workers," *Human Organization,* no. 12 (Spring 1953); Chris Argyris, *The Organization of a Bank* (1956); Floyd Mann and L. K. Williams, "Organizational

We would nonetheless like to believe that there is a particularly interesting area for study here, provided it is approached from a "culturalist" perspective. The cultural dimension, so generally forgotten in the study of the problem of social classes, takes on fundamental importance in this perspective.

In our opinion, the quite perceptible differences which we note between various Western societies concerning the place and even the role of white-collar employees constitute a decisive argument in favor of such a perspective. All comparisons clearly suggest it.

While there is a striking parallelism between the union behavior, social attitudes, and in all likelihood the role and social status of well-defined blue-collar groups, such as printers, miners, and dock workers, considerable differences appear among white-collar employees and even greater differences among civil servants. French public administration is the sector in which unions have the greatest influence. Practically the opposite is true in Germany and in England. Tradition decreed that the French civil servant vote to the left and the German *Beamte* to the right. The German *Beamte*, even in the most humble posts, had a status which distinguished him from the rest of the population, while the term "civil service" and the prestige attached to it was, in England, reserved for members of the upper class.

Among white-collar employees, the contrast, while less important, remains nonetheless profound. The terms *Angestellte*, *employé*, *white-collar worker* or *blackcoated worker* do not have the same meaning in current vocabulary. *Angestellte* is a specialized well-defined term; *employé* is a general term which common usage has made quite well-defined; *white-collar worker* and *blackcoated worker* are no more than metaphors, for which one can substitute only the professional term *clerk*, a much more limited term which has not acquired any sociological meaning. Many authors, however, ignore this distinction and rank white-collar employees, foremen, and skilled laborers in the *lower middle class*. To these differences in vocabulary correspond differences in status and in prestige (more pro-

---

Impact of White-Collar Automation," contribution to the 11th conference of the Industrial Relations Research Association (1959).

nounced in Germany, less so in England), and differences in unions' behavior[28] (separate unions in the Germanic tradition; integrated unions in the English labor movement; apparently integrated unions in France, which in practice however retain a somewhat different orientation, to the extent that union pluralism, with an ideological base, expresses at least in part social differences such as the white-collar—blue-collar difference).[29]

Technological development and the diffusion of training are not the only issues. The ambiguity in the white-collar employee's situation depends on the degree of evolution of society; but it is at the same time marked and formed by the system of domination and the prevalent model of relations between social categories. Characteristics peculiar to each manifestation of this ambiguity depend, in the last analysis, on certain fundamental cultural traits characteristic of each society. In modern industrial societies, the influence of technology on the mode of social organization seems to be fully exercised only in relation to the lower categories. For nonmanual workers, technological determinism is much less compelling; among these workers we may be confronted with systems of organization which manifest considerable differences.

Such systems cannot be easily analyzed, for to do so requires that we simplify highly complex collections of variables and leave more room for accidents of history. By studying the history of the actual functions of the French white-collar and civil service union-movement, we will nevertheless determine to what extent fundamental cultural traits of French society deeply affect the social climate and the reactions of the white-collar world.

28. The DGB, the German trade union federation, now encompasses white-collar employees organized within industrial unions, but the problem of white-collar particularism continues to give rise to many discussions which are rarely entered into in France or in England. One of the most important postwar strikes, that of the metal workers of Schleswig-Holstein, had its deep-rooted cause in the discrepancies in the treatment of white-collar and blue-collar employees.

29. The heart of the CFDT was until a few years ago the old Federation of white-collar employees, while the FO is the bastion of civil service unions.

3 Union Activity

In modern societies, union activity constitutes the most immediate and most spectacular response by a subordinate group to its situation. It expresses in a very crude way both the psychology and the strategy that the group uses in its relations with ruling groups and with other subordinate groups.

Before presenting the necessarily very partial results of our inquiries, we would like to devote ourselves to a rapid analysis of the union history of white-collar employees and minor civil servants. This will allow us to bring to light the ambiguity in their behavior as a social group, and the importance of cultural influences in determining that behavior. On the other hand, we will also make use of this opportunity to describe in advance, in very rough terms, the political and social context within which the attitudes and the behavioral patterns which we will study are to be found.[1]

The Lessons of History

The Origins

Nonmanual unionism in France had three principal sources, of equivalent influence, whose mutual con-

1. For a detailed analysis of the history of white-collar unions we refer the reader to a chapter entitled "The Case of France" which we drafted for the work edited by Adolf Sturmthal, *White-Collar Unionism in Seven Countries.*

trasts well express the contradictions in the behavior of white-collar employees: a revolutionary and anarcho-syndicalist source among commercial salesworkers, a secular and Freemasonic source in the civil service, and a Catholic and bourgeois source in the first Christian unions. Each of the three movements which issued from these sources expressed, at some point, in a categorical way, one of the possible choices open to the white-collar world: bourgeois collaboration or proletarian revolt, corporatism or minority ideology. But none of them succeeded in maintaining this purity; their positions were often reversed and they tended more and more to converge.

Large stores were the site of unionism's first appearance. The large Parisian department stores, as is well known, date from the years 1850–60. The first to appear in the world, they introduced a concentration of responsibilities and a revolution in methods which amounted to a complete upheavel in one of the traditional areas of activity of the petite bourgeoisie.

This economic revolution had deplorable social consequences. Work schedules were heavy, working conditions punishing, and discipline extremely severe. The reaction of the employees was immediate. Societies for mutual assistance were formed beginning in the 1860s.[2] There was also the development of very strong agitation in favor of Sunday rest; after a series of meetings held at the Grand Orient, one of the Freemasons' temples in Paris, a Chambre syndicale des employés de commerce was established in 1869, the same year as the First International. Beginning in this era, anarchist and Proudhonian influence was intermingled with Masonic, Republican, and anticlerical influence.

The Chambre syndicale fédérale des employés, which was firmly established in 1882,[3] had a difficult and stormy existence. Its principal demands were for an eight-hour day and Sunday rest. In general, its activities were spectacular but

2. On this period consult: *Les employés de commerce parisiens* (pamphlet edited by the Chambre Syndicale fédérale des employés, CGT, 1937).

3. Already in 1879, the anarchist leader Emile Pouget, who was later to become the number-two man in the CGT office during the heroic times of the Charter of Amiens, had organized a union of drapery-store employees. He was at that time a salesman in a large department store.

quite ineffective, at least in the short run.[4] Three essential characteristics made it special. It was, first of all, an almost exclusively Parisian movement which could never gain any serious foothold in the provinces. Secondly it was an extremely small movement, having no particular mass influence except during times of crisis and in the heat of a general action. Finally, it was a revolutionary movement, directly open to the most extreme influences.[5]

This labor and proletarian orientation expressed the aspirations and the situation of the small minority, that is the ruling group of the union, which was both isolated from the masses in the profession and part of the intellectual revolutionary milieu in Paris. It expressed the constant temptation of that milieu, but not by any means the adherence, even partial, of its members.

The second current of nonmanual workers' unionism, and by far the most vigorous, originated among the lower strata in the civil service, especially among mailmen and teachers. This clientele, which was to come to unionism en masse, was more serious, more prudent, and less anarchist than the fringe group of rebels which had such a deep effect on the unionists in the large department stores. From the start, the civil service movement was a general provincial movement; it was not a movement of the Parisian intellectual minority, like the unionism of the department stores, nor was it a movement of militants without troops, like the blue-collar movement.

The mailmen were the most active. Having for some time already been organized into mutual assistance associations, they created in 1900, with the help of Millerand, the socialist minister, two general associations, one for agents and the other for subagents, which very quickly succeeded in gaining the adherence of three-quarters of the employees.[6] Their action

4. Among other actions, it organized the great strike of the Dufayel department stores (1905), which was one of the most spectacular conflicts of the era.

5. The Chambre syndicale would participate, for example, in the establishment of the CGT.

6. At this time the recruitment procedures and the chances for promotion in the postal ministry were already remarkably egalitarian and democratic, and the postmen's unionist revolt aimed only for

was moderate and reformist thanks to Freemasonry (they were in direct and clandestine contact with the highest state authorities), but they were also involved in discussions with the revolutionary CGT and gave some thought to a possible affiliation with that group.

The violence of the reaction by the government, under the direction of Clemenceau and his undersecretary of state for postal services, Simyan, accentuated for a time the revolutionary character of the movement. The two successive general strikes which broke out in 1909 excited considerable emotion and were spectacularly supported by the CGT.[7] After Clemenceau's departure, the last obstacles to unionization of the profession disappeared. From that point on, unionism among postal workers was to develop smoothly, to the point of actually controlling the entire system of human relations which made up the postal administration.

The other civil service movements followed, in a more moderate form, the same fundamental pattern: a general organization of the majority developing easily, because of the existence of an egalitarian administrative spirit, and guarantees already given by the administration; the maintaining of

---

the elimination of arbitrary political and administrative influences which continued to affect them.

7. Ordered by Clemenceau in 1906 to take his rebellious personnel in hand, Simyan became involved in disputes with his employees for two years. He finally decided to proceed with a complete reform of the system of promotions, a move which would have put postal workers at the mercy of the minister's orders. After a strike of the Parisian central telegraph office which gave rise to police brutality (March, 1909), a general strike was voted by the association and soon was extended to all of France. Forced to beat a retreat, Clemenceau succeeded in achieving a return to work without committing himself to anything but half-promises. Simyan, retained in office, began once again to fire the militants, after a cooling-off period of several weeks. The second general strike which was then triggered ended in failure despite the appeals for solidarity by the CGT. Reprisals by the Administration were severe—eight hundred agents were immediately fired—but only a month later the Clemenceau government fell, and the postmen had their revenge. Since then, no government has dared to raise again the question of civil servants' adherence to unions. The crisis of this period is succintly described by Edouard Dolléans, *Histoire du Mouvement Ouvrier* (Paris: Armand Colin, 1953), 2, pp. 158–63. On postal workers in general one can consult B. Laurent, *Postes et Postiers* (Paris: Octave Doin, 1922).

contacts both with the republican and anticlerical leaders of the civil service and with the revolutionaries of the CGT; playing these ambiguities off against each other; and finally succeeding in imposing itself by using political resources.[8]

If the two movements—civil service on the one hand, commercial employees on the other—testified, despite all their ambiguity, to the "proletarian" choice of one part of the white-collar world, the third movement, the Catholic social movement, was, at least originally, a movement in favor of social order and of bourgeois society. The new initials CFDT symbolized the rupture of this movement's last connection with the bourgeois world. This CFDT, whose independence and combativeness everyone had for some time taken delight in emphasizing, actually began as a very conservative placement bureau organized in 1885 by the Brothers of the Christian Schools, a religious order in charge of the most important of the French Catholic grade schools, for their old students. The Syndicat des employés de Commerce et de l'Industrie, which succeeded the placement bureau in 1892, was created with the help of Catholic employers' associations. Its origins were for a long time a great handicap to this organization, and at the time it was considered practically a scab union. But with the change in atmosphere brought on by the end of the Dreyfuss affair and by the arrival of a new generation of young catholic liberals such as Marc Sangnier, the SECI decided to transform itself and to extend its scope in order to become the rallying point for all Catholic workers. It kept its distance from the ecclesiastical hierarchy, and began to prepare to make common cause with the labor movement.[9]

8. The other civil service movements were not nearly as militant as that of the postal workers. Teachers, however, followed a similar path. Their leaders were sent packing by Clemenceau at about the same time as the first leaders of the postal workers in 1906 and 1907. Beginning in 1910, their movement became radicalized, and in 1912 their union was dissolved by the government because they had voted at their congress to support an antimilitarist motion.

9. On the foundation and initial development of the SECI, see Paul Verdin, *La fondation du syndicat des employés de commerce et de l'Industrie* (Paris: Éditions Spes, 1929). On the period that followed, see R. P. Stephane Piat, *Jules Zirnheld, Président de la C.F.T.C.* (Paris: Bonne Presse, 1948).

The Turning Point of the 1920s

White-collar employees played no small role in the great wave of strikes which shook France, as well as most other western societies, in 1919 and 1920. They participated in the general strike of May 1, 1919. In May and in June, one after the other, most of the large department stores went on strike and, for the first time, even the banks were forced to close. And, for the first time also, Christian employees supported a strike movement. The successes achieved were, however, only temporary. No stable organization was able to constitute itself, and new adherents withdrew as quickly as they had come. In October, 1919, the general strike of large Parisian stores, though impressive from the point of view of size and duration (it lasted a month), ended in semidefeat; from 1920 on, the white-collar union movement, torn by dissensions just like the labor movement, went from one defeat to the next.

But while the material results achieved by the movement in the years 1919–20 may seem meager, they had great psychological importance. For it is from this period that we can date the deep allegiance of the French white-collar world to the workers' cause. To be sure, this unity would remain extremely vague and would accommodate itself to much opposition. Officially, however, it could never again be brought into question. The Catholic unions, which had until then remained dubious, had at last shown that at the decisive moment they took sides with the strikers. Even the white-collar employees in banks, those last bastions of bourgeois respectability, had followed.

The years following were marked by the disastrous consequences of union divisiveness. They were nevertheless decisive years for the civil service and for the development of the special relationship which the French union movement maintains with the state. The CGT majority, disencumbered of communist elements,[10] was actually able to establish within

10. Following the epoch-making division of the French socialist party, the Communists had built a rival federation of trade unions, the CGTU (Confédération Générale du Travail Unitaire). Up to the reunification of 1935, the CGT was dominated by socialist-inclined or moderate ex-anarchist leaders.

the civil service an informal though limited alliance with the left-center government of the 1920s. Thanks to this alliance, the moderate CGT and its civil service unions would become one of the pillars of the secular republic. The group, which had hardly made a move during the 1919–20 period of crisis, obtained, as a result of the famous Chautemps memorandum, complete union freedom. In exchange, it provided highly useful support for the electoral campaign of the moderate left cartel in 1924.

These successes completely upset the equilibrium of the traditional labor movement. The role of civil service unions within the CGT became all the more considerable as the rest of the movement declined. Even from the point of view of numbers, civil servants made up the CGT's strongest groups; in 1932, the three great federations alone—Fédération générale des fonctionnaires, Syndicat national des instituteurs, and Fédération postale—comprised 35 percent of the membership of the CGT, and were at the same time the only groups which could reasonably expect to muster the support of the vast majority of the members in their respective professions. Perhaps even more important was the number of trained and responsible militants among them, capable of adapting themselves to the needs of the labor movement. Protected by the statutory rules of the civil service, these militants could easily find enough free time to accomplish the secretarial work indispensable to the survival of the movement. We find them everywhere—for example, assuming the duties of secretary to departmental and local unions. Their intellectual roles, as educators and as mediators between the world of labor and the political and administrative world, were thus essential. Even within the CGTU, their contribution was far from negligible.

The Crisis of 1936

The alliance between white-collar and blue-collar employees, forged during the strikes of 1919–20, was put to the test and definitively sealed during the great social crisis of May–June, 1936, when most of the large department stores, a half-dozen Parisian insurance companies, and innumerable commercial firms were occupied by strikers, as were the suburban factories.[11]

The hard core of the white-collar movement during this period consisted of the personnel of large department stores. Bank employees obtained an advantageous collective contract but did not go on strike, and the entire civil service stayed out of the conflict.

On the union front, the combat was directed with great vigor by the Chambre syndicale des employés de la région parisienne, which was affiliated with the reunified CGT. The CFTC and its white-collar federation was kept out of the collective negotiations for the large stores and could not take any serious part in the discussions, except for those concerning insurance companies and banks. For CGT employees, as for laborers, the years 1936–37 were years of triumph. Membership in the chambre syndicale exceeded one hundred thousand, and the Fédération nationale approached 300,000 members. In Paris itself, unionized workers in department stores numbered thirty thousand, and were more than twenty thousand in each of the other two branches—banks and insurance companies.[12] As in the rest of the union movement however, the tide quickly turned. After the failure of the general strike of November, 1938 (in which the CFTC refused to participate), membership in the Fédération dropped quickly. When war came, unionism had not yet succeeded in rooting itself deeply in the white-collar milieu.

The movement of 1936 had decisive political repercussions. During a very tense era, it firmly established the resistance of the intermediate strata to the temptation of fascism. (This had not been the case in the countries of central Europe.) Right-wing leagues, in particular the *Croix de Feu* and later its

11. On this period, one can consult the CGT pamphlet, *Les employés de commerce parisiens;* Jacques Danos and Marcel Gibelin, *Juin 1936* (Paris: Éditions ouvrières, 1952); L. Bodin and J. Touchard, *Front populaire, 1936* (Paris: Coll. Kiosque, 1961); Val Lorwin, *The French Labor Movement* (Cambridge: Harvard University Press, 1954); H. Ehrmann, *French Labor from Popular Front to Liberation* (New York: Oxford University Press, 1947).

12. From the point of view of militancy, white-collar employees were by no means second to blue-collar workers. In 1937, the strike in the commercial firm La Soie was one of the most spectacular of the entire period, the occupation of the premises lasting 155 days.

political offshoot the *Parti social français*, made fruitless efforts to organize "Syndicats professionnels" which would be opposed to the class struggle in the white-collar milieu, which these groups considered an ideal area for their activity. In the end they had little success despite, or perhaps because of, the importance of the support which they got among employers. Elsewhere, in the area of union politics, the crisis gave rise to a general regrouping of forces. Surprised at the outset, the CFTC could not deny its CGT adversaries the empirically clear monopoly that they had arrogated to themselves as representatives of the labor class. But the CFTC knew how to react shrewdly and not place itself in direct opposition to the movement (it did not attack the CGT directly except on the issue of union freedom). This very moderate tactic perfectly suited the state of mind of white-collar strikers, who basically wanted to affirm their independence, and therefore take part in the action, but did not at all want to become ideologically and socially involved in the revolutionary battle. The Christians were thus very quickly able to regain lost ground. During the same period, the labor unions came more and more under the control of Communist militants and became radically dissociated from the civil service unions, which were faithful to their socialist ties. These oppositions and internal tensions laid the groundwork for the actual division of forces, in which ideological orientations overlaid, in part, the differences in mentality and the prejudices of social categories.

On one side, blue-collar and manual workers have identified much more with the Communist party; on the other, nonmanual workers have divided between the secular and socialist tendencies predominant among civil servants and the Christian tendencies predominant among white-collar employees in the private sector.[13] The CGT union organization in the large department stores was the only one not to fall victim to the logic of this regrouping. Its success constituted the only strong tie of the white-collar group with the unified labor movement.

13. This rough distribution does not take into account the crisscrossing of tendencies and of positions. But it is worthwhile not to lose track of this general orientation on which certain reflexes are based. The remarkable developments of the CFTC within the labor context reverse, in part, the general tendency—but only in part.

But it was to pay afterwards the price of divisiveness. It lost all its influence in the national organizations and all its possibilities for action as soon as enthusiasm had waned.

On the material side, the gains achieved by white-collar employees during the years 1936–37 were generally inferior to those achieved by blue-collar workers, but the guarantees they obtained were considerable and in the end proved to be more durable than certain more obvious advantages secured by blue-collar workers. For example, differences in salary between males and females were reduced and equality assured in a number of branches. Indemnities payable in case of dismissal at last completely transformed the dependent situation of the white-collar employees.

Liberation, Nationalization, and Contemporary Movements

The period of the Liberation saw the renewal of the general alliance between white-collar and blue-collar employees, but at the same time it saw the complete transformation of the relations between employers and unions in nationalized enterprises; these developments helped to give a special character to a whole sector of the white-collar world.

The militants within both the white-collar and the civil service milieus had played a large role in the small resistance groups which everywhere laid the groundwork for the renaissance of the labor movement. They were also at the very forefront of union politics at the end of the 1940s. But, as is well known, the union enthusiasm of the Liberation period did not last long, and quickly gave way to a merciless power struggle between unionists of Communist persuasion and their various adversaries.

The split of 1947 placed most of the socialists among the civil servants, but at the price of a general collapse of the union movement. The nationalized sectors were the principal battleground. The Communists succeeded in organizing white-collar as well as blue-collar employees in the nationalized electricity and gas authority; they were less successful in their efforts with mine workers, and in banks and in insurance companies they were held at bay by the CFTC.

The combat took place at different levels, because there

were then positions to be filled on boards of directors and even at the top levels of new enterprises. A few of the union leaders became businessmen (primarily in insurance companies). Many others saw themselves offered parapolitical and para-union posts. These individual successes created a new atmosphere peculiar to the post-Liberation Parisian white-collar world. Multiple contacts existed between militants and political and economic leaders, and these contacts gave considerable influence to the movement. But the *struggle for positions* helped to completely demoralize the unions; their momentary influence was also deeply compromised by the complete absence of participation in policy-making on the part of those who were unionized. Nationalization was a complete failure on the psychological level; it was greeted with hope if not enthusiasm, but after a few years evoked nothing but indifference and cynicism.[14]

During the period of regression—or we might say the period of return to normality—of the labor movement which we have known since 1948, the union movement has once again slowly become a pressure group, with a large audience but with limited possibilities for action. In this moderate atmosphere, the civil service unions have regained the leadership. Their leadership role has, however, been paralleled and sometimes surpassed by the unions in nationalized enterprises, which were also well organized and relatively protected by public power. In any case, the greatest social disturbance of the entire period, the general strike of civil servants of August, 1953, was launched by the militants in the postal and telecommunications services.

In the private sector, leadership passed from the largest department stores to the banks and nationalized insurance companies. The two principal strikes, those of 1947 and 1957, were strikes by bank employees.

The repression of the Hungarian revolt in November, 1956, and the ascent to power of General De Gaulle weakened the

14. The results of our research provide clear testimony to this indifference in the cases of insurance companies and banks. The majority of the employees are neutral or opposed, not a single deeply committed partisan appears, and a significant minority does not even know that the enterprise is nationalized.

influence of the Communist party in labor circles only momentarily. On the other hand, the losses suffered in the white-collar and civil service milieus could not be recouped, and the general opposition between manual and nonmanual workers became even more accentuated.

White-collar and Civil Service Unions Today

Union Geography

The diversity of origins and traditions, and the accidents of history, which we have just described contributed to the development of a highly complex white-collar and civil service union movement. A brief description of its divisions and of its range of influence in the major areas where it is active is indispensable.

The Civil Service

The civil service is by far the most "unionized" sector of the French economy. Union membership is on the average about 40 percent, as compared to only 15 percent in the private sector. Moreover, the percentage for the civil service is relatively stable, while in the private sector considerable fluctuations are possible. On the other hand, civil service unions are extremely divided. They number more than four hundred relatively autonomous national organizations. To be sure, these organizations are regrouped into federations centered around three head offices (*centrales*).[15] But the ideological competition is redoubled by the competition between categories and administrations so that, on the whole, the union movement in the civil service comes out looking like a mosaic of small groups, each jealously guarding its autonomy, and in muted battle with the others. This degree of complexity, relatively rare in the French union movement, gives a very special character to unionism in the civil service.

Judging from the results of elections to collective bargaining commissions, it appears that the CGT and the CGT-FO have

15. As is well known, there also exists a federation of autonomous unions. Moreover, each of these three federations has created a general organizational arm for the entire civil service, a Cartel for the FO, a Fédération générale for the CFTC, and a Union générale for the CGT.

about comparable influence (they receive almost a third of the votes, the CFDT 20 percent and the autonomous groups 10 percent). But this overall distribution masks very different situations. The CGT has preponderant influence mostly in the labor-oriented lower categories, for example, among the postmen. They have a majority in a number of large administrations, such as the sales tax (*Contributions indirectes*) and penal administrations, which traditionally have had open recruitment.[16] In contrast, the CGT-FO specialized in the middle categories. Its members are the majority in most of the service administrations and it is the largest union in a certain number of large administrations which have a tradition of "respectability," such as the income tax and the treasury. But the FO's influence is much greater than a comparison of size of membership would tend to suggest. Its federations and its unions actually have considerable power in the functioning of the administrative machine as a result of their traditions, their relations with the managers of the civil service, and the weight of their recommendations regarding promotions. No protest movement can succeed without their accord, and once a movement is triggered there is a very good chance that the FO will have a decisive role in negotiating its resolution. Most of the time, however, this influence is quite hidden and therefore quite vulnerable to criticism. Moreover, it carries with it heavy responsibilities and deprives the leaders of the FO of much of their freedom. The more they are associated with the government of the civil service, the more they lose contact with their troops. The development of autonomous unions, whose leaders and whose militants were formed within the FO, was a serious warning to them. The growth of the CGT and of the CFDT at their expense now constitutes yet another threat.

As for the CFDT, it is altogether new in this sector. It has already organized part of the female personnel of certain administrations during the 1920s, but its great development dates from the years after the Liberation, when the violence of anticlerical tradition began to die down. It benefited from

16. There was no split in these unions, which stuck with the CGT. As a result, their leaders maintained their independence from the Communist party.

the general growth in the number of females in the civil service, and from the youth and aggressiveness of leaders and militants not as satisfied with themselves as their counterparts in the FO were.

These remarks do not apply to the teaching profession, whose members are civil servants, but which actually constitutes a completely separate sector. From the point of view of unions, the contrast is especially sharp because, as is well known, teachers are the only important professional group in France which has succeeded in maintaining unity, and whose union organization includes the vast majority of the members of the profession. The FEN (Fédération de l'Éducation nationale), with its 200,000–250,000 members, is in fact the most important union federation in France.[17] Since 1947, it has been an autonomous federation, affiliated with neither the CGT nor the FO. It enjoys great power within the profession as a result of its unity,[18] but also and above all because it exercises very tight control over promotions and is in a position to offer its members a variety of services. It is, however, a very cumbersome corporate-minded machine, whose great responsibilities make it cautious and not susceptible to change.[19]

The Large Department Stores

Since the war, the Parisian department stores, which as we have said had been the birthplace of nonmanual unionism in France, have ceased to play a role in the union movement. Their personnel now seem to be totally indifferent. Directors who are much more aware of human problems have succeeded in keeping the unions in check, while at the same time con-

17. To be sure, the FEN is face to face with a competing organization, the SGEN, which is affiliated with the CFDT. The SGEN is a minority organization which has considerable intellectual influence, but which does not yet count for much on the practical level.

18. Like the federation of civil servants, the FEN includes many different national unions, forty in fact; but it is dominated by the SNI (Syndicat national des instituteurs) which by itself comprises 60 percent of the total membership. Elementary school instructors are 90 percent unionized, while professors in secondary and technical schools are only 50 percent unionized.

19. The revolutionary events of May, 1968, have not basically altered their situation, although they may have called in question the legitimacy of the leadership of the FEN.

forming to legal obligations. "Comités d'entreprise" handle social work and vacation colonies. Committee elections and social security measures allow one to estimate the respective influences of the three central union offices, but the unions have no practical effect when it comes to decisions that affect work life. The number of dues-paying union members is very small.

By virtue of historical traditions, unionism in the large stores is still dominated by the CGT and the CGT-FO. The FO has more members in the provinces, especially in the southwest and in certain cities such as Marseilles. The CGT is stronger in Paris, but each large store is a special case.[20] The CGT has lost a lot of ground in this sector since 1956. On the other hand, the FO seems to draw from the same sector its most dynamic group of young militants.

Banks and Insurance Companies

While it is very much a minority in the large department stores, the CFTC is generally at the head of the movement in banks and in insurance companies. In this sector, which is of particular interest to us since it constitutes the framework for the research which we will present, unionism is now far more powerful than in the department stores, and more influential than in many labor sectors. Nationalization is responsible for this seemingly paradoxical situation.[21] It is really impossible for the directors of nationalized enterprises directly to oppose unions; and as for enterprises which have remained private, they have long had a tendency to align themselves with nationalized enterprises in matters of working conditions and relations with unions, for fear of attracting attention and bringing up again the problem of their status.

White-collar employees in this sector are therefore relatively well protected. They receive regular salary increases as a function of seniority; they enjoy a relatively rationalized system of promotions; and, finally, their union freedom is re-

20. Of the two largest Parisian enterprises, one, le Printemps, is dominated by the CGT, and the other, Les Galeries Lafayette, by the FO, but in neither does management seem to give much attention to the union.

21. It should be noted that in certain areas in the process of development, such as South America, bank unions have paced the entire union movement.

spected. On the other hand, salaries are often not up to par. Heads of these enterprises are actually under the direct control of the finance ministry, and employees have practically no means of making themselves heard. Their only recourse is to excite public opinion by means of a strike or, even better, a large demonstration.

The type of unionism which prevails in banks and in insurance companies is relatively similar to the type we have analyzed among civil servants: the same complex relations with heads of the enterprise, the same stratification, the same difficulties of communication. But certain characteristic traits do exist. In the first place, the size of the membership is less, about 30 percent of the total personnel; in the second place, the differences between enterprises are considerable.[22] In the third place, supervisory and middle-management strata are in general much less active in unions than their counterparts at the same level in the civil service; the general hierarchical system accentuates the split between executives and their subordinates, and does not favor the intermediate levels as much; finally, quarrels between unions constitute a much greater handicap for the overall movement, this competition having developed before unionism was able to attain a position of strength.

In France as a whole, the CFDT unions are by far the most powerful. But the CGT unions are sometimes on top in Paris, and the FO unions are in the majority in certain enterprises and in such sectors as the stock market and social security.[23]

22. Later we will see that in our sample of six insurance companies, three have a union membership of less than 20 percent, and the other three have 40 percent to 50 percent. In this respect, there seems to be no difference between private and nationalized companies.

23. Since 1962, the CFDT has been organized, as the CGT and the CGT-FO have been for some time, around a national federation consisting of major branches such as banks, insurance companies, social security, and a certain number of minor branches such as publishing, journalism, notaries, export-import, and retail business. In the various industries, white-collar employees henceforth belong to the same unions as blue-collar employees. The CFDT's resistance to this regrouping, which lasted until 1962, was highly characteristic of white-collar employees' attachment to the traditional barrier between social groups. This attachment has still today far from disappeared and was for a long time the driving force in the old CFTC federation of white-collar employees which comprised all white-collar employees in all industries.

The Operation of White-collar and Civil Service Unions

Like nonmanual unions, French white-collar and civil service unions are forever affected by the same operational difficulties: pluralism, centralization, fund-raising problems, and the preponderant importance of voluntary militants for the survival of the organization.

Pluralism constitutes one of the most irritating difficulties in French union life. Nowhere is there to be found a factory, an administration, or even an office, where the many different union tendencies are not represented. One organization's success in a particular sector in no way constitutes, for the other organizations, a reason to leave responsibility for that sector to that organization; rather, it is an invitation to enter into competition with that organization. If an organization is not strong enough in a particular sector, it will at least maintain one or two correspondents, and a half dozen members will suffice to officially constitute a section. Elections, which have for a long time been politicized, help lend importance to political choices concerning even such matters as place of work, and thus create divisions among personnel.

These divisions and the competition which they bring with them are a trying burden for union action. They make for demagogy and irresponsibility. This problem seems to be even more particularly acute in the white-collar milieu, where there is more distrust and the cultural and political levels are higher on the average. Save in the exceptional case of the FEN, white-collar employees and lower civil servants have a tendency to consider union militants as groups of competing advocates who are at their disposal any time they have a problem. They refuse to identify with their cause, and indifferently make use of one group or the other, and of one group against the other.

Centralization seems likewise to be even more highly developed among white-collar employees, as a result of the complete domination of the Paris region in their areas of activity.

White-collar employees in banks and insurance companies who had formed a separate federation within the CFTC in 1950 and 1954 in order to protest against this particularism once again reunited within the new federation when it agreed to give up the members it had in the industrial sectors.

All the unions are directed from Paris by "permanents" living in Paris. In the provinces, there are no more than a few such permanent full-time staff members, and no provincial center purports to have, as do centers for certain industrial sectors, any special influence.

The poverty of French union organizations is proverbial. In this respect, white-collar employees, blue-collar employees, and civil servants are in the same boat. The number of permanent full-time staff members is extremely small. One lone staffer serves several thousand members, who in turn never constitute more than a third of the total employed in the sector covered. In the United States the ratio is one staff member to every seven hundred union members, and in England and in northwestern Europe one to two thousand or three thousand members, who in turn constitute at least 50 percent of the total work force.[24]

The situation is a little better in the civil service, because of the facilities which the administration makes available for union work. From this point of view, which is in practical terms of capital importance, civil service unions are highly favored, and the white-collar milieu is generally treated far better than the blue-collar milieu.[25] But this situation introduces deep psychological differences. Union work is really accomplished in a completely different atmosphere in the civil service milieu and even in the white-collar milieu. Whatever may be the ideologies professed, more intimate collaboration exists between management and the unions. Time spent on union work calls for a minimum of tolerance on the part of bosses. White-collar and civil service unionism thus appears to the observer to be far more involved in collaboration with management, far more sensitive to the actual situation, in a word far less intransigent and revolutionary.[26]

24. In relation to the number of workers rather than to the number of union members, permanent full-time staff members are thus fifteen times more numerous in the United States and four times more numerous in England. On this subject see: Seymour M. Lipset, The First New Nation (New York: Basic Books, 1963), pp. 170–203.

25. In the civil service, part-time workers are usually officially recognized in determining union representation.

26. This atmosphere is very noticeable in the companies we have studied.

Like blue-collar unionism, however, white-collar and civil service unionism suffers from the excessive importance of voluntary militants, whose rigid ideological motivations make it difficult for the organization to adapt itself flexibly to the real problems at hand. Actually, white-collar militants are more susceptible to other motivations; unionism may offer them direct or indirect chances for promotion. But the existence of such perspectives hardly diminishes ideological pressure, and creates on the other hand a climate of distrust and suspicion among both adherents of the movement and nonunion members. Only practical on-the-job responsibilities may make it possible to break the vicious circle. But these are as nonexistent in the office as they are in the workshop.

Means of Action

In France union activity among white-collar employees and civil servants presents two contrary aspects: on the one hand, regular and official activities involving contacts and negotiations with employers and with public authorities; on the other hand, unpredictable explosions, which bring into question established human relationships and force a certain amount of change. Unions make use of these explosions, which are the main source of their power, but they can neither mobilize the popular force which is indispensable to them nor even foresee its reactions; in any case, they cannot take advantage of it in their negotiations except in a very indirect way.

In the nonmanual sector, the official activity is generally more highly developed and more complex, while popular explosions are rarer, more disciplined, and can be controlled more easily. Demonstrations and one-day actions, which partake of both styles at the same time, have gained considerable importance at least in the civil service and, to a lesser degree, in banks and insurance companies.

The official activity exists at different levels, but is especially well developed at the highest national level. Union leaders are obliged to spend the greatest part of their time in representative activities, on commissions and on councils. This is a heavy burden for them, but one to which they must give priority, since these activities allow them to stay well informed and to make maximum use of their negotiating powers.

The actual negotiations are very deceptive. In the non-manual area, the unions are in a weak position, except when the state is involved, but it is precisely in this case that salaries are most inadequate.[27] This paradox may be explained by the complexity of the union process and by the often forgotten fact that, while the highest and lowest categories in the civil service are certainly badly paid, the intermediate categories are in an advantageous position compared to those in the private sector, at least when it comes to the definition of occupational positions. The unions are powerful, but only in a negative and conservative sense. They prevent the question of the advantages of status and the guarantees enjoyed by civil servants from coming up, but they cannot easily help their members to take part in the new opportunities offered by the expansion of the economy.

White-collar employees in banks and in insurance companies are in fundamentally the same situation. In these areas, management can easily pretend that the barriers to salary increases and to reorganization of the occupational structure come from the state. A general climate of economic and social stagnation has been established here from which it is difficult to break out.

General Perspectives

As we have already noted, if only the general factors which govern the evolution of techniques and of occupations were at issue, there should be no differences between the reactions of white-collar employees in different countries. In particular, they should show the same disposition to become involved in union action, and do so in the same manner. Yet this is by no means the case. If we compare the actual union behavior of French, English, and American white-collar employees, the range of differences is surprising.

The brief analysis which we have just presented brings out the following characteristics in particular.

27. A second paradox should be noted. In this domain, the only one where there can be no collective contract because the sovereign state can make decisions only in a unilateral manner, one finds in the end more direct negotiations between employers and employees than in the sectors where this direct mode of industrial relations is recommended by legislators.

1. White-collar and civil service unions are in France part and parcel of the union movement. They have never, as in Germany, constituted separate unions, and they have long ago resolved their problems of allegiance. In moments of crisis, they have always come down on the side of "workers."

2. They have always been directed from Paris and in a Parisian perspective, thus partaking of the French complex about centralization and accentuating the white-collar and civil service milieu's fascination with bourgeois culture.

3. There has always been a profound split between unions in the public sector and unions in the private sector, not only in the political sphere, but also in the area of habits and behavior patterns. The creation of an intermediate category, the nationalized sector, resulted in a noticeable rapprochement, while the ideological motivations of the basic cleavages tended to decrease.

4. The modes of action of white-collar and civil service unions are, like those of the other French unions, unpredictable and sometimes incoherent. Great waves of short-lived enthusiasm may engulf the entire milieu, only to be followed by long periods of lethargy. No conscious policy can develop, and everything happens by improvisation.

5. In France, white-collar and civil service unions do not have substantial power, but neither are they, as in England or in America, the least-developed sector of the union movement. They can certainly not be characterized as laggard—quite the contrary—and the civil service is actually the only solid bastion of French unionism.

6. Like all other workers, white-collar and civil service employees are divided in union matters by ideological lines of cleavage, but these lines of cleavage mask deeper and more confusing distinctions between hierarchical and functionally separated social groups; and within the general theoretical unity to which everyone subscribes, one can rediscover differences which testify to the persistence of class barriers.

The origin of such peculiarities seems to us to call for some explanations, given the fact that the social origins of white-collar employees are not very different from one country to another.

We believe that these differences are essentially due to the importance of the human relations which are a necessary part of office jobs. As we have already emphasized, office jobs, in contrast to blue-collar occupations which depend quite narrowly on necessary technical arrangements, depend much more on national cultural factors. Every Western society has elaborated its own specific organizational models for solving its management problems; despite the development of common techniques, office activities remain much more different than technical activities. The social status and the possibilities for action of office workers can be completely different depending on where they fit into these models.

In Germany for example, where social distances remain quite pronounced, and where the weight of authority has traditionally been heavier than in Anglo-Saxon countries, and more easily accepted than in Latin countries, the poor communication between social categories has allowed white collar employees to retain their privileges more easily. But the German *Angestellte* himself suffered from this lack of communication, and quite naturally sought to organize for collective action. His union action had to be conservatively oriented in the social and political area, however, because of the persistence of his privileges and because of his psychological solidarity with those in authority.[28]

In England, and even more in America, where manual workers saw their right to be heard by their bosses recognized very early, intermediate groups such as white-collar employees have not been accorded much attention by the upper classes and have never solidified into a conscious category. They have never had any social prestige, or any particular political significance; their unions have never been separate unions and have always followed in the wake of labor unions.[29] The labor move-

28. It would be worth the effort, from the point of view of the sociology of knowledge, to analyze the German intelligentsia's peculiar passion for the problem of white-collar employees; this passion seems to be related to factors peculiar to German society. The same phenomenon, however, reappears in Poland where a whole series of works have been devoted to it by Professor Szepansky and his students. On this subject, see Jolanta Kulpinska, "la Sociologie industrielle en Pologne," *Sociologie du Travail* 5, no. 1 (January 1963).

29. Perhaps this explains the reluctance of a man like David Lockwood to abandon the field of rational economic process. The problem of social privilege is not as apparent in England.

ment, on the other hand, is sufficiently respectable for white-collar employees to belong to it, and though they often represent the voice of moderation in the movement, their collective politico-social action, when exercised, is oriented to the left.[30]

In France, social distance has never been as great as in Germany, and white-collar employees have never organized themselves into separate groups. But communication between social categories has remained difficult; there can be no negotiation without long and frustrating detours, and without state intervention. This situation gives a certain advantage to white-collar employees and to civil servants, who are as a result given better "consideration." In a social collectivity where communication is poor, individuals and groups who communicate well are much more highly valued than they would be in a collectivity where human relations are easier. These two divergent factors explain why white-collar unions are, in France, comparatively more vigorous than their American and English counterparts are, and why, on the other hand, they are not separated from the rest of the labor movement as their German counterparts were, and to some extent still are. French white-collar and civil service employees who, more than in Germany, lost the prestige related to social distance and the economic privilege which tends to go along with it, nonetheless retained a role much superior to that of English "blackcoated" workers. This situation also makes it understandable why French white-collar employees and civil servants have always leaned to the left in the political sphere, while their German colleagues traditionally remained more susceptible to right-wing and nationalist propaganda. Finally, in this context, civil servants have the greatest natural advantage, their success deriving from the difficult balance between protest and neutrality which proximity to the organs of state has allowed them to work out.[31]

30. This collective action occurs, in fact, only in England, where it has moreover been much less moderate since the end of the last war. The differences between the United States and England, in this respect as in many others, are great. We will be excused for not detailing them in such a brief discussion as this.

31. One might object that civil servants are not very well paid, but this is the case in all Western countries. Besides, French civil

In France, the peculiar strategy of communications and negotiations between social groups has given rise to one last totally original characteristic, which our analysis of the union movement has brought to light, and which now bears some consideration; namely, the existence of a tremendous gulf between the private sector and the public sector. Everywhere in the Western world one finds differences and contrasts between these two sectors. But nowhere has this characteristic become nearly as marked as in France. What is involved, it seems to us, is not merely superficial group solidarity, but two opposing systems of cultural participation and social integration which coexist in France, one a paternalistic type prevalent among white-collar employees in the private sector, the other an egalitarian type enjoyed by civil servants. Each of the two types naturally falls within the general model of communications which we have described. But between them lies a gulf which must be considered one of the essential facts of social and political life in France. To the fundamental psychological situation which we outlined in the last chapter, there correspond two series of divergent roles and two images of the world, opposed to each other in certain respects. These roles and these images are built up around the peculiarities of each of the systems of promotion, one based on the principle of impersonal and egalitarian competition and on anticlericalism, the other on networks of paternalistic recommendations and on the right-thinking (*bien pensant*) conformity.

We have come a long way from the system of patronage which, only fifty years ago, governed the allocation of many jobs in the private sector. The loyalty demanded by today's employer cannot be compared to the veritable moral allegiance required by his predecessors. But personnel departments continue to search, consciously or unconsciously, for candidates who come closest to the "respectable" image they have of the

---

servants enjoy substantial advantages of various sorts, in particular, considerable independence. If the desire to defend their status has generally taken precedence over pecuniary demands, it should not be forgotten that the middle categories, which comprise a large part of the civil service, especially among men, receive very favorable treatment after a certain level of seniority is reached. Finally, the weight carried by civil service and teachers' organizations in French political and social life is unparalleled anywhere else in the world.

good office worker or the good salesgirl. Many of them continue to worry about a candidate's family and to avoid those who seem to come from a working class milieu.[32] Selection and promotion still depend greatly on recommendations, on appearance, and on external bearing. Public administration ignores these subtle pressures that impose conformity, but social barriers have nevertheless not yet vanished there either. The difference between the two sectors does not lie in the absence of stratification, but in the fact that the values which legitimate stratification are different in each.

The existence of this contrast, however superficial it may seem, has profound implications for the possibility of union development as well as for political reorganization. Despite the rapprochement and the interpenetration which we have witnessed since the Liberation, the contrast in mentality and clientele remains one of the essential bases for union politics, even for French politics as a whole.

32. Until a few years ago, this was still the practice in one large Parisian department store.

PART TWO
The World of Work and the Company

4 The Population Studied and Research Procedures

Our reasoning will be based on facts drawn from research we carried out in 1957 on six Parisian insurance companies.

We have no intention of presenting a detailed description of the insurance company environment. Bringing out its peculiarities and comparing them to those of other milieus interests us less than understanding how, within a sector that is quite characteristic of the world of office workers, individuals adapt to their given conditions and to the situation; how they view these situations and, in reacting to them, give them structure and form.

Certain general points of information are, however, necessary in order to pinpoint for the reader the characteristics of the milieu within which we will operate, and the research procedures which we have followed. The value and the significance of the data which we have collected depend just as much on the characteristics of the population as on our methods.

The Insurance Company Milieu

Sixty thousand persons were then employed directly or indirectly in the insurance profession in France. This number, steadily on the rise since the Liberation, includes door-to-door salesmen, agents, brokers and their employees, in addition to employees in central offices. Our research covers only this last group, which makes up less than half of the total.

Jobs in head offices are one of the best examples of modern administrative work: activities there are very abstract and have already been rationalized to a great extent, because semiautomatic production circuits have been installed; on the other hand, white-collar employees are organized into highly structured functional units, which are a far cry from the traditional small service enterprises customary in the nineteenth century.

While agents and brokers are scattered all over France, the vast majority of employees in head offices work in Paris within a narrowly circumscribed area, essentially the ninth arrondissement. The seven companies studied were all localized in this business quarter, close to the main boulevards. All those interviewed were thus subject to the influences of the same metropolitan environment.

Demographic Characteristics

The six companies on which the research proper was based represent three thousand persons out of the twenty thousand white-collar employees in Parisian head offices. The 358 subjects interviewed (301 white-collar employees and 57 supervisors) are not exactly representative of all insurance company employees, or even of the subgroup formed by these six companies. They were not chosen by direct random lottery; instead, we took a stratified sample in which the major job categories are underrepresented and the minor categories overrepresented, in order to allow for more precise comparisons. As far as all the major variables which interest us are concerned, however, the employees interviewed have exactly the same characteristics as the collectivity of their Parisian colleagues, and we may therefore consider them quite representative of this collectivity.

Males, for example, make up 48 percent of the sample, which was in 1957 the mean percentage for the entire profession. The population involved is also relatively young; half the subjects are less than thirty years old and only 23 percent are over forty-five. Their family situation corresponds to this age distribution: the number of bachelors is considerable (33 percent); only 42 percent have children; the only notable fact in this regard is that at any given age of parents, families have less children than the national average.

The 57 supervisors we interviewed are naturally older (65 percent of them are over forty-five years old). The vast majority are males (77 percent) and, though their number of grown children is less than average, their family responsibilities are nonetheless heavier than those of their employees.

Geographic and Social Origin

Most insurance company employees are from Paris. More than half the subjects interviewed were born within the city limits, or in the suburbs; only a quarter of them, however, are from old-time Parisian families. Analogous percentages are found in all similar enterprises and in particular in banks.[1] This geographic origin contrasts sharply with that of lower civil servants in Paris, among whom less than a quarter are Parisian.[2]

Another contrast: While the civil service does the vast majority of its recruitment in the central and in the southwest areas, insurance company employees from the provinces come by and large from the northern half of France, in particular from the departments of the North (20 percent) and the West (25 percent).

Social origin is difficult to establish, because of the imprecise terms generally used by subjects to describe the professions of their parents.[3] The general picture that emerges from their responses is nevertheless precise enough: 20 percent of the parents of subjects interviewed had professions of more or less bourgeois standing (lower liberal professions, small entrepreneurs, lower and middle executives); 11 percent of the parents were shopkeepers, 25 percent white-collar employees or lower civil servants, 9 percent had one white-collar parent and one blue-collar parent, 30 percent were blue-collar workers

1. A survey made in 1955 and the study conducted in 1959 gave the same results.

2. See Michel Crozier, *Petits fonctionnaires au travail* (Paris: C.N.R.S., 1956), especially p. 17.

3. Precision on this point is practically impossible when the problem of social origin is not the primary focus of interest in a study.

and only 4 percent were farmers. As will be noted, the percentage of white-collar employees with blue-collar origins is rather high; almost 40 percent had at least one blue-collar parent. But this assertion must be refined, since those parents were rarely blue-collar workers in a large industry. A precise analysis of the hundred interviewees in our preparatory study revealed that the blue-collar professions related in this way to the white-collar milieu are almost exclusively artisan-type professions (plumber, cabinetmaker, sanitary supervisor, linotypist, carpenter), or professions involving responsibility (straw boss, foreman).[4]

The educational differences which we have been able to establish repeat almost exactly those which we have just presented in examining the parents' professions. Twenty percent of our interviewees have had a secondary education (7 percent have higher education),[5] one-third have the intermediary high-school certificate or have received equivalent education, and 40 percent have not gone beyond a primary school certificate.

Supervisors have almost exactly the same education and the same social origin as employees. On the other hand, marked differences between the two groups appear when one compares the social milieu within which their members actually develop. Supervisors never have working class wives[6] and their wives work much more rarely. Above all, they claim to have many more friends, and these friends are from a higher social stratum.[7]

4. It is remarkable that our results from this preliminary study are almost identical with those derived from the full-scale study: 25 percent of the subjects could be classified as belonging to a bourgeois or petit-bourgeois milieu, 30 percent as white-collar—civil servant, 40 percent as blue-collar or general laborer, and 5 percent as peasants.

5. Exclusively among qualified clerks, who sometimes have a law degree.

6. Among married male supervisors, 69 percent of the wives are housewives; 26 percent are white-collar employees or civil servants, and 5 percent are supervisors. Among married male white-collar employees, these percentages are 31 percent, 48 percent, and 4 percent respectively. Moreover, 9 percent of these white-collar employees have wives who are blue-collar workers; this percentage is, on the other hand, much higher among women, who, in 20 percent of the cases, have a blue-collar husband.

7. Forty-five percent of them have at least one friend in a liberal profession or at a higher level, and 30 percent have one friend at a middle level—a teacher or equivalent profession. The corresponding

Professional Characteristics

Our interviewees distribute professionally as follows: Clerks (*employés aux écritures*), 27 percent; claims adjusters (*rédacteurs des services "sinistres"*), 13 percent; policy writers (*rédacteurs des services "production"*) 20 percent; archivists and file clerks, 12 percent, and keypunchers, 9 percent. These six categories effectively constitute the essential job categories of the profession. But we have eliminated all ancillary categories and have greatly overrepresented the two categories of policy writers and archivists, mostly at the expense of clerks.

This is a population which, despite its low age, has relatively high seniority in the company, since more than half of the personnel have more than six years of seniority, and only 9 percent have less than one year.

Hierarchically, only 65 percent of our interviewees are classified as office workers in the technical sense of the term; the others are classified as supervisory personnel *(agents de maîtrise)*, but this title does not imply any supervisory responsibility, and we have considered them for the purposes of our research as office workers in point of fact. As for the supervisors we interviewed, they have the rank of submanager, associate-manager, or department manager.

Finally, salaries of the subjects interviewed, like those of the majority of their colleagues, are relatively low. Moreover, notable differences exist between categories. In our sample, the range of remunerations was as follows (in 1957): 29 percent of the subjects earned less than 35,000 francs (old francs, naturally) per month; 26 percent earned from 35,000 to 40,000 francs; 31 percent from 40,000 to 55,000; and only 12 percent more than 55,000. Supervisors' salaries ranged between 50,000 and 120,000.[8]

---

percentages among white-collar employees are only 22 percent and 17 percent respectively.

8. Differences between companies, while not negligible when it comes to white-collar employees, are quite substantial when it comes to supervisors. In 1970 the differences would range from 2,000 to 5,000 new francs, or from $400 to $1000.

Research Procedures

The companies that comprised our research sample were chosen with the help of the leaders of the profession (Fédération des sociétés d'assurance and Comité d'action pour la productivité dans l'assurance). But our choice naturally depended more on the reception accorded to us by the presidents and directors of insurance companies than it did on theoretical considerations. We were nevertheless able to put together a sample of large and middle-sized companies that were considered quite representative of the profession as a whole. It included four nationalized companies and two private companies, two fire insurance companies, one life insurance company, one liability insurance company, and two specializing in both fire and liability insurance. Number of employees ranged from two hundred in the smallest company to more than eight hundred in the largest. Not represented in our sample were only the very large enterprises (the three or four companies that employed more than a thousand persons)[9] and the many small companies employing less than a hundred persons.

The full-scale study was preceded by a long preparatory study carried out over a period of several months in only one company, which opened the way for a very thorough follow-up.[10] The standardized questionnaire which was used in the six companies in the full-scale study was developed on the basis of the results of the preliminary study.

The full-scale study lasted six months. It involved neither staggered nor extended periods of observation. But, before proceeding to the interviews, we had long conversations with representatives of management, and with representatives of all

9. Actually, quite a large number of groups of affiliated companies that carry the same name employ more than a thousand persons, but they are not integrated, and each company in the group, at least from our point of view, has a completely autonomous existence. Mergers have changed this picture in the late sixties and now the very large companies have become the dominant factor. Five out of the six companies studied are now part of bigger concerns.

10. See Michel Crozier and Pierre Guetta, *Une organisation administrative au travail,* mimeographed (Paris: I.S.S.T., 1957).

the unions. In almost every company, under the aegis of the Comité d'entreprise,[11] we organized meetings to explain the objectives and the modalities of the study. The interviewees, fifty per company, were not chosen at random; rather we chose, in agreement with management and with the unions, and on their advice, forty work groups, six per company, representing the six major professional categories, and we interviewed all the members of these forty groups and their immediate bosses. Representatives of the Comité, usually one union, one management accompanied us in each company at the beginning of the interview period and participated in the discussions we organized with each of the groups, in order to explain what we were about to do and to help in answering questions. Thanks to this long and thorough preparation, and to the generous help readily offered to us by the unions, we were extremely well-received everywhere and our refusal rate was no more than 6 percent to 7 percent.

The experience acquired during the preliminary study allowed us to develop extremely precise questionnaires, which presented those interviewed with well-defined choices. The interviews were nevertheless conducted orally. They ran about an hour and a quarter on the average, and the complete interview cycle took about two weeks per company.[12] The interview with supervisors, which could not be prepared in the same way during the preparatory study, involved a rather large number of open-ended questions and raised some problems of coding.[13]

Our analysis will be based exclusively on the present study, but we will refer frequently to three other parallel studies which we conducted before and after this one. The results of one of these studies, conducted in 1954 and relating to a public administration, have already been published.[14] The other two,

11. The French Comités d'entreprise are statutory committees grouping representatives of workers and management on a parity basis.

12. Preparation for each company took about the same amount of time.

13. Data processing was accomplished by means of punched cards. The Guttman scales which we used were prepared by hand using a reduced sample, but the subjects were later classified mechanically by the machines.

14. See n. 2 above.

conducted in 1958–59 and in 1960, one a study of the administrative departments of a large nationalized bank and the other concerning a Parisian ministry, have so far been the subject of only research reports. These references will allow us to make certain comparisons, and to gain some perspective on the insurance company environment.

5 Adaptation to Work

The Problem

The study of a social group which defines itself above all by the type of work its members perform must begin with an attempt to understand the nature of this work and the manner in which those who perform it experience the role they have chosen or which has been imposed upon them. Any theory that aims to explain the relations between classes or social categories is really based on the following postulate. There is a very close relationship between the political and social game as played by each group and the material or affective common interests which develop among the members of each group from their work situation or, at the very least, from the distortions and prejudices which that situation creates among them.

In any case, it is through work, and because of the roles played in work, that the particular identity and personality of a social category may be formed. To be sure, we subscribe to the idea that the individual's work counts less than his recognized position in society. But the rewards and the consideration he receives do not depend exclusively on the social system. As great as the part played by social prejudices and economic exploitation may be, the differences in treatment between various hierarchical and functional categories correspond, to a large extent, to a hierarchy of functions and responsibilities, well tested and accepted as necessary by those subject to it.

In order to understand the social personality of the white-collar employee and of the civil servant, it is thus indispensable to first study his personality at work. Even if, after study, the contrasts and contradictions which we will uncover do not turn out to really condition his personality outside of work, they will prove to be indispensable interpretive elements.

The natural development of relationships between researchers and those studied reproduces quite exactly this general approach to research on socio-professional groups. It really seems that the conditions and modalities of work, the role it implies, and above all the interest taken in it and the satisfaction derived from it, constitute a sort of obligatory point of departure. The interviewee himself never fails to be surprised that such questions are not asked of him. His social life extends beyond the world of the company but it is through his work experience that his relationship with the world takes on its immediate and easily expressible public significance.

All the research we have carried out, both in insurance companies and in banks, or in public administrations, has conformed naturally to this model, and it seems to us that this logical analysis of the communication between researcher and research subject, conducted at the actual place of work, allowed us to establish more natural and comprehensive relationships with our interlocutors.

But, if work and the work experience constitute a privileged domain of interpersonal communication which is particularly important to those interviewed, it is far from easy to interpret the materials drawn from it. For man is influenced by his environment, not only in the substance of his judgments, but also in the very categories he uses in judging. His frames of reference and his aspirations also condition the significance he attaches to questions asked of him. If we pose a question concerning the possibilities for initiative at work to a bookkeeper and to a ministerial staff member, we must be aware that the meaning of their responses is not the same; what the bookkeeper calls initiative would, for the ministerial person, be no more than routine application of operational procedures.

Must one then give up the attempt to make comparisons? We do not think so. When a sociologist raises questions about satisfaction, he is not trying to learn whether "the soup is good"; he is trying to understand how the response expresses the subject's relation to society, the reality of his role in society.

If, however, we adopt such a relativistic viewpoint, the interpretation of responses to a questionnaire is no longer as simple as we might have thought when we attempted to apply opinion studies in the company domain. It is not really sufficient, in this case, to accumulate rough statistical facts; one must also attempt to understand the dynamics of human relations which express themselves through the responses. To accomplish this, the usual sociological analysis by correlations which assume a homogeneous universe must be completed by a comparison of objective reality to images of that reality, or rather to the whole series of contradictory images of the same reality which subjects present to us as a function of their different roles and situations.

The Nature of the Tasks

Office work is in practice much more diverse than it appears to be from the outside. The job performed by a bookkeeper in charge of entering credits and debits for clients' orders is very different from that of a claims adjuster who must determine the basis for settlement of a claim, or that of an employee with all the coupon-clipping operations for policies which clients have placed in the hands of a bank.

The administrative departments of insurance companies, which were the subject of our research, provide excellent examples in this respect. They possessed at that time two major characteristics which are rarely as distinct in other professions: on the one hand diversity of occupations and of qualifications and, on the other, the existence of a universally accepted social order which assigns to each category a definite place in the continuum of rank and prestige. We will describe one by one the functions of the six major occupational categories which constituted the basis for our sample, placing particular emphasis on the problems of adaptation which they seem to raise a priori for personnel.

File Clerks

File clerks were at the bottom of the social scale in insurance companies. But their position was, more often than that of their colleagues, a transitory one, and the somewhat peculiar nature of their tasks had, besides many inconveniences, certain advantages.

To begin with, the file clerk does his job standing up. While all others are seated side by side, under the eye of a supervisor, in windowed offices with connecting doors, the file clerks stays on his feet and moves about. Therein lies, in a certain sense, his glory, but also his servitude.

For his work is tiring. Over the course of a year he will shift nearly five hundred thousand dossiers. If he works in the archives, in the basement, he must constantly answer the telephone. A mistaken reference or a misfiled dossier inevitably leads to a lot of searching, often under pressure. If he is assigned to do research for the departments, he will have to run from one department to the other, go up and down the five stories of the building in order to find the mislaid dossier. Most of the interviewees emphasize the arduous physical demands of the work. One of them, for example, told us with somewhat bitter humor: "We are always on our feet; when we had a twenty-four hour strike, it gave us a rest."

Many other factors contribute to giving this group its particular physiognomy. Its salaries are the lowest. The social origin of its members is more homogeneous and more "of the common people" than those of other categories. Most file clerks are young and consider other employees "old fogies." Finally, their geographical situation isolates them. The archives are generally located in the basement or at least on a separate floor. Communication is by telephone or by a sort of dumbwaiter. It is a closed world. But, within that world, file clerks enjoy a certain amont of autonomy. Each file clerk is assigned an area for filing; within that area the battle against disorder is his alone. He must have a good memory, and a good sense of organization. Certain file clerks develop into veritable filing virtuosos, admired by those who use them. Often they have a sense of great responsibility. "The archives," says one, "are the brains of an insurance company."

Meanwhile, the isolated and mechanical aspect of their work ("You are no more than a cog"), its elementary nature compared to the more intellectual job of those involved in paper work, and finally the total dependence on other departments, are painful things for the "filer-archivist." For the "filer-researcher," the situation is a little more satisfying. Low salary, low status, fatigue, heteronomy—all apply to his case as well. But his world is more open. He circulates from department to department, learns something in each, establishes relationships, and acquires an understanding of the overall operation of the company which the archivist can never get. Finally, he has many more opportunities to use his intelligence and much more of a chance for promotion. If he is capable and is favorably noticed, he may one day get to handle policies.

By the very nature of their function, filers are the most dependent of all employees. That explains why among them one finds the strongest demands for autonomy. One of the questions we posed during our preliminary study was: "Do you believe that employees can by themselves develop the best way of accomplishing their work?" Filers responded "Yes" twice as often as clerks and ten times as often as policy men.

Keypunchers

We move now from an exclusively masculine occupation to an exclusively feminine occupation, whose status is hardly any higher, but whose characteristics are totally different. Keypunching is physically just as demanding and even more routine than filing. But it is conditioned not by individual demands made in an atmosphere of urgency, but by the rules of productivity. The file clerk is on call; he must always be available. In contrast, keypunchers have a regular job to perform which does not imply personal subordination. In relation to file clerks, they have about the same position as semiskilled machine operators in relation to laborers.

The constraint imposed upon them is above all that of productivity. This constraint is directly concretized in the modalities of their salaries. In general, keypunchers work in small groups. Of the departments we studied, the largest comprised about twenty persons. Their small number, their special skill, and the fact that they are often trained on the outside by manufacturers of statistical machines, gives them a place apart in the company. Their occupation is extremely well defined, being the same in all professions and in all companies. Moreover, the demand for their particular qualification is very high in other businesses. For all these reasons, keypunchers are much less subject than their coworkers to the pressure of the habits and norms of the company where they work. Their frame of reference is different and the atmosphere within their group shows it. They are at one and the same time more demanding and more detached—in a word, freer. Finally, the relationship they maintain with their company is essentially a financial one, with productivity exactly measured on the one side, and premium pay on the other.

Typists

Like the work of a keypuncher, the work of a typist is in some ways analogous to that of a machine operator. All of these occupations are professions in only a limited sense of the term; manual and mechanical, they require experience, and the hierarchy "office machine operator, typist, stenographer-typist" is directly related to the machine which the employee operates. With the typist, however, we get into the area of language, that is, into an area where social and cultural differences begin to play a role. Adaptability and powers of comprehension and communication are of greater importance. Nevertheless, this special situation tends to disappear as, on the one hand, the ability to communicate and to adapt to a bourgeois style of reasoning become more widespread and, on the other hand, typists' jobs themselves become more standardized.

Insurance is one of the professions which has developed farthest along these lines. Except for a small minority of secretaries, typists are pretty much separated from other employees, and their work, which is no longer directly coupled with that of other departments, can be organized on a completely independent basis. At the same time, the present day general use of dictating machines has completely separated stenographer-typists from those who used to give them dictation. On the other hand, for most of these employees, this mechanization practically does away with the qualification of stenographer, without replacing it with any other, because the use of dictating machines, though requiring a sometimes difficult adjustment, is in fact within everyone's reach. Finally, the work is now much more clearly defined, with norms and definite standards of productivity to be met.

Insurance company typists work on policies, riders, receipts, bookkeeping, and mail. These production jobs (policies, riders, receipts) and bookkeeping jobs each require a certain type of experience which consists mostly of becoming familiar with certain models which are then applicable to almost all cases. Replying to mail is also handled by means of dictating machines, except for certain really complicated affairs where a department head may call for a stenographer; nevertheless, correspondence work has the greatest variety to it, and those assigned to it are generally better typists who have had more education and are prouder of their qualifications.

Within the company, typists constitute a relatively isolated group which no longer has any direct relationship with clerks or with file clerks, and less and less of a relationship with policy writers and claims adjusters.[1] Yet they do not have, as do keypunchers, a well-defined external frame of reference and, in fact, depend much more directly on the company within which they have obtained their experience, and where they have generally become quite narrowly specialized.

Clerks

Clerks form the largest group, both in banks and in insurance companies. They also constitute the most heterogeneous group. Actually, the basis for this group is not a common function as among file clerks, or a common technique, as among keypunchers or typists. It would seem at first glance that the traditional appellation *employés aux écritures* ("clerks") is a catchall designed to encompass a large variety of jobs, which would be difficult to distinguish and for which the use of cate-

1. This makes it understandable why typists rarely consider themselves white-collar employees, have no desire for a different position, and have a tendency to adopt as their frame of reference either the "worker" milieu or the "intellectual" milieu (the policy men's milieu is, in fact, the only one with which they have contact).

gories and of coefficients (not counting, in insurance companies, the titles of overseers) would introduce sufficient differentiations. More than anything, being a clerk signifies being clearly defined as neither this nor that, but rather as belonging to a mass of multifaceted personnel who have developed a more or less large number of bureaucratic skills which are called for according to the rhythm of work and needs.

The use of a common appellation nevertheless corresponds to a sociological reality. Both in their origin (they have the most white-collar and civil service parents), and in their demographic behavior (marriage within the group and birth control), clerks are the ones who come closest to the traditional idea of office worker. Within the organization itself, located at an equal distance from file clerks with "proletarian" tendencies and claims adjusters and policy writers with "bourgeois" tendencies, clerks constitute, one might say, a sort of middle class within the middle class. In insurance, they are the essential element, the solid base of the system, not only because of their numerical predominance, but also because of their stability. For it is among them that one finds those with greatest seniority; policy writers and claims adjusters change, clerks remain.

When one examines the role clerks play, one is struck above all by the great diversity of their functions. Each detail is simple, but the articulation of the whole is extremely complex, so that only a rare few have an overall grasp of the general process. Fundamentally, the operations involved are counting, collating, noting, checking, inscribing, recopying, and filling out forms, stub-books, and ledgers.[2]

Not only are the tasks diverse, they are also multiple. Rarely does an individual, over the course of a year, have only one function. Most employees interviewed were involved in several

2. Here are the activities of the forty clerks interviewed, as disclosed by responses during the preliminary study (in order of frequency of operations): verification work (receipts, riders, policies, dossiers, memoranda, agent accounts, and the like); assorted filing; calculation of rates, premiums, and commissions; establishing or analyzing various facts and clients' situations; keeping books, recording receipts and claims; keeping accounts; reproductions services; card-indexing; graphing statistical tables minor correspondence, complaints; special contract work; cashier work.

small jobs, either at the same time or successively during the course of the year. In any case, tasks are periodic; although there are peak periods for some of them, rotation of personnel is commonplace.

This variety and multiplicity does not fail to affect those subject to it. When clerks discuss their work, two expressions come out all the time: "It's special," "There is a lot of detail." Actually, everything is "special," for formalism dominates. As in the incantations of a primitive civilization, there is a rigorous order and a prescribed intonation for each word, lest it lose any of its effectiveness; similarly the method of performing each operation is learned separately with no possibility for generalization. The competent man is still the one who has been through a lot, who has been exposed to many departments, and who has handled many different cases. Only as a function of his experience can he respond to the demands for information made by his coworkers or by his subordinates. His knowledge remains initiatory.

Possibly this will no longer be the case in a few years, when the process of rationalization now taking place in all administrative organizations as a result of the introduction of automation will have run its course. For the moment, however, even in organizations with the highest degree of standardization, these operational characteristics prevail.

Policy Writers and Claims Adjusters

Policy writers and claims adjusters[3] comprise a very special group in the insurance environment. In banks and in public administration, redaction work is entrusted to executive staff members or to a few highly specialized persons altogether separate from the world of employees. In insurance, on the other hand, we are involved with numerous groups located at the very top of the reward and prestige hierarchy, but nevertheless made up of general operational personnel. There is, however, a whole series of gradations between specialized clerks, who already have a little law background, and highly qualified policy writers and claims adjusters, capable of developing the procedure to be followed in a matter that is under contention.

3. Collectively referred to in French as "les rédacteurs."—TRANS.

The simplest positions are the "production" jobs we have mentioned, which involve drafting contracts and riders. Policy writers determine which documents are necessary at the request of agents in the field, after having taken into account all relevant factors in the light of rules and tables supplied to them. They are generally the youngest staff members in this group, and the ones with the least education. Next to them, "correspondents," older and more experienced than they, generally overseers, write to clients and to agents to ask for specifications and additional information.

The claims departments handle the more difficult problems raised in the settlement of accidents and damages insured by the company. The work involves discussions, negotiations, and decisions, handled by letter or, more rarely, orally. The most competent claims adjusters, those charged with handling contested claims, often have law degrees.

Compared to other employees, all these men have a privileged position. It is true that their salaries are relatively low, their working conditions often mediocre, and the productivity demanded of them considerable. Still, most of them have the feeling that they are doing work which is more important and more enriching. They are located, one group at the beginning (production) and the other at the end (claims) of the professional cycle. That is why, for them, the work is more concrete and more significant. At one end insurance is sold to a client, at the other end claims are adjusted. Everyone has a clear conception of his role. This shows up in the description they give of their work; it is much simpler and more comprehensible than the descriptions given by clerks. While the latter have a tendency to see their work in terms of particular operations, the former state it more easily in terms of function. For example: "I sell the merchandise," or "I prepare the work for the lawyer."

Moreover, these staff members enjoy a rather high degree of autonomy. They are "individuals." Each one handles his own affairs and must assume his own responsibilities. They are unanimous in declaring that they must have a professional outlook, while in the other groups one employee out of three, at least, thinks this is not necessary.

The work load for policy writers and claims adjusters is,

however, usually very heavy. Whether it be in the tumult and noise behind the "counter" or in the studious silence of the office, the number of matters that must be expedited is such that it is impossible for them to slow down in the least. Work breaks are not formal as among typists, there is no boss to declare a "coffee break," the number of breaks they are able to squeeze out is reduced to a minimum. The pressure to produce dominates the workday; conversations, asides, daydreaming, hardly exist. Also, fatigue is acute and widespread; it is clearly more intense among this group than among all other employees. To be sure, the awareness of fatigue is quite appropriate to the serious, competent, and efficient role that policy writers and claims adjusters see themselves as playing.

Patterns of Development

The development of techniques leads to the disappearance of artisan-type jobs, such as clerical tasks which are easily done by machines, as soon as one can demand of the public that it adjust to a minimum of rules which permit the rationalization of operations to be accomplished. The beneficiaries of this development have so far been the more routine jobs, such as keypuncher or office machine operator, or jobs requiring higher qualifications, such as policy-men or counter-men. In the long run, it seems likely that we will see the complete disappearance of routine jobs themselves, which we can imagine being completely replaced by machines as soon as—and it will be soon—these machines become capable of directly deciphering the documents that give rise to the operation. All that will survive then are supervisory and programming jobs, auxiliary jobs of verification and correction, and specialized jobs involving direct human contact or an indirect, but highly technical, human relationship.

For the moment, however, the introduction of electronics affects only those involved with office machines, and then only partially, and directly affects only 2 percent or 3 percent of all employees. The revolution that is heralded will not have its full effects until another decade has passed. The employees we interviewed had absolutely no awareness of it.[4]

4. This was written in 1963. The picture has now changed substantially.

Attitudes toward Work

Methods and Perspectives in Studies of Satisfaction

The first idea that came to the mind of psychologists and sociologists who wanted to understand attitudes toward work was to ask those concerned a series of questions with the aim of measuring their satisfaction. Common sense was here coupled with an especially acute preoccupation with qualification in a discipline in the process of development. A subject's satisfaction really seems to be a clear datum, easily measurable, and allowing all the comparisons between individuals, between groups, and between companies that one would like.

But, underlying the somewhat naive positivism of the first researchers, one can discover many relatively contestable postulates. It was thought, for example, that all attitudes were sufficiently expressed by the idea of satisfaction, and that in order to have a reasonable view of a person's motivation for his behavior, it was sufficient to present for assessment by him a review of all the facts which might affect him. It was thought, besides, more or less consciously, that all the individual satisfactions could be added up to give a general result, *morale*, and that the entire objective of fundamental researchers in this area was to discover the weight carried by each individual satisfaction in the common result. Prejudging their conclusions, practitioners of applied research presented employers with proposals for company analyses which would display on a graph the weak points of their organization, and also give overall scores summarizing the different types of satisfaction.[5]

Such postulates were imposed because of the methodological shortcuts they allowed. They led to the development of a quantitative industrial psychology. Factor analysis seemed to be the technical solution to all problems.

Unfortunately, experience would soon show that such simplifications were not effective in practice, and that premature quantification might even be an obstacle to understanding. Research for or about latent factors of morale would in the end

5. See, for example, Robert K. Burns, "Attitude Surveys and the Diagnosis of Organization Needs," The University of Chicago Industrial Relations Center Research Reprints Series, no. 42 (1955).

prove to be vain and illusory. At the same time, on the theoretical level, the development of dynamic psychology would lead researchers like Daniel Katz and Robert Kahn to level devastating critiques against the notion of morale itself.[6] The "integrationist" outlook which this notion assumes has since then appeared totally anachronistic, from the point of view of group psychology, as well as from the point of view of sociology.

Since the 1950s researchers have turned their attention more and more to the problems of interpersonal relations and organizational equilibrium. And no one any longer expects to understand the conditions of integration of a system as complex as that of a human organization by superficially determining the individual satisfaction of its actors.

Questions relating to satisfaction have, however, continued to be universally used, for they provide a measuring instrument, limited to be sure, but irreplaceable. No general conclusions can be derived from their sum, and an index of contentment makes no sense. But the social psychologist can make good use of comparative responses on matters of satisfaction in understanding the influence of norms and attitudes on patterns of behavior. The sociologist interested in problems of organization will compare the level of satisfaction that underlies interactions and reciprocal perceptions in groups he studies. Finally, for anyone who wants to understand phenomena of change, the evolution of satisfaction over time constitutes an indispensable type of measurement.

But the spirit in which such questions are asked is altogether different. It is no longer a question of getting measurements that are valid in and of themselves or through purely statistical exploration, but of gathering comparative elements susceptible to diverse interpretations.

Our inquiries were deeply influenced by these changes in perspective. In the end, they developed within the perspective of the study of organizations. We abandoned the analysis of the interplay between aspirations and expectations on the one hand and satisfaction on the other, in order to concentrate on intergroup and intercompany comparisons. This relative

6. A critical analysis of this notion will be found below, pp. 135–38.

simplification allowed us to get a more precise view of those factors related to the internal structure of the company—that is, to the social hierarchy—which condition employees' adaptation to their jobs; it also enabled us to understand somewhat better the importance of work in a social-status perspective. In a very indirect way then, by studying office workers' satisfaction with their jobs, we will be able to come back to our theoretical discussion of the position of white-collar employees in society.

Interest in Work and Satisfaction with Position

In a work whose empirical data came precisely from a study carried out in an insurance company, social psychologists of the Survey Research Center of the University of Michigan distinguished four major dimensions in attitudes toward work: the satisfaction due to the intrinsic content of the job, the satisfaction of belonging to a particular organization, the satisfaction due to the salary received or the prestige of the job held, and the pride in belonging to a particular work group.

Instead of these four dimensions, the analysis we performed during our exploratory study would suggest two: interest taken in the work and satisfaction derived from the position occupied.[7]

Satisfaction in matters of salary and consciousness of professional status cannot really be reduced to these two dimensions. But then again, satisfaction with salary and the feeling of belonging to a particular work group appear to be two relatively minor aspects of the universe of attitudes toward work.

The measure for interest in work which we finally retained seems very close to the one adopted by the University of Michigan study. To develop it, however, we made use of more descriptive questions which a preliminary hierarchical analysis had shown us would reflect subjective assessments very exactly. Note that the equivalence of the phrases "The work is interesting" and "I like the work" is not simply an accident of vocabulary. The possibility of using descriptive language really

7. A detailed analysis of the conclusions we drew from that study may be found in Crozier and Guetta, *Une organisation administrative,* pp. 40–48.

implies that, at least in part, we are touching upon a social phenomenon. I like this work because, objectively—that is, in the social representations which have currency—this work is considered likable. Thus it makes no difference whether I say "I like this work" (subjective expression) or "This work is interesting" (objective expression).

We measured "interest in work" with the help of a Guttman scale which included the responses to two questions describing interest in work, one in abstract terms, the other concretely, and the response to a third question on the advantages of the position which revealed spontaneous choice of interest in work.[8]

"Interest in work" thus defined in objective terms contrasts sharply with satisfaction with position, whose more subjective character clearly appears in reading the central question of the scale which we used:

Which of the following statements would you be most likely to use in speaking of your position?
1. I like it a lot, it suits me perfectly.
2. It's a good job, I really can't complain.
3. It's no great shakes as jobs go.
4. What can you do, any way you look at it it's a dirty job.

The scale includes two questions evaluating the correctness of the decision made in coming to work for the company[9] and two questions on whether it is good to be an insurance company employee.[10] In the end, these questions correspond to both the second and the third dimensions used by the University of Michigan study (satisfaction of belonging to the company and satisfaction with the status of the job). However,

8. The formula used for the concrete descriptive question clearly expresses the meaning of what we were measuring.

"Finally, among the following statements (about your work), which one comes closest to what you think?

"1. It can be fascinating if you make the effort.
"2. It's often interesting, you learn things. The job has its agreeable aspects.
"3. It's mostly monotonous.
"4. It's really not interesting at all. Anyone could do it."

9. "Taking everything into account, did you do a good thing in coming to work for this company? Would you advise a friend to do it?"

10. "Is a position as an insurance company employee a good one? (yes; fair; as good as any other; mediocre)."

they take on a somewhat different meaning precisely because of their similarity. What is actually being measured, this time, is not simply the interviewee's evaluation of belonging to the organization that employs him, or his evaluation of the prestige of his qualifications, but an even more subjective balance between his own aspirations and the characteristics of his job.

General level of satisfaction

First, let us look at the overall results for the two key questions and for the two scales that test interest in work and evaluation of position (see tables 1–4).

TABLE 1

Interest in Work

Very Interesting	Interesting Enough	Not Very Interesting	Not at all Interesting
25%	37%	29%	9%

TABLE 2

Interest Scale

<table>
<tr><td>Group 1</td><td>Group 2</td><td>Group 3</td><td>Group 4</td><td rowspan="4">Errors and unclassifiable</td></tr>
<tr><td colspan="3">Do not say their work is very interesting.</td><td>Say their work is very interesting.</td></tr>
<tr><td colspan="2">Do not mention interest in work as one of the advantages of their position.</td><td colspan="2">Mention interest in work as one of the advantages of their position.</td></tr>
<tr><td>Choose the statement: This work is monotonous and not at all interesting.</td><td colspan="3">Choose the statement: This work is fascinating or this work is often interesting.</td></tr>
<tr><td>22%</td><td>29%</td><td>24%</td><td>19%</td><td>7%</td></tr>
</table>

TABLE 3

Evaluation of Position

It Suits Me Perfectly	I Can't Complain	No Response	It's No Great Shakes	It's a Dirty Job
9%	41%	17%	28%	2%

TABLE 4

Scale of Satisfaction with Position

<table>
<tr><th>Group 1</th><th>Group 2</th><th>Group 3</th><th>Group 4</th><th>Group 5</th><th rowspan="5">Errors and unclassifiable</th></tr>
<tr><td>Declare that they did not do a good thing in coming to work for an insurance company and that they would not advise a friend to do so.</td><td colspan="4">Do not declare that they did not do a good thing in coming to work for an insurance company and that they would not advise a friend to do so.</td></tr>
<tr><td colspan="2">Say that it's no great shakes as jobs go.</td><td colspan="3">Say that I can't complain, or I like it a lot.</td></tr>
<tr><td colspan="3">Say that their family thinks the job of insurance company employee is a fair position or no great shakes.</td><td colspan="2">Say that their family thinks it is by and large a good position.</td></tr>
<tr><td colspan="4">Personally believe it is a fair position or no great shakes.</td><td>Personally believe it is a good position.</td></tr>
<tr><td>6%</td><td>16%</td><td>26%</td><td>19%</td><td>18%</td><td>16%</td></tr>
<tr><td colspan="6">NOTE: The order of factors is significant, especially the fact that the employees interviewed declare that they have a much less favorable view of the prestige associated with the position of insurance company employee than their family does.</td></tr>
</table>

These results are hardly surprising. They confirm, at least as far as interest in work is concerned, the figures we ourselves obtained in an earlier study of a public administration, and correspond quite exactly to those obtained by other researchers and to those we ourselves later obtained for comparable jobs.[11]

TABLE 5

Interest in Work by Type of Company

<table>
<tr><th></th><th colspan="3">Very Interesting</th><th colspan="3">Interesting Enough</th><th colspan="3">Not Very Interesting</th><th colspan="3">Not at all Interesting</th></tr>
<tr><td>Accounting firm</td><td colspan="6">67%</td><td colspan="6">33%</td></tr>
<tr><td>American insurance companies</td><td colspan="4">31%</td><td colspan="4">38%</td><td colspan="4">31%</td></tr>
<tr><td>Exploratory study, Parisian insurance company</td><td colspan="3">24%</td><td colspan="3">55%</td><td colspan="3">16%</td><td colspan="3">5%</td></tr>
<tr><td>Study of six Parisian insurance companies</td><td colspan="3">25%</td><td colspan="3">38%</td><td colspan="3">29%</td><td colspan="3">9%</td></tr>
<tr><td>Study of administrative departments of a large bank</td><td colspan="3">21%</td><td colspan="3">57%</td><td colspan="3">17%</td><td colspan="3">5%</td></tr>
</table>

11. See Herzberg, Mausner, Peterson, and Capwell, *Job Attitudes: A Review of Research and Opinion* (Psychological Service of Pittsburgh, 1957).

We have been able to make the very general comparison that follows (see table 5) by making use of our own studies and the relatively comparable study carried out by the Survey Research Center of the

The overall picture that emerges from these figures is that of persons relatively lukewarm toward their work and their positions, but whose opinions are nevertheless varied and do not correspond at all to the image of the downtrodden small bureaucrat, robot of modern civilization, disseminated by the literature of the years between the two wars.

Work vs. Position

But what do these figures really mean? We will attempt to understand them by doing a comparative analysis of the factors which influence the responses given by our subjects to the two types of questions asked.

Immediately we are faced with a curious paradox. Though these responses seem to be closely interdependent, they contrast sharply on one essential point. "Professional category," the general factor which conditions them the most, has an opposite influence in the two scales. An examination of the cross-tabulation shows this very clearly. First of all, as might be expected, there is a positive relationship between subjects' scores on the two scales. Subjects interested in their work have a much better chance of being satisfied with their position than their colleagues, and vice versa. For example, 40 percent of those who say their work is very interesting are satisfied with their position, and only 10 percent of them are dissatisfied. By contrast, among those who say their work is monotonous, we find 41 percent who are malcontents as compared to 27 percent who are satisfied.[12]

On the other hand, if we tabulate scores obtained on each of the two scales as a function of subjects' professional category, we get two tables that are diametrically opposed (see tables 6 and 7).

Obviously, there are noticeable variations from one category to another, since the percentage of interviewees who are not very interested in their work ranges from 21 percent to 76 percent, and the percentage of those satisfied with their posi-

University of Michigan on an insurance company; on this subject see: Crozier, *Petits fonctionnaires,* p. 68; Morse, *Satisfaction in the White-Collar Job,* p. 56; Crozier and Guetta, *Une organisation administrative,* p. 39. The study of the bank has not yet been published.

12. The probability of independence is less than 01 percent.

tion varies between 15 percent and 54 percent. But while, in the case of interest in work, claims adjusters are the most interested and typists and keypunchers the least interested, when it comes to satisfaction with position, claims adjusters are the ones who complain the most, and typists and keypunchers complain the least.

These variations in opposite directions are all the more surprising if we compare these results to the responses given to a question of the same order, but a neutral one, on satisfaction: "Taking everything into account, would you say that you are by and large happy or by and large unhappy?" The distribution of responses to this question remains constant whatever the professional category, which tends to prove that the psychological profile of our interviewees is pretty much the same in every case, at least as far as aptitude for satisfaction is concerned. In a comparable psychological area, membership in a particular professional category has an opposite effect depending on whether the image evoked is that of work or position.

In such an environment, whose homogeneity from the point of view of essential psychological factors we were thus able to verify, we went on, in order to establish firmly the profound

TABLE 6

Interest in Work by Professional Category

	Categories 3 and 4, Interested	Categories 1 and 2, Little Interested	Unclassifiable
Claims Adjusters	59	23	18
Policy writers	60	37	2
Clerks	48	44	7
Typists	21	76	3
Keypunchers	27	69	4
Archivists	31	61	8

NOTE: We have reorganized categories 1 and 2 to make reading easier. N = 301.

TABLE 7
Satisfaction with Position by Professional Category

	Categories 1 and 2, Little Satisfied	Category 3 Make No Statement	Categories 4 and 5 Satisfied	Unclassified
Claims adjusters	31%	33%	15%	21%
Policy writers	21%	34%	30%	12%
Clerks	20%	20%	47%	12%
Typists	22%	25%	35%	17%
Archivists	19%	28%	37%	17%
Key-punchers	16%	12%	54%	19%

NOTE: We have reorganized categories 1 and 2 to make reading easier. N = 301.

nature of the paradox, to an analysis of variance which proved to have great statistical significance.[13]

We can thus affirm that the contrast between interest in work and satisfaction with position cannot be due to chance but rather constitutes one of the essential characteristics of this environment. *The more one rises in the professional hierarchy, the greater the tendency to be interested in one's work and to complain about one's position* (see figure 1).

If we extend the comparison to supervisors, taking into account hierarchical differences and not just professional qualifications, we find exactly the same schema. Almost all the supervisors in our six companies declare that they are interested in their work, but only 40 percent of them are satisfied with their position.[14]

13. Significant at the 01 level ($F = 5.04$ for 4 degrees of freedom).

14. The studies we conducted of the administrative departments of a large Parisian bank and of a Parisian ministry roughly confirm these results. In truth, we do not find the same contrasts between professional categories because, in the bank and in the administrative

FIG. 1. *Comparative means of scores of the various professional categories on satisfaction at work, cheerfulness at work, and satisfaction with position.*

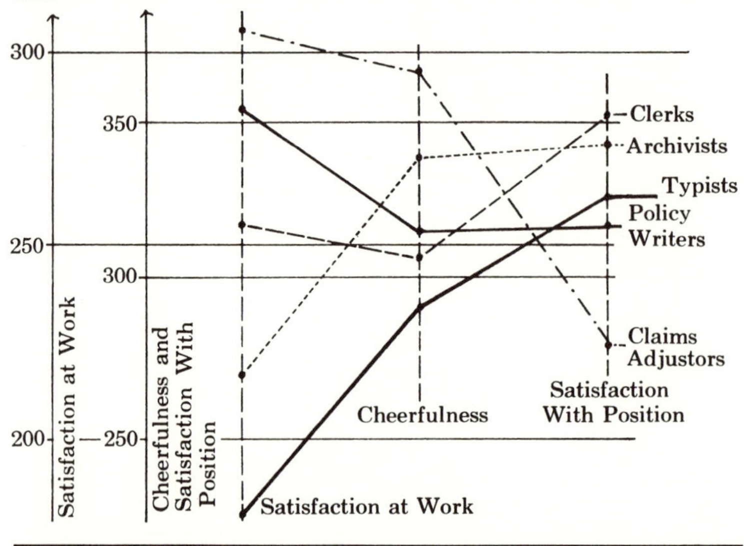

An analogous, though somewhat weaker, contrast appears when we compare by company. The differences between our six companies so far as the distribution of opinions concerning interest in work is concerned are relatively small.[15] But they are much greater when it comes to position, and work in opposite directions. The two companies where interest in work is highest are also those where complaints about one's position are most prevalent, while in the two companies where interest in work is lowest, workers seem more satisfied with their positions.[16]

Let us now try to probe more deeply into these similarities

departments, these categories do not have notable differences in prestige. But as for differences between hierarchical categories, they are more acute and follow quite exactly the schema which we have established.

15. It is important to emphasize this, since on the other questions the variations from company to company are in general quite considerable.

16. The analysis of variance, however, is not as conclusive as it is for professional categories; the contrast is not altogether significant statistically.

and contrasts by moving on to a comparative analysis of the influence of the most significant variables on these two reactions. Evaluation of work and evaluation of position, first of all, vary in the same direction when tabulated by sex and by seniority. Men are slightly more satisfied than women, and those with greatest seniority are more satisfied than those who have just come into the company. Nevertheless, the curve that describes satisfaction at work as a function of seniority is not a level one; it presents a curious and, if one may say so, classical profile, since it has been constantly rediscovered in analyses carried out in numerous countries. Upon entering a company, one is relatively satisfied; then the initial years, primarily the second through the fifth, constitute a rather painful experience corresponding to the loss of first illusions; after that, with the attainment of greater and greater seniority, one becomes more and more involved and satisfied. The curve of satisfaction with position as a function of seniority presents a companion profile, though it is less pronounced (see figure 2).

FIG. 2. *Curve of interest in work and of satisfaction with position by seniority.*

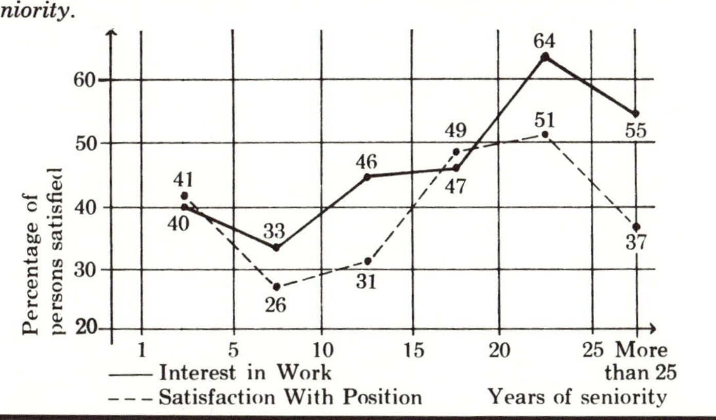

Interest in work and evaluation of position are similarly, and positively, related to the feeling of autonomy at work, to the impression of not being tightly controlled, to a positive evaluation of the office one belongs to, one's boss and the company's social policy.

On the other hand, certain opinions and attitudes seem to

be related exclusively to interest in work. In particular, these are the favorable attitudes manifested regarding chances for promotion, participation in the joint-management committee, and information on the progress of the company.

Evaluations of position are influenced by two variables which seem to have little effect on interest in work—profession of parents and level of education. Employees whose parents had a prestigious occupation and those who received a higher-level education are much more likely to be discontent with their position.

These same evaluations are related to the responses which we obtained to a series of questions that aimed to test the social aspirations and the cultural level of employees. There again, the more one has social aspirations and a high cultural level, the more one is likely to complain.

What might be the meaning of such a constant contrast? In light of this entire body of relationships, a first hypothesis could be formulated. Interest in work seems to express adherence to a profession and the esprit de corps that accompanies it. This sort of disposition is a function of the prestige of the occupation itself. It is regular, hierarchical, and relatively predictable. It varies little from company to company. One can maintain that there is a rather close parallel between the prestige accorded by third parties to each occupation and the interest manifested by members of that occupation.[17] The satisfaction a subject feels with his position expresses a relationship with a world of a totally different order. It is no longer a question of the place occupied by the subject in the hierarchy of functional prestige, but rather of the game which

17. This is also what emerges from certain American studies. See, for example: Donald Super, "Occupational Level and Job Satisfaction," *Journal of Applied Psychology* 23 (1939): pp. 365–77; "The Fortune Survey," *Fortune*, May and June, 1947; Lawrence G. Thomas, *The Occupational Structure and Education* (New York: Prentice Hall, 1956); Nancy Morse and Robert Weiss, "The Function and Meaning of Work and the Job," *American Sociological Review* 20 (1956): 191–98; Gladys Palmer, "Attitudes Toward Work in an Industrial Community," *American Journal of Sociology* 63 (1957): 17–26; for an overall review of the problem, see Robert Blauner, "Work Satisfaction and Industrial Trends in Modern Society," in *Labor and Trade Unionism*, ed. Walter Galenson and Seymour Martin Lipset (New York: Wiley, 1960), pp. 339–60, especially pp. 343–44.

he plays with society in order to obtain the best possible treatment. The dimension we touch upon here is in certain respects also a social dimension—but in a completely different sense from "interest in work." What is involved is an individual assessment of a phenomenon of hierarchization which is itself collective; in the case of interest in work, it is more a question of a collective evaluation of an individual phenomenon of adaptation.

In fact, what is presented to us in this contrast is not so much a difference of domain as a difference in points of view. Certainly the two notions are relatively ambiguous; the implicit interplay which we find between them cannot be understood unless we consider the conditions for adaptation to work as a social phenomenon.

Adaptation to Work as a Social Phenomenon

What is the social meaning of these attitudes toward work whose complexity was just revealed? First of all, it is important to note that our subjects' evaluations bring out, to a great extent, purely psychological dispositions. The importance of these dispositions is emphasized by the stability of responses to the question we posed regarding the impression of well-being.[18] These responses do not vary as a result of the subjects' social situation or their place in the organization. Hardly anything affects the responses at all, except for familial factors (marriage, widowhood, divorce). They are, however, very closely related to evaluations of work and of position. It is reasonable to think that, for many individuals, these evaluations correspond to particular psychlogical dispositions.

A Swedish psychologist, Uno Remitz, devoted himself to an extremely thorough statistical study to measure these diverse influences precisely.[19] His work should have been particularly interesting for us, from a comparative point of view, since it treats a sample of bank employees. But it is limited and relatively deceptive from this point of view, because of its exclu-

18. This question, it will be remembered, ran as follows: "Taking everything into account, would you say that you are by and large happy or by and large unhappy?"

19. *Professional Satisfaction Among Swedish Bank Employees* (Copenhagen, 1960).

sively psychometric orientation. In any case, his conclusions are worth taking into consideration. According to him, only 10 percent of the variance in matters of attitude toward work can be attributed to external social factors, while factors internal to the company might at the very most account for an additional 10 percent. Four-fifths of the variance would express, according to him, the existence of a unique factor, "disposition toward satisfaction," which, like intelligence, could be isolated as a measurable individual factor.

One could contest the methods followed and maintain that with different questions—ours for example—the results would have been somewhat different and that in particular the part of the variance due to social factors would have risen greatly.[20] It remains nonetheless true that psychological dispositions seem to have a considerable effect on good or poor adaptation to work.

If we agree that social factors can in any case explain only part of the individual differences, what is the meaning of the relatively notable differences which certain variables of a social order seem to introduce?

As a point of departure for our research in this area, we took the results of one of our earlier studies relating to an office worker milieu, relatively similar in its work to the milieu of insurance company employees. We were able to show, with a reduced sample, that satisfaction at work depended directly on the agreement between social status outside work and social status at work. Employees with higher social origins were not satisfied at work unless they had a role and a position which assured them higher status, while their colleagues from among the common people were satisfied whatever their position.[21]

This analysis could not be repeated however in the present study. Perhaps the relationship between the aspirations en-

20. When he attempts to specify the differences between individuals disposed to satisfaction and those disposed to dissatisfaction, Remitz brings to light the following characteristics. The dissatisfied ones are more active, more ambitious, more vulnerable, less "sure," and more capable of contact; the more satisfied ones are less active, slower, and more stable. It is hardly credible that such characteristics could be completely independent of social factors external or internal to the company, even if, in a functional or less hierarchical society, stratification carries less weight.

21. Crozier, *Petits fonctionnaires,* pp. 74–75.

gendered by the external milieu and the image of reality one develops are much more complex in the insurance company milieu than in the clerical agency milieu which we worked on originally. In the clerical agency, a Paris branch of a large public agency, we were involved with personnel whose jobs were all equally standardized. Any small difference that remained was greatly valued. Besides, the employees, all women and relatively young, constituted a homogeneous milieu within which social differences took on greater importance. Finally, the number of employees whose social milieu was definitely superior to the prestige of their work was very considerable. For these three reasons, the influence of social stratification may have seemed to us decisive while, in the study of the six insurance companies, this influence was masked by the complexity of the hierarchy of positions, the greater variety of personnel, and the limited amount of real downward mobility.

At the clerical agency, we did not find any interesting distinction so far as the problem of position is concerned, because great discontent—which could be considered completely abnormal—prevailed.[22] Thus a statistical comparison is impossible. But nothing stops us from comparing the two experiences in an attempt to draw out of them a wider interpretation.

The general conclusion one can draw from the results at the clerical agency—namely, that preoccupation with a suitable place in the hierarchy determines the nonpsychological differences between our subjects—can help us to develop a broader interpretation of the different reactions of higher and lower professional categories in the matter of work and of position.

One can, in fact, formulate the following hypothesis. Either of the two ways of playing the game predominates according to hierarchical level. At the lower level, employees feel too threatened. They do not have the security necessary to complain about their position. They reason exclusively as a function of the past or of the risks against which they are insured. Their job is their protection and that is enough to make them satisfied with it. They feel weak and disarmed; consequently they tend to forego a struggle that is too much of a mismatch and

22. We did not pose really precise questions which would have been suitable to reveal the attitudes which we have just analyzed in insurance companies.

to accept their place in the social hierarchy. On the other hand, they will complain more easily about the work, because making noise in this way is less dangerous and more fruitful; it allows them to affirm superiority to their condition, and to proclaim that they are capable of doing better, without meanwhile taking the risk, in protesting against fate, of admitting that they have not done very much with their lives.

The more one rises in the hierarchy, on the contrary, the more readily one takes this risk, to the extent that one feels freer and psychologically stronger. The prestige of one's work, however, its recognized interest among one's colleagues and among the public at large, make it difficult to complain about the work. On the contrary, the affirmation that they like their work constitutes, for higher-level employees, a means of affirming their superiority. Moreover, adherence to a trade and esprit de corps provide enough psychological and even practical security to the individual to allow him to be more venturesome in discussing the advantages of his position.

The qualified clerk complains of the conditions imposed upon him by the company in the name of the importance and the dignity of his trade, while the typist tends, on the contrary, to authorize her demands for more interesting work by invoking her faithfulness to the company.

These two ways of playing the game, which are only half-conscious, have no more than a partial effect on choices. But they are what tip the balance, and are of considerable importance. We find an indirect but nevertheless significant expression of this in vocabulary, when we hear the clerk declare that he "works in claims" and the typist that she "works in insurance."

The reality of this game is indirectly confirmed by our findings on the rivalries which become manifest between groups. It seems that each group tends to despise and reject inferior groups, and readily chooses interest in work as a means of affirming its superiority. We became aware of the depth of this feeling when we presented to the interested parties in the bank results comparable to those we have just presented. Members of higher-level categories received as a traumatic shock the news that their colleagues in lower-level categories were really interested in their work; this was the point whose significance they made the greatest effort to minimize even when quantified results were submitted.[23]

At the same time, our hypothesis allows us to explain the paradox one finds in the comparisons between companies. In two of the companies, interest in work seems to be distinctly higher. This favorable situation is explained by greater decentralization, which allows more autonomy to lower echelons. In at least one of these two cases, this result was achieved by deliberate management policy. Yet, contrary to expectations, the atmosphere did not improve—just the opposite happened. Employees who are more satisfied with their work have a tendency to complain more about their position, as though their dignity, given greater recognition by their organization, only serves to reinforce their opposition to that organization.

Finally, the importance of the interplay between groups can help us understand the peculiar nature of the results which we obtained in the case of the bank. The nearly complete absence of a prestige difference between different categories has, in effect, opposite consequences. On the one hand, there seems to be greater satisfaction with one's work at the operational levels. But on the other hand, there also appears to be much more indifference and much less involvement in social matters. So, in this white-collar milieu at least, the more clear-cut the stratification, the more individuals tend to participate. Moreover, dissatisfaction seems to grow with participation.

Through these analyses, the white-collar world emerges as one dominated by stratification—hierarchical stratification in the bank,[24] social stratification in the clerical agency, professional stratification in insurance. White-collar employees seem to need this stratification; its reduction in the bank and in the clerical agency engenders more indifference and apathy, and leads those involved to polarize over finer and even artificial

23. One thing that emerges from an analysis of the open-ended conversations carried out during the preparatory study is that liking one's work is clearly a sign of aristocracy; this trait is readily denied to inferiors, while complaining about one's position is perfectly appropriate.

24. The great importance of hierarchy at the executive level compensates for the absence of a prestige difference between various white-collar categories.

differences. This stratification always expresses itself on the job. Hence our interviewees' very great involvement in the prestige and prerogatives of their occupation. Hence their uncertainty and their contradictory ways of playing the game. Each of them suffers in these ways, but nevertheless none of them can overcome the incompatibility between the need to participate and the fear of getting involved. From the point of view of the organization itself, stratification offers a solution. If its constraint is so easily accepted, that is because, indirectly and in a less trying manner, it assures the participation necessary.

In any case, we are still far from the hypothesis of H. P. Bahrdt, according to which modern white-collar employees are in a process of transition from the world of constraining control to the world of cooperation.

6 Interpersonal Relations

The Problem

Work constitutes the primary and most obvious dimension of the social life of the members of a company. It is the most neutral and most impersonal element of their positions, and the one upon which they first project their problems. But the fact that their attitudes in this area express themselves directly and naturally does not mean that these attitudes are the only important ones held by the members. Man's relationship to society is not in effect limited to this sort of direct and individual negotiation between contributions given and advantages derived that these attitudes reflect. In studying these attitudes, we get only a partial and very inadequate view of the manner in which the different actors experience their situation. In addition to the task, even taken in the larger sense, with the limitations and advantages of a psychological order which it involves, one must also take into account, to the extent that it is decisive, the necessary insertion into a social system which provides man with an indispensable natural milieu for interaction.

The problem of human environment and, to be more precise, interpersonal relations with colleagues, superiors, and subordinates, thus constitutes a second dimension, just as indispensable as the dimension of work. This environment is influenced by the servitude imposed by the work and partakes of a certain functional character. But it also constitutes a completely autonomous dimension, which reflects at one and the same time the system of social relations and the cultural system of society as a whole. We have already noted that, through this environment, these two systems influence and color, in turn, attitudes toward work. Also, it is not the least bit surprising that sociologists of work have more and more moved from the analysis of adaptation to work to the analysis of interpersonal relations, from psychotechnical analyses to social psychology and sociology, while practitioners have overcome their preoccupation with selection in order to confront problems of ambiance and atmosphere.

The influence of human environment can be studied in two ways. One is the direct and descriptive approach: collecting information on the opinions, the attitudes, and the behavioral patterns of employees involved in relations with their colleagues, their bosses, and their subordinates. The other is the indirect approach: bringing out the differences in opinions, attitudes, and behavior which are manifest among and between members of different groups.

In our research, we have tried to use both methods. In our first exploratory work, we were struck by the existence of stereotypes whose distribution seemed to depend basically on membership in various work groups. It will be remembered that, to analyze this phenomenon, we developed a research design which allowed us, in interviewing all the members of forty work groups, to have a representative sample of individuals as well as to compare all the opinions expressed within any one group. Thanks to this design, we could make double use of the responses of the subjects questioned. Taken individually, the responses allow us to describe and evaluate the quality of interpersonal relations; taken within the group framework, they provided us with a means of measuring the influence of the group on overall attitudes and behavior patterns.

At the beginning we thought that the primary group had a decisive influence on the diffusion of styles and stereotypes that affect the way in which situations are experienced. But our hypothesis was not verified. We were forced to recognize that, for a large number of questions—in particular for those concerning work, and those that relate to the cultural world and to social aspirations—membership in a particular group hardly seemed to have an effect.[1] The influence of the group proved to be overwhelming, however, so far as ambiance, human relations, and the problems raised by the direction and organization of work were concerned; these influences appeared to have a lesser, though notable, effect on evalutions of position and of chances for participation and integration into the company.

We will endeavor to develop this last point more thoroughly in the next chapter. Here we will concentrate on interpersonal relations as they may be studied from the individual angle and from the angle of the group, beginning with the descriptive aspect and the problem of relations between colleagues.

Relations Between Colleagues

The Office Atmosphere

The elementary social cell is, of course, the office, that is, a unity of place, a separate room with its desks and its file clerks. People in the same office know each other, at least by name, and live together eight hours a day. The department also generally constitutes a coherent social group. It may encompass several different locations and sometimes even be distributed over several floors, but it has a single, centralized management and its own particular job to do. To avoid confusion, our sample included only offices, that is, groups that had, in addition to a single management and a single job, an inescapable framework for interaction.

In insurance, as in many office jobs, the very nature of the functions generally decrees that work relations more often take the form of coexistence than collaboration. Employees work side by side, each doing his own job separately. So we have the policy men with their daily pile of dossiers, and the typists with their tapes or their magnetic belts. One may,

1. Our mistake, as far as work was concerned, was due to the coincidence of group and professional category influences which jointly affected the fundamental situations experienced by our interview subjects. In comparing the same professional groups in six different organizations, we were able to determine that the professional factor overrides the group factor.

however, find, both among clerks and among those who work on machines, two- and three-man teams.

What is the style of relations between colleagues? Long observation of offices during the exploratory study showed us noticeable differences in atmosphere within any one professional category. We saw offices where relationships are formal, cold, and even somewhat stilted, where no one wants to commit himself to anyone; and offices where the atmosphere is much more easy-going, where camaraderie and good fellowship are the rule, at least on the surface.

Nevertheless, we can generally say that relations between colleagues lack warmth. Our interviewees are quite reserved in the matter of camaraderie; they expect cordial relations with their colleagues, but prefer that a certain distance be maintained. Eighty-five percent of them never get together with their colleagues outside of work, and the 15 percent who do seem to apologize for it. The general order of the day seems to be "every man for himself," "we see each other enough during the week." Yet when one questions them about the character of employees, they do not fail to criticize them—as well as themselves—for their coldness, their egoism, and their distant character.

Distance and coldness are perhaps means of maintaining possible conflicts within acceptable limits. There seem, in fact, to be numerous occasions for conflicts. During the exploratory study, conflicts of sex, conflicts between generations, and professional conflicts were calmly described to us.

Conflicts which result from men and women cohabiting the same office are numerous. "You can't always get along with men," say certain female employees. "Women, they're the plague of the department, they carry on so!" reply the men, in even greater proportion.

Generational conflicts are, however, even more numerous. If one believes the comments collected in the open-ended interviews, the old-timers bully the young, try to limit them and to dampen their exuberance, while the young rile the old-timers and shock them easily. The young's reactions are often brutal.

"There are many oldsters," one of them tells us, "who have

their little manias." "They're always bringing up the good old days, they never stop saying: 'In my time. . . .' "

As for the old-timers, they complain about the irreverence of the young. In general sense, the two groups hardly enjoy living together; when they have the chance, the young prefer to be with the young and the old stick to their own group. A few even go so far as to propose radical segregation, the young with the young, the old with the old.

Professional rivalries are indicated less often than conflicts between sexes and between generations. They are nevertheless no less important, and the fear of favoritism seems to be very widespread.

"There are a lot of people around here who are out to make it any way they can." "There are secret payoffs, people have it in for each other." "Some people get together with their submanagers after work, there is petty gossip, wheeling and dealing." "The less you say about it here, the better."

No more than indicative value should be attached to these descriptions, evaluations, and hopes on the part of employees. A statistical analysis of their individual responses, which related not only to good or bad atmosphere but to their personal feelings toward their colleagues, definitely does not confirm their own hypotheses. Many of them, for example, believe that size of the group is an important element in determining atmosphere. They think it is easier to get along with one's neighbors in a small office. This romantic vision, akin to the myth of the happy villager, does not correspond at all to reality as we were able to determine it. Small offices do not have a better atmosphere than larger ones; quite the contrary is the case. Similarly, it was impossible for us to conclude that there are any clear differences in atmosphere between male and female offices, between young and old offices, between homogeneous and heterogeneous offices.[2]

On the other hand, our results concerning factors which influence individual feelings were much more precise. In particular, three fundamental elements of group life clearly stood

2. Our sample of forty groups was too low to permit examination of such complex variables; but if these problems were as crucial as our interviewees think, differences would have appeared.

out: Affective atmosphere, formalism of interpersonal relations, and professional pride of the group.

Affective Atmosphere

We sought to obtain an evaluation of office atmosphere by posing the following questions to our subjects.

If you were to describe the atmosphere in your office, which of the following statements would be most appropriate?
1. The atmosphere is very good, everyone gets along very well.
2. The atmosphere is good, people behave properly.
3. The atmosphere is not bad, but sometimes there are scenes, and jealousies.
4. People don't get along very well.

We were able to make the results more precise by blending them with responses concerning atmosphere which were given to a general question on the advantages and the inconveniences of the position. And finally, we used the combination or quasi-scale shown in table 8.

TABLE 8
Evaluation of Office Atmosphere

Category 1	Category 2	Category 3
State that the atmosphere is very good. Choose the atmosphere as one of the advantages of the position.	State that people behave properly or that the atmosphere is not very good. Choose the atmosphere as one of the advantages of the position.	State that people behave properly or that the atmosphere is not very good. Do not choose the atmosphere as one of the advantages of the position.
19%	21%	57%

As we have already noted, there are perceptible differences between groups, but it is not possible to establish a model to explain these differences, which are not related to either size of group, or professional category, or sex or age distribution. At best, we can note that typists, on the average, evaluate the atmosphere in their office as slightly worse than do their colleagues, while archivists evaluate it as definitely better. Differences between companies are, on the other hand, more considerable than we had expected. Office atmosphere is evaluated as poor by 73 percent of the employees of one company[3] (and good by 7 percent) while the distribution in another company is 41 percent and 37 percent.

Who are the malcontents? Age and sex seem to have some influence. Women and old people complain more. Above all, employees of more bourgeois origin, or those who have higher aspirations, are much more likely to be discontent. We find, for example, that among employees who from a list of professions which they would consider acceptable for an eventual spouse choose only those at the highest levels, 80 percent are malcontents.

Individual factors seem, however, to carry much less weight than collective factors. We did not find any close relationship between evaluation of atmosphere and overall evaluation of managers. But the decisive importance of the manager's personality comes out clearly in the definite connection between evaluation of atmosphere and the degree to which the interviewee gets along with his manager. The worse one gets along with one's manager, the better the chance that one will evaluate the atmosphere as poor. This effect becomes even more profound if one compares the atmosphere in groups with liberal, authoritarian, and bureaucratic management styles.[4]

Formalism in Relations between Colleagues

We asked our interviewees whether they used the informal *tu* or the formal *vous* in addressing their colleagues in the office,

3. Interestingly, this is the company with the fewest employees, where the prevalent atmosphere is the most traditional.

4. In the section that follows, which is devoted to hierarchical relationships, we will analyze in detail the significance and the import of these relationships. We simply note in passing that in groups with a good atmosphere, that is, groups where at least three-quarters of the employees consider the atmosphere good, we find 50 percent of the managers liberal, 38 percent authoritarian, and 12 percent with a bureaucratic style or a laissez-faire approach. In groups with a poor atmosphere, that is, those where at least three-quarters of the employees consider the atmosphere fair or poor, we find 17 percent liberal compared to 27 percent authoritarian and 56 percent laissez-faire. Of the laissez-faire managers, 80 percent lead groups where there are complaints about the atmosphere. Conformity, fear of compromising

whether they called them by first name, and whether they ever went out to have a cup of coffee with them. These diverse objective behavior patterns were, with a relatively small number of errors, well-ordered on a scale which allows us to characterize quite accurately the formalism of relations between employees.

Differences by professional category are perceptible, but smaller than one might expect (see table 9). Archivists are much less formal than their colleagues (they are never found in categories 4 and 5) and keypunchers address each other as *tu* more readily, but on the whole we find relatively similar distributions. Curiously, the company seems to have an effect, even though we cannot show any peculiarities in the social composition of the various personnel groups.

TABLE 9

Relations Between Colleagues

<table>
<tr><th>Category 1</th><th>Category 2</th><th>Category 3</th><th>Category 4</th><th>Category 5</th><th rowspan="4">Un-classifiable</th></tr>
<tr><td>Address everyone as tu</td><td colspan="2">Address only some persons as tu</td><td colspan="2">Address no one as tu</td></tr>
<tr><td colspan="2">Call everyone by first name</td><td colspan="3">Do not call everyone by first name.</td></tr>
<tr><td colspan="4">Sometimes goes out for a cup of coffee with his colleagues</td><td>Never goes out for a cup of coffee with his colleagues</td></tr>
<tr><td>12%</td><td>19%</td><td>32%</td><td>13%</td><td>9%</td><td>15%</td></tr>
</table>

On the other hand, individual characteristics are the basis for more notable contrasts. Women are much more formal than

oneself, and minimal devotion to the company charcterize the laissez-faire bosses, as we shall see later, and make them much less likely to create a good work atmosphere.

men, and old people are much more so than the young. Employees whose parents were business people or who came from a higher-level environment use *tu* less often than sons of laborers, and those who had greater education do so less than those with only primary-school education. Finally, and above all, employees who have a higher cultural level and those who have higher social aspirations are definitely more formal than their colleagues.[5]

Professional Group Pride

Besides the questions on affective relations and on modes of interaction, we posed two questions which were designed to determine the interest our subjects had in their office as a functional group.

We asked them whether they thought their office was on the whole "better" or on the whole "not as good" as other offices, and whether it would make any difference to them if they changed departments. The results showed us, as should have been expected, that the vast majority of employees were at least passively devoted to their office.

But it should be noted that the responses obtained are related, much more directly than the questions on atmosphere, to the responses regarding managers.[6] In this case it was no longer simply a matter of direct influence of authority-style, but of an easily perceptible individual equation between office pride and a favorable evaluation of the manager.

Office pride seems to be very little affected by variables other than relations with the manager. At best, we can note that clerks and archivists are much more often disposed to change departments than their colleagues. Nor does office pride have much of a relation to the other attitudes we tested. What is involved here is a much more narrow dimension than we had at first imagined, something more related to the climate

5. These relations are statistically significant to about .01 percent.

6. Naturally the responses to these two questions are closely related to each other. Among those who say that their office is better, 73 percent would be annoyed to change, and no one would change gladly; among those who think their office is not as good as others, the proportions are 10 percent and 23 percent respectively.

of success established by the manager than to relations between colleagues.

Hierarchical Relations

Managers occupy an important place in an employee's social universe. They are the source of reprimands and compliments, encouragements and criticisms. They are responsible for distributing work. Besides, the manager has the "know-how," and his willingness to communicate it can be the crucial factor in determining an employee's development and future in the company. Finally, for the young, ambitious employee, he is the example of success. Being accepted or rejected by one's manager therefore takes on exceptional importance. Even if we put aside his role as dispenser of rewards, the manager's mood constitutes, by virtue of his physical presence alone, an important element of the prevailing atmosphere. It is impossible that his existence be of no concern to the employee. His methods, his idiosyncrasies, his preferences, his human warmth, even his tone of voice, are all details which touch the employee to the quick.

When our interviewees describe their career, they do not say, "I did this, then that," but rather, "I worked for X, then I went to work for Y," or "Z made me come to work for him." Manager and function are very closely intertwined in the minds of subordinates. Beyond this, it is function more than title that defines the manager in the hierarchy. The manager is the person *for whom* one does the work. Theoretical administrative organization corresponds only imperfectly to actual organization. In a situation where executives are often overly numerous, power, in a certain measure, belongs to whoever wants it or can take it. Without a doubt, in many cases "force of circumstance" gives rise to beneficial adjustments, but not always. We also find a good number of cases of power vacuums and cases of dispersion of power.

This sort of situation (which is not general) seems to be characteristic of a bureaucratic environment which has remained traditional. It is due to the absence of a well-determined policy with regard to personnel, but especially to the predominance, at all echelons of the hierarchy, of technical functions over human functions and leadership functions, a condition which often allows executives to avoid their responsibilities to their subordinates.

This situation is highly noticeable to employees. If one makes a list of the grievances of employees with regard to their managers, one notices that these grievances are less personal than one might have expected. They have a rather general import, and concern the functioning of the department more often than they concern some personal injustice that was committed.

What, in effect, do employees reproach their managers for? In more than half the cases, for faults which management could just as well attribute to them: technical incompetence, human incompetence, or both at the same time.

Here are a few harsh judgments in this area taken from our exploratory study.

"Mostly, they are old fogies who have been here for twenty or twenty-five years. They made it by virtue of seniority and are not very competent. Mine would do best to retire to the country."

"Mr. X is not a real manager. He does his work, but he does not have a manager's temperament. All in all, we are badly managed, badly compensated, badly encouraged."

"Our manager has a lot of style, but he does not have the makings of a manager at all; a few years ago there was a real mess here. What an employee hates most is to be criticized in front of everyone; that's not the way to do things."

"My manager didn't train us, we trained him."

These judgments often come from young and particularly critical employees who, besides, do not mean to apply them to *all* managers. A critical point of view is not, let us note carefully, an index of bad morale. Most employees who adopt a critical point of view are well integrated, on the whole satisfied, and impatient to be put to the test.

But, more than awkwardness or weakness, it is managers' indifference—or at least their apparent indifference—to subordinates' work and to their problems that shocks employees.

"They do not consider what they are doing." That is the

big grievance. "They are too far away and make no effort to come closer." "As soon as they have their petty comforts, their little ivory tower, the rest is a joke to them."

Employees tend to think that managers, once promoted, and so at last free of the demands of day-to-day business matters, and sheltered from worries, want only to avoid getting in trouble. They are then seen as turncoats, as *deserters*. As another employee puts it:

"The minute you become an executive, you are no longer yourself; you are obliged to act in a certain way."[7]

Reciprocal evaluations by managers and employees

To determine more precisely the attitudes of employees toward their managers and thus allow us to confront the latter with the attitudes and behavior patterns of the former, we asked them a series of standardized questions. We will not waste much time on the distribution of opinions, since this presents nothing exceptional. Let us note that 58 percent of the employees declared themselves mostly satisfied with their managers, compared to 19 percent who found them fair and 17 percent who frankly declared themselves discontent.[8] On the question about the advantages and inconveniences of their position, 32 percent spontaneously chose the response "good managers" as an advantage, and 16 percent chose "bad managers" as an inconvenience. In a second series of questions, where we attempted to make employees specify the behavioral traits they approved of in their managers, the following positive traits emerged: knows his work well (chosen by 53 percent of the sample), orderly (48 percent), agreeable (41 percent),

7. If we ask employees whether it is better that executives be chosen from their ranks rather than from the outside, a third of them refuse to answer, have reservations, or do not take a stand. There are certain ambiguities in the way in which old-timers speak of an executive they knew when he was just an employee like themselves. Often they are proud of his success—they participate in it in a way; in any case, they have borne witness to the mysterious transmutation that turns the passive employee into an element of management. But some can also revolt, deny the mystery, as does the employee who declares, "I don't think it's good to be directed by someone who was hired after me."

8. The percentage of employees who are more or less discontent is 31 percent in the bank, 24 percent in the clerical agency, and 24 percent in the ministry as well. See Crozier, *Petits fonctionnaires,* p. 87.

forceful (36 percent), a man of merit (33 percent), just (33 percent), candid (32 percent), cordial and friendly (23 percent). Meanwhile, on the negative side, the following appeared: meddlesome (18 percent), overdemanding (15 percent), lacks dynamism (10 percent), distant (6 percent).

These choices are organized into three scales. The first scale includes the positive choices "cordial," "friendly," and "agreeable" and at the other end of the extreme, the negative choice "meddlesome." The second includes, at one end, the positive choices "energetic" and "knows his work well" and, at the other, the negative choice "lacks dynamism." The third scale includes the positive choices "man of merit" and "orderly" and the negative choice "demanding." These groupings show us which points employees are particularly sensitive about. Especially dreaded are managers who control closely, the "meddlers," those who are more interested in productivity than in quality of work or in group harmony, the "overdemanders," and those "who lack dynamism" because they do not know how to make decisions or how to direct. Such qualities as candor and justice do not seem to be crucial for employees.

All these evaluations vary considerably from one company to another and from one position to another. But a more thorough analysis allows us to show that it is at the work-group level that important differences emerge: the manager's personality thus seems to have a determinant influence.

Extremely interesting complementary evaluations on the part of managers correspond to these evaluations by employees. While employees express their discontent openly, managers issue unfavorable evaluations of their subordinates less frequently. But if one takes into account the difficulty a manager might have in evaluating his work-group unfavorably, since such an evaluation might be taken as an admission of failure or powerlessness, and if in consequence one considers that not saying "I have a very good group" is practically equivalent to saying it is mediocre, the correspondence is striking.

If we now compare employees' evaluations of their managers with managers' evaluations of their work-groups, we get the results shown in table 10.

We find a relationship of the same order, and just as clear-

TABLE 10

Evaluations of Each Other by Managers and Subordinates

Groups in which	the manager declares that his team is very good	the manager declares that his team is good	the manager declares that his team is not very good	Total
The vast majority of employees are satisfied with their manager	64%	36%	0	100%
Groups that are divided and groups that are discontent	32%	54%	12%	100%

Note: Only 33 groups could be used for this confrontation. N = 33.

cut, when we compare employees' feelings with the image their manager has of those feelings. When employees are hostile, the manager almost always perceives this hostility and expresses it in his response. This reciprocity of feelings, based on a relatively clear perception of reality, will come as no surprise to the social psychologist. It makes evident the importance of the affective aspect in the manager-subordinate relationship, but tells us nothing about the factors that determine the quality of this relationship. A study of leadership styles will allow us to deal with a variable which is, from this point of view, much more decisive.

Leadership Style

All the executives of the groups studied were interviewed at length on what they considered to be the proper way to behave towards subordinates, and about their personal experience in this matter. From their responses we attempted to extract, by using both content analyses and statistical cross-tabulations, a small number of relatively stable behavioral models.

This method allowed us to rediscover, in an empirical manner, the classical distinctions established by American social psychologists between authoritarian executives, liberal executives, and laissez-faire executives.[9]

The primary contrast was between authoritarian executives and liberal executives; this contrast emerged as relatively clear-cut from the responses obtained to two questions, one concerning the use of fear and the other facility in exercising authority.[10]

If, from these two questions which are closely related to each other, we establish an attitudinal scale, we can distinguish two coherent groups that have a large number of common characteristics when we analyze their responses to other questions.[11]

One group, which encompasses 30 percent of the total, comes out as having a tendency toward liberalism, while a second group, encompassing 38 percent, comes out with a definitely authoritarian orientation. Here are characteristic extracts from interviews in each group.

The authoritarian executives: "To make yourself feared

9. We refer here to the famous experiments by Kurt Lewin and to all the work they stimulated. See in particular, as part of a very abundant literature, Lewin, Lippit, and White, "Patterns of Aggressive Behavior in Experimentally Created Social Climates," *Journal of Abnormal and Social Psychology* 1 (1939): 217–19; Coch and French, "Overcoming Resistance to Change," *Human Relations* 1 (1948): 512–33; D. Katz, N. Maccoby, Nancy Morse, *Productivity Supervision and Morale in an Office Situation* (Ann Arbor, Michigan, 1950).

10. A majority expressly advocate fear as a means of leadership, while a smaller group definitely opposes it. Between these two extreme positions, a third group, also a minority, backs off in the face of any categorical option.

In the results concerning authority, we have a more nuanced distribution. Forty per cent of the subjects adopt noncommittal attitudes of the type, "It's O.K., things work out all right." Two groups, both smaller, declare categorically that it is easy to exercise authority, but the first insist on collaboration with personnel, while the second turn the question into one of personal prestige, declaring for example, "When I've decided something, it must work, I make sure of it . . ." Finally, 20 percent of the interviewees complain of difficulties due to the criticism, the inattention, or the inexperience of employees.

11. In fact, we were able to establish many quasi-scales in Guttman's sense, all of which come back to the same point: the distinction of the authoritarian group from the liberal group or from both other groups together; but no organization into a general scale proved to be possible.

seems to me indispensable, personnel must think twice before acting. . . . You can't allow limits to be exceeded. Yet, setting one brutal example seems to me preferable to constant fear. In any case, they [the employees] must realize that you will not abuse your authority, but that you will maintain it. They must be made to feel that authority is always there, particularly the day they need you.

The liberal executives: "Maybe you get more by making yourself feared, but then you aren't very well-liked. As for me, I get what I want and I don't make myself feared. . . . I propose a method. If theirs is better, I accept it. . . . I reject the formula, 'oderint dum metuant.' "[12]

Authoritarian executives are the only executives who perceive the existence of a certain hostility on the part of their subordinates. Conversely, liberal executives, when they indicate difficulties, often have the impression that their employees are intimidated.

As far as methods are concerned, differences express themselves first of all in the matter of encouragement and complimenting. The rule among liberal executives is to encourage and compliment employees "from time to time" or "frequently." In contrast, a very great majority of authoritarian managers admit that they compliment only "rarely" or never.

The same differences are manifest in the matter of employees who are late to work. This little detail is, in fact, one of the most rigid regulatory principles; management attaches great importance to it and supervisors are charged with paying particular attention to promptness. A quarter of the managers interviewed adopt a tolerant though watchful attitude, while almost half show themselves to be, on the contrary, resolutely interventionist. Liberal managers, naturally, show a marked preference for tolerance, while authoritarian managers are, on the contrary, the most significant fraction of interventionists.

As far as work load is concerned, attitudes are altogether symmetrical. The "tolerant" executives recognize that their employees complain, at least sometimes, of having too much work, while the authoritarian executives (like, moreover, the rest of the sample) ignore the complaints of their workers.

12. "Let them hate me as long as they obey." The quotation was made in Latin to the interviewer.

Obviously there are a few exceptions here and there, but they are rare, and it really seems that liberal and authoritarian executives do not perceive the same elements of the situation, in terms of needs, complaints, and diverse activities in the work team, or at least that they do not attach the same importance or give the same meaning to each of these elements. Liberal managers do not appear to notice late arrival or attach relatively little importance to it; on the other hand, they are attentive to the reactions of their group in the matter of work load. Authoritarian managers note lateness and consider it an important matter, but do not perceive complaints in the matter of work. What we are faced with here is a phenomenon of selective perception: style of leadership orients attention to one particular sector of reality, while the other sector stays in the shadows.

Liberals and authoritarians contrast sharply in two other areas, both significant: evaluation of the work team and the feeling the manager may have of being irreplaceable. Liberal managers are more likely to think that they could be replaced.[13]

The Laissez-faire Supervisors

Almost a third of the supervisors interviewed fall outside the authoritarian-liberal contrast. At first, the existence of this third group posed a difficult problem. One might have thought that what we were really dealing with here was a group of individuals with divided opinions, or a group which had highly nuanced or neutral viewpoints. But an attentive examination of their comments shows that what is involved is much more an evasion of the problem than a hesitation to express oneself on it. Were we then dealing with an irregular collection of subjects who were on the defensive, or overly scrupulous, or who considered the questions asked of them too simplistic? The other comments made by these supervisors and the evaluations made of them by their subordinates suggest instead that they are a third group, relatively homogeneous, whose style of

13. While only 15 percent of liberal managers declare that no one could replace them, this percentage rises to 40 percent among authoritarian managers and authoritarian managers declare more frequently that they have a "very good work team."

leadership, evidently negative, corresponds to the attitude they manifested when confronted with the problem—a difficult problem for them—which this questionnaire constituted. In fact, the contrast between the members of this third group and the rest of the sample is, on quite a few points, much stronger than the contrast between liberal supervisors and authoritarian supervisors.

Let us look, for example, at the way their subordinates describe these supervisors. It will be remembered that we presented employees with a series of possible descriptions, phrased in their own words, and asked them to choose among these the ones that would apply best to their own manager. If we compare the responses obtained as a function of styles of leadership, we note that 84 percent of the managers whose employees complain that they lack dynamism and fear responsibility fall within this third "intermediate" group. Generally the supervisors in this group are called meddlesome and overdemanding, while their colleagues, whether they be liberal or authoritarian, are called forceful and are regarded as "cordial, orderly, and men of merit." This verdict is quite clear-cut.

Another comparison draws attention to the defense mechanism which not choosing or making conventional choices seems to constitute for them; they act in this way not because of uncertainty, but out of a desire to escape a disagreeable reality. We compared the evaluations made by supervisors to those made by employees with regard to the atmosphere that prevails in the work group. Supervisors' evaluations are naturally much more optimistic than those of their employees. Still, 45 percent of the managers perceive quite accurately the affective climate in their team, while 27 percent make a noticeable error in their evaluations and a third group consisting of 27 percent make a response contrary to that of their teams.[14]

Half the supervisors who were so completely mistaken about the atmosphere in their department are members of the third group. Moreover, we know that 80 percent of the members of this group head departments where the vast majority of em-

14. We categorized the groups as having a good or bad atmosphere depending on whether 75 percent of the members responded that the atmosphere was good or bad; groups with no strong majority opinion either way were considered to have a mixed atmosphere.

ployees consider the atmosphere poor, while these members themselves show unflagging optimism regarding the feelings of their subordinates (not one of them, for example, says that his employees are not at ease with him). In this perspective the supervisors of this third group appear to be men who do not get involved, because they make a point of avoiding responsibilities by refusing to see reality as it is and by always choosing impersonal solutions which compromise them as little as possible.

Yet this avoidance of contacts and of responsibilities provokes highly unfavorable reactions among subordinates. Finally, there is a much greater difference between the results achieved in the matter of human relations by conventional or "laissez-faire" supervisors and those achieved by the rest of the sample, than there is between the results achieved by authoritarian supervisors and those achieved by liberal supervisors. We become aware of this by comparing the attitudes of employees and supervisors in the three groups (see table 11).

TABLE 11

Supervisory Style and Employee Attitude

	Subordinates Are Discontent	Subordinates Are Divided	Subordinates Are Satisfied
Liberal supervisors	25%	28%	47%
Authoritarian supervisors	28%	36%	36%
"Laissez-faire" supervisors	56%	27%	17%

Origin of leadership styles; influence of the organization

This analysis of styles of leadership and their consequences has allowed us to bring to light one of the fundamental elements of interpersonal relationships between superiors and subordinates. But we still have an overly "psychological" interpretation, and what remains now is to ask which factors influence the development of these leadership styles. Thanks to the special design of our study, which gave us the opportunity for both intergroup and intercompany comparisons, we can present at least the beginnings of an answer.

Neither psychological characteristics, sex, age, seniority, or education seem to have much of an influence on supervisors' choice of leadership styles. On the other hand, the type of work done by the group they lead has a quite noticeable influence, and the organization to which they belong has a decisive influence.

The difference introduced by type of work is the kind that might be expected. In the policy-men groups, managers have a tendency to be more liberal; in the clerk and archivist groups, they are more authoritarian. But these differences remain weak (44 percent liberal managers among policy-men compared to 28 percent in the other professional categories) despite the importance of influences which tend to reinforce them (the need of a manager in a production department to depend on the good will and the professional conscience of his collaborators,[15] and the high level of education of supervisors and subordinates in these groups, which make it more difficult to use authoritarian procedures).

The profound difference between supervisors working in different companies thus appears all the more remarkable in this milieu which remains, in all other respects, very homogeneous.

Our study involved six companies. Three of them have relatively balanced distributions between the three leadership styles which we distinguished; but the three others are each heavily weighted in favor of one particular style.

Of these three, the first is an old, traditional company, somewhat smaller than the others (it employs only two hundred persons compared to a mean of five hundred). Authoritarian supervisors make up 75 percent of this group, compared to a

15. In imperfectly rationalized companies, such as insurance companies, managers cannot assure proper functioning of their departments without relying on the good will of their subordinates. We asked them, "What is most important for the functioning of a department—tight organization and control of work, or the professional conscience of employees?" "Professional conscience" was the answer given by 65 percent of our interviewees, compared with 5 percent answering "organization and control."

mean of 28 percent among the five other companies. This contrast corresponds well with the observations of our researchers on the respectable and paternalistic style of the organization, and the prestige enjoyed by its management.[16]

The second is a modern company of eight hundred persons whose liberal orientation, though strong—since 55 percent of its supervisors are liberal compared to 25 percent among the other companies—was much less easily predictable. What we have here is a company in full process of great commercial expansion where employees and supervisors alike are subject to the constant stress of change, both in methods of work and in organization. This expansion and rationalization has brought about a greater specialization of tasks; on the other hand the rhythm of work is more sustained and productivity is definitely higher than elsewhere. One might have thought that under such circumstances supervisors would be led to adopt a more authoritarian attitude. But the effort imposed by management is not translated in this way; the atmosphere has, in fact, remained relatively cooperative, and modernity of work methods has favored a liberal orientation rather than an authoritarian orientation.

The third company is one with a laissez-faire style, where 62 percent of the supervisors fall into the group consisting of those who refuse to take responsibilities. It is a relatively modern and active company, but its organizational structure seemed confused. At all levels, authority seemed to be poorly accepted. Unions, quite strong in the company,[17] shared in this uncertainty. This company had already been reorganized several times without yet being able to find its equilibrium.

These three companies are not representative of the white-collar milieu, or of the insurance company milieu. But the fact that completely comparable organizations, with the same functions and personnel of the same origin, in a milieu that is generally considered very homogeneous, should end by developing styles of hierarchical relations that contrast so sharply,

16. It is in this organization that we find by far the largest number of employees who know the name and a few personal traits of their director-general.

17. As they were, moreover, in the two other companies with liberal and authoritarian orientation.

shows the preponderant importance in this area of the variable "company." This will become all the more striking when we discover the projective tests, designed to reveal the existence of authoritarian traits among the supervisors interviewed, have brought to light only very weak variations from company to company.

The importance of hierarchical rank

The study we conducted in insurance companies related only to employees and their immediate supervisors. By using this approach, we intended to concentrate on the most immediate fact of the employees' human environment, but we tended to ignore the considerable importance in administrative organizations of the length and the complexity of the bureaucratic chain.

During two earlier studies of the administrative departments of a large bank and a Parisian ministry, we attempted to study different hierarchical levels and to compare their conceptions of leadership. A new element appeared in the course of the present study: the importance of hierarchical rank, which can be considered both as a cultural factor (the higher one is in the hierarchy, the more one is called upon to partake of the cultural values of the upper classes), and as a factor that pertains to the system of organization itself (the higher one is in the hierarchy, the more one has a role that involves discussion, compromise, and arbitration between contradictory demands).

We posed the following question concerning style of leadership to our interviewees:

What is preferable for a manager:
—to control from up close, since one can never depend on one's subordinates;
—to keep hands off to some extent, because a subordinate who is left with no responsibility works poorly?

The answers were extremely coherent and completely different from those that are generally expected (see table 12).

This breakdown repeats perfectly the American research results used by Seymour Lipset in *Political Man* (New York, 1959) to support his theory of working class authoritarianism.

TABLE 12

Preference for Tight Control by Hierarchical Rank

Bank		Public Administration	
Department Manager	7%	Office Manager	14%
Department Submanager	12%	Office Submanager	24%
Section Manager	17%	Group Manager	44%
Group Manager	23%	Agents and Clerks	45%
Employees	43%		

Presented in this way, this breakdown appears to be almost a fact of culture.

But we can also note that it corresponds perfectly to another breakdown which we were able to establish based on responses to a projective question on the ideal manager. The question was framed as follows:

What is, in your opinion, the ideal manager?
1. One who impartially distributes tasks and rewards, avoiding hasty judgments.
2. One who makes an effort to act diplomatically, adapting his methods to each person's personality.
3. One who avoids being authoritarian and makes an effort to help employees perfect their methods of work themselves.
4. One who knows how to make clear and forceful decisions which employees must follow and respect.

Naturally we contrast those who chose statement 2 with those who chose statement 4 (see table 13).

TABLE 13

Preference for Manager

	Choose the Diplomatic Manager As Ideal	Choose the Authoritarian Manager As Ideal
Department Manager	55%	15%
Section Manager and Group Manager	32%	32%
Employees	10%	45%

Yet this second table brings out a fundamental difference in roles. Already at a middle level, the supervisor must take into account the diverse interests and the contradictory attitudes of those he must direct and with whom he must collaborate. He must necessarily act as a temporizer and as a diplomat. This behavior is viewed with much disfavor by his subordinates, who accuse him of lack of candor and declare their preference for a forceful manager, who makes clear and categorical decisions (but naturally in their favor[18]).

In this way, we discover the existence of another variable which conditions the relation between superiors and subordinates. Beyond differences between particular organizations, there exists a constraint which is of a general nature and is related to the complexity and the weight of the hierarchical order.

Conclusions

The results which we have just presented can be used in a number of different perspectives. For example, they open up interesting possibilities for understanding the practical problems of training which arise in companies,[19] and they can also offer a contribution to the theory of organization. But our objective in this work is not to present general conclusions on human relations in organizations but to describe in depth the peculiarities of office workers' behavior and the logic of their attitudes.

From this point of view, a certain number of general remarks come to mind.

First of all, a comparison of the responses to questions regarding relations between colleagues and those concerning relations between executives and subordinates, seems to indicate that formal relations have noticeably more importance

18. For a more thorough discussion of these results, we refer the reader to Michel Crozier and Jacques Lautman, "La contribution du sociologue à l'étude des problèmes de formation," *Sociologie du travail* 5, no. 4 (1963): 329–43.

19. Such is the objective of a research report which we published in 1959. See Michel Crozier and Bernard Pradier, *Groupes et chefs, les relations hiérarchiques dans six compagnies d'assurances parisiennes,* mimeographed (Paris: ISST).

than informal relations. The entire field of social psychology was renewed by the discovery of informal relations at the primary-group level. But the progress made as a result of this discovery led to neglect of the importance of formal factors and of the significance which may be assumed by differences between predominantly formal and predominantly informal systems. Relations between colleagues are not without influence on atmosphere, but it certainly appears that our office workers remain relatively isolated and on the reserved side, that they have practically no relations outside work, and that they do not form blocs at work. The superior-subordinate dialogue is, in the end, of greater importance in determining work atmosphere than interactions between colleagues.

The second characteristic to be noted is, in our opinion, the involvement of office workers in the organizational system of which they are a part. This characteristic is a corollary of the first. All the results seem to show that subordinates do not form a world apart, but rather are deeply affected by the hierarchical system to which they belong, which they in turn influence and mold. The behavior of upper management is the determinant factor for executives' leadership style, and this leadership style is in turn a decisive factor for interpersonal relations in general and for atmosphere. To be sure, the influence at one remove which is exercised on employees at the bottom is not as perceptible as the pressure felt by members of the executive staff. Passive resistance among the mass of subordinates is considerable, and we do not rediscover among employees in the six companies the differences which we were able to note between their supervisors. These differences nevertheless exist and are all the more significant since they are manifest against an extremely homogeneous background. The administrative world, at least in this smaller sector, is certainly a world deeply influenced and penetrated by the attitudes and behavior patterns of the managerial classes.[20]

Involvement in the organizational system is matched by a

20. The few comparative studies between white-collar and blue-collar employees which we were able to consult all show that white-collar employees are always more sensitive to action on the part of management, whether it be favorable or critical; as for blue-collar employees, they are always more indifferent.

great vulnerability to the defects of that system and, in particular, to the heaviness and the lack of realism of the bureaucratic communication networks. This characteristic which was present in our six companies and which was emphasized, for example, by the importance of laissez-faire supervisors, came out even more emphatically in our earlier study of the administrative departments of the bank. The number of hierarchical levels and the distribution of roles among these levels engenders an atmosphere characterized by lack of realism and fear in human relations, which in turn provokes the need for control and reinforces, in a sort of vicious circle, the organizational system that gives rise to it.

Elsewhere we have analyzed the genesis and the consequences of this bureaucratic phenomenon.[21] Here we simply indicate that the behavior of office workers and their attitudes are deeply marked by this role which is imposed upon them. Contrary to the blue-collar group, separated and protected as much as oppressed by the class barrier, white-collar employees do not resist by means of solidarity[22] but rather by indifference and apathy, or eventually by demanding forceful and authoritarian supervisors.

The heavy weight of hierarchy and the complexity of communications are nevertheless not due only to the concentration of modern production units and to the development of their administrative organs; they are also related to the difficulties of a cultural order which men encounter in establishing a complex system of roles and communications. Two dimensions seem in the end to dominate interpersonal relations among office workers: a general dimension of a cultural order, which takes into account the weight of a bureaucracy and of the general atmosphere of centralization; and a dimension of a structural order specific to each company, which introduces the very notable differences in leadership style and in atmosphere that have already been noted.

21. See Michel Crozier, *The Bureaucratic Phenomenon* (Chicago: University of Chicago Press, 1964).

22. There is much to be said, though, for the real importance of working class solidarity. Certain groups of blue-collar workers with strong traditions and high prestige do have solidarity, but isolation, apathy, indifference, and incoherent revolts predominate in many sectors.

Can we go still further and draw from these findings some initial conclusions on the role of the office worker in modern society? In our first section, we noted the growing ambiguity of human relations which is brought about, in modern societies, by the participation of all individuals in complex collectivities. Office workers, we hypothesized, are the subordinate group most involved in this complexity, and therefore the group which should orient itself most easily toward greater tolerance and openness to others. The results which we have just analyzed do not invalidate this hypothesis, but they show that these rational developments are not as yet accompanied by the indispensable psychological—or, if you will, cultural—progress.

The French white-collar employee, fashioned by the oppressive structure of companies, opens himself with difficulty to the tolerance necessary for the smooth functioning of more complex collectivities. He resists ambiguity and takes refuge in formality and obedience. Meanwhile, at a deeper level, adaptation slowly takes place. And during the course of a long series of communications of results in the bank, we were able to determine that the usable human resources among white-collar employees are, as of now, much more substantial than managers had imagined. These managers had themselves been formed by the general mold, which often still appears to them to be the only way of getting effective results.

7 Participation and Integration

Complexity of Relations between Individual and Organization

The study of work and of human environment do not cover all the human problems of an organization. If we wish to understand the social personality of insurance company employees at work, we must confront the problem raised by their participation in "companies," that is in coordinated and rationalized collectivities. The tie between the individual and the organization is relatively abstract, and it is through the concrete realities of work and of work group that the problem is raised. Nevertheless, it cannot easily be avoided, since the pressure of the organization on its members and the very nature of the dialogue it establishes with them affect all their attitudes and behavior patterns. Whether this influence is direct, as in the matter of human relations and leadership style, or indirect and much more limited, as in the matter of adaptation to tasks—that is, to well-crystallized social roles—it constitutes one of the essential dimensions of the human equilibrium of the social system formed by the company.

The problem of relations between individual and organization was for a long time conceived in the unitary perspective of "integration." We have already criticized the applications of such a perspective in the matter of satisfaction at work and "morale." But it is important to emphasize that this perspective was, in fact, equally inadequate in its area of choice. The analysis of relations between individual and organization in terms of integration arrived at rigid conclusions which all later research, little by little, invalidated. Beginning with the principle that every human being has a need to belong and to participate, the first investigators who devoted themselves to the problem thought that anything that contributes to reinforcing the "integration" of an organization is good, and anything that contributes to diminishing it is bad.[1] This Manichean conception was well received, because it seemed both clear and practical. If you admit that all individual relations in an organization fall, more or less, along one dimension, you should easily be able to measure the cohesion of a collectivity and the degree of participation of members, compare organizations to each other, and discover the factors which determine better or worse integration and, therefore, also determine the morale and human equilibrium of society.[2]

Such postulates could not fail to meet violent criticism from workers' unions; the applications that were made of them gave rise to accusations of manipulation and met with resistance which was difficult to surmount. The failure on the scientific level was just as clear-cut. It was quickly seen that participation in the organization did not necessarily correspond to favorable judgment of its management, and that one could in fact participate just as well through conflict as through integration. At the same time it became clear that traditional integrative measures—pensions, social advantages, and so on —could certainly diminish the rate of turnover of personnel by creating greater devotion to the company, but that it had

1. The term "integration" current among authors of the 1940s evoked the idea of an organization and subordination of all efforts to the community constituted by the company. Consciously or unconsciously, "integrationists" looked forward to a fusion between economic organization and social life.

2. This is the thesis upheld by Elton Mayo in his famous book *The Social Problems of an Industrial Civilization* (Boston: Harvard Business School, 1945). It influenced many American authors in the 1940s and in the beginning of the 1950s. The best critique of this thesis is, in our opinion, that of Clark Kerr and Lloyd Fisher, "Plant Society, The Elite and the Aborigenes," in *Common Frontiers in the Social Sciences* (Glencoe: Free Press, 1957).

no influence at all on their real activity and on their willingness to become involved and to participate.[3]

In order to study more comprehensively the problem of relations between individual and organization, one must therefore adopt a less narrow view, and take into account the complexity and the ambiguity of participatory relations. Generally the starting point is too often the idea that every individual always wants to participate in the leadership of collectivities of which he is a part, and that it is only the resistance of leaders or of the social system which prevents him from doing so. Participation is in fact dangerous, because it gets one involved; one can better safeguard one's independence by submitting to orders than by seeking to participate in the elaboration of decisions.[4] This is what explains the paradox encountered so frequently in French public administrations, that of forced participation. Subordinates, basically ready to participate in the functioning of the organization, are afraid to let this be known, because they do not want to risk finding themselves involved; they participate, at least apparently, only to the extent demanded of them and, by virtue of this fact, are hampered by constraint. On the other hand, between the participation-with-alienation that is to be found in identification with the leader or in the religion of the organization, and the conscious and voluntary participation in decisions that get one involved, there exist a whole gamut of situations to which members of an actual organization must accommodate as part of reality, as demanding as these members may be in the matter of democracy. Let us note in passing that there can be no conscious and voluntary participation unless the entire chain of command is implicated. If one is content to play only on the

3. The term "participation" seems to be in style now, just as the term "integration" was ten years ago. There is the risk that it will give rise to just as much confusion. One could actually say that man always participates, at least in an indirect or empathic manner, in the orientation of collectivities of which he is a part. But the demands for participation that are now so often expressed have no meaning unless what is involved is conscious and voluntary participation without alienation, that is a relationship which excludes affective manipulation either through enthusiasm or submission. Unless we specify the contrary, it is in this limited sense that we will use the term here.

4. We have developed this point in the *Bureaucratic Phenomenon,* pp. 269–73.

direct relationship between individual and organization, one will get participation only by virtue of either enthusiasm or manipulation.[5]

Traditional measures for integration are naturally powerless to grasp the complexity of these relations. Individuals' assessments are only one aspect. In order to make satisfactory judgments, one must understand the nature of these individuals' interplay with the organization, and interpret the implicit and explicit negotiation they carry out with that organization. The method of organization analysis we have used elsewhere,[6] one based on the confrontation between the formal and the informal, between feelings and behavior patterns, between reciprocal judgments of each other by various protagonists, could not, unfortunately, be used here, given the extensive and descriptive nature of our research. But, though we could not apply the method, we wanted at least to be inspired by its spirit. It was not possible for us to study the overall hierarchical chain and the reciprocal relations of different groups, but we were nevertheless able to pose general questions which brought to light the direct individual-organization relationship. The responses we collected, however partial, revealed to us a process much more complex than that of forces of integration.

Analysis of these responses will allow us to pose the problem of conflictual participation, by introducing evaluations of the union and of the joint-management committee as intervening variables; these responses will also allow us to show the contrast between real taste for information, discussion and knowledge, on the one hand, and, on the other hand, a more general and more passive devotion to the company. Finally, based on the data we collected on behavior patterns characterized by indifference and apathy, we can, at least partially, envisage the effect of the hierarchical chain.

Knowledge of Company Life and Interest in Management

We asked the subjects interviewed a large number of questions on what they knew, what they thought, and what they ex-

5. Enthusiasm and manipulation allow the short-circuiting of intermediate strata. But their results are never more than temporary.

6. See *The Bureaucratic Phenomenon,* especially pp. 150–156.

pected of their companies and of the role they played in them. The responses we got fell into two groups, one corresponding to the more intellectual questions which implied knowledge or desire for knowledge, and the other corresponding to the questions about feelings or evaluative judgments in which relations characterized by negotiation or passive loyalty were tested.

The first series was not, in fact, very homogeneous. Our questions related to both the degree of knowledge about the problems of the company and to the interest manifested in its management. In the area of pure information we asked, for example, what the profits of the company were during the last year and who was its director-general. In the area of management, we asked each of our subjects whether he ever thought about problems of organization of work, or talked about them with his friends or with his managers; whether he took up the defense of his company when he heard it attacked by the public, and whether he thought his company had a good reputation.[7]

It was not possible to organize the responses to all these questions on a single scale, but we were nonetheless able to make up two quasi-scales, the first testing the degree of information of subjects, and the second the interest they manifest in company management (see tables 14 and 15).

These two scales are related to each other and the responses as a whole seem to correspond quite definitely to one universe, but errors are numerous and coherence is relatively weak.[8] We can nonetheless make use of the results obtained to analyze the factors which affect employees' knowledge of company life and the practical interest they have in its affairs.

As for the overall results, they distribute as shown in table 16.

Differences by company are relatively weak as far as knowledge on the one hand, and, on the other hand, a more general, gory are more considerable (members of higher categories—claims adjusters and policy writers—are definitely better

7. Other questions tested the desire for information, and sources of information.

8. The questions on the desire for information and on the reputation of the company could not be organized, nor are those concerning current modes of information.

TABLE 14

Degree of Information

<table>
<tr><th>Group 1</th><th>Group 2</th><th>Group 3</th><th rowspan="3">Errors and Unclassifiable</th></tr>
<tr><td>Have some knowledge of the company's profits</td><td colspan="2">Know nothing about profits</td></tr>
<tr><td colspan="2">Have some knowledge of the personality of the director-general</td><td>Know nothing about the director-general</td></tr>
<tr><td>26%</td><td>56%</td><td>15%</td><td>3%</td></tr>
</table>

informed and much more interested in problems of management). Education works in the same direction and, as might have been expected, men take a much greater interest in company life than women.[9]

Other noticeable differences illustrate even better, perhaps, the significance of this knowledge and interest. Employees who are well informed about the company are also those who are the best informed in the area of policy. They are much more likely to be unionized and to be interested in the joint-management committee.[10] Finally, they generally have higher aspirations and wider contacts. The same relations are found again, only somewhat less clearly, as far as interest in management is concerned.

In a general way, despite their relative lack of rigor, all these results point in the same direction: The more one rises in the professional hierarchy, the more one also has, by virtue of family and milieu, wide horizons and the more likely one is to be interested in the affairs of one's company. The results we obtained in questioning supervisors reinforced this schema even more. On the intellectual plane at least, the likelihood of participation by employees seems to be a function of their professional and social level.

9. The responses to the questions on the reputation of each company, evidently profoundly distorted by the differences (highly perceptible) between companies, nevertheless conform to the same model.

10. Probability of independence less than .01 percent.

TABLE 15

Interest in Management

<table>
<tr><td>Group 1</td><td>Group 2</td><td>Group 3</td><td>Group 4</td><td rowspan="4">Errors and Unclassifiable</td></tr>
<tr><td>Defends the companies without reservations</td><td colspan="3">Does not defend the companies without reservations</td></tr>
<tr><td colspan="2">Talks to his friends and to his managers about problems of organization</td><td colspan="2">Does not talk about problems of organization</td></tr>
<tr><td colspan="3">Sometimes thinks about problems of organization</td><td>Never thinks about problems of organization</td></tr>
<tr><td>19%</td><td>18%</td><td>31%</td><td>27%</td><td>5%</td></tr>
</table>

Loyalty to the Company

This is absolutely not the case when it comes to loyalty to the company in the more traditional sense of integration, or when it comes to the feelings of employees concerning their relations with the company. We posed two questions on this subject, one of which aimed to get at the employee's judgment of the contribution the company makes to him and the other to reveal what he thinks he owes the company.

The first question was formulated as follows

Do you think that the company does all that it can for its personnel? Which of the following would you say is most accurate?
—It makes a great effort.
—It makes a certain effort.
—It doesn't bother itself much about it.
—Things are very bad.

And the second:

If you wanted to describe the way you see your relations with the company, which of the following statements would suit you best?

—I do my work conscientiously, but the rest is of no concern to me.
—I must take to heart the interests of the company. I owe the company a lot, it keeps me alive.
—Given the working conditions we have, there's no point in being overzealous.

As far as the employee's judgment of the company's generosity and the conscientiousness he shows about his own effort are concerned, it is not the employees who are most qualified, best educated, and whose aspirations are highest who are the most cooperative, but rather employees who are less well-educated, less qualified, and have less of a bourgeois orientation.

Let us look at our results a little more closely. The responses to the two questions are closely related,[11] but this overall relationship is rigorous only for the choice "the company does not bother itself much about its personnel" on the first question, and for the choice "I must take to heart . . . " on the second question. One can construct a good scale of loyalty to the company with these two fragments of questions and the responses to a third question on the attention given to general expenses of the company.[12] The peculiarities of this relationship are significant. The contribution-retribution equivalence, which many social psychologists and sociologists insist upon,[13] does not really come out except in two cases: when the employee indentifies himself in a traditional way with the organization to which he is devoted, or else when he is, on the contrary, violently discontent. In all other cases, that is, for the vast majority of employees, there is absolutely no equivalence.

A comparison of the results even allows one to discover a few unexpected differences. For example, the feeling of loyalty to the company varies little from company to company; on the other hand, the judgment made of the company's efforts varies

11. Probability of independence less than .01 percent.

12. We asked our interviewees: *"There is also a lot of talk about reducing general expenses. In your opinion should the employee make an effort to accomplish this?"*

13. For example, George Homans. On this subject see the application made of his theory by Roethlisberger, Zaleznik, and Christensen, *The Motivation, Productivity and Satisfaction of Workers* (Boston: Harvard Business School, 1958).

a great deal. In one company, 36 percent of the subjects interviewed say, "It makes a great effort," and 9 percent "It does not bother itself much about it." In another company almost the opposite is the case: 10 percent say, "It makes a great effort," and 35 percent, "It does not bother itself much about it." Differences by sex are just as notable. Women say much more often, "The company makes a great effort," and much less often, "I take to heart." As far as professional categories are concerned, the breakdown is clear-cut on judgment of the company, but is reversed, at least in part, when it comes to feelings, due to the absence of zealousness manifested by typists and keypunchers.[14]

TABLE 16

Attitudes Towards Companies

<table>
<tr><th>Group 1</th><th>Group 2</th><th>Group 3</th><th>Group 4</th><th>Errors or Unclassifiable</th></tr>
<tr><td>Take the interests of the company to heart</td><td colspan="3">Declare themselves conscientious or show no great zeal.</td><td rowspan="3"></td></tr>
<tr><td colspan="2">Are careful to reduce general expenses</td><td colspan="2">Indifferent to the problem of general expenses</td></tr>
<tr><td colspan="3">Declare that the company makes at least some effort for its personnel</td><td>Declare that the company does not do much at all for its personnel</td></tr>
<tr><td>20%</td><td>33%</td><td>20%</td><td>13%</td><td>13%</td></tr>
</table>

Which organization the employees belong to has little effect on these results (we find just about the same distribution in

14. This anomaly, which corresponds to the particular status of these categories in the company, may explain at least in part the differences between males and females.

each company);[15] they are noticeably influenced by seniority and by age, but in the expected direction.[16]

On the other hand, the contrast we have shown between an active intellectual interest in the organization (involving knowledge and discussion) and a passive sort of loyalty are manifest even more clearly than for the separate questions, first, in regard to the variables relating to origin and position and then, especially, with regard to social and cultural aspirations.

As far as the variables "origin" and "position" are concerned, we discover that subjects whose parents have a relatively higher profession are less loyal to the company. Actually, the differences are weak; they are also relatively weak as far as education is concerned (the better one is educated, the less one is loyal to the company). But they are definitely stronger—the finding is a surprising one—when we introduce salary as an intervening variable. Subjects in the two highest salary levels have little loyalty to their companies (the proportions are 62 percent and 53 percent respectively, versus a general average of 33 percent). Finally, classification by professional category is highly suggestive; it is almost exactly the inverse of what we get for level of information[17]

TABLE 17

Percentage of Subjects Quite Loyal and Very Loyal to the Company (Categories 1 and 2 of the Scale)

Keypunchers	73%
Clerks	63%
Archivists	61%
Typists	44%
Policy writers	43%
Claims adjusters	36%

15. This similarity between the results in each company may be surprising when we recall the very noticeable differences obtained on the two key questions of the scale. This is explained by the fact that many of the "it does not bother itself much about its personnel" responses become errors on the loyalty scale.

16. The curves which show loyalty to the company as a function of seniority and of age are altogether similar to those we have already presented for work and for position.

17. Only typists are really an exception.

Even more notable differences exist in the area of social and cultural aspirations. First of all, the more one is conscious of one's social standing, the less one is loyal to the company; among those who are in the highest category in a scale measuring perception of "social standing," 33 percent are loyal to the company while 51 percent have little loyalty; those in the lowest category of the scale are 58 percent loyal, 29 percent have little loyalty.[18] The same relation is found in two other scales measuring, in one case, aspirations in social matters and, in the other case, cultural level. Tables 18 and 19 show this perfectly.

The loyalty scale is positively related, if not to the scale measuring information (the differences do go in the same direction, but are quite weak), at least to the scale of interest in management. We rediscover quite exactly the same model we have already seen with regard to the satisfaction with position and satisfaction with contrast work: Two measures relating *grosso modo* to the same individual universe (here the relationship of individual and organization) are related to each other at the individual level, but vary inversely in relation to a few of the most important variables which define the situation of those involved. The lesser homogeneity of our results did not allow us to attempt an analysis of variance; the differences found are noticeably less clear-cut. Nevertheless, it seems reasonable to admit that what we are touching upon here is a phenomenon of the same order, which, as a better-handled questionnaire would have allowed us to demonstrate statistically, was not due to simple coincidence.

If this is so, let us try to reflect on the significance of this new contrast, so comparable to the first. As in the world of work, it may be that a good part of the choices which we gathered are determined by individual variance. But as for the rest of the differences, whose importance is considerable,

18. In the highest category the key question related to the professions judged suitable in the choice of a mate; included in this category were only those who judged only the higher professions that were presented to them (pharmacist and teacher) as suitable. In the lower category the key question involved a comparison with the father's position; ranked in this category were those who thought they had a position which was definitely better than that of their father. For an analysis of this scale, see below, pp. 181–82.

TABLE 18
Loyalty to the Company as a Function of Social Aspirations

	Loyal to the Company	Little Loyalty	Unclassifiable	Total
Weak social aspirations (hope their children enter non-intellectual professions, do not go to the theater, or to see operettas, do not look for friends in professions with higher prestige)	65%	20%	15%	100%
Higher social aspirations (would like their children to enter intellectual professions, say they are interested in theater, have friends in professions with higher prestige)	39%	52%	9%	100%

N = 301

we would tend to attribute them to the dialectic between security and psychological vulnerability to which we have already referred. Employees of modest origins and circumstances, who do not have sufficient educational background and those who have low aspirations, are above all else sensitive to the protector-protected relationship which the company offers them. They are devoted to the company, but in a passive way, and refuse to become interested in its activities in a positive manner, because they do not feel either intellectually or morally able to risk it. Employees who are educated and

TABLE 19

Loyalty to the Company as a Function of Cultural Level

	Loyal to the Company	Little Loyalty	Unclassifiable	Total
Low Cultural Level	76%	19%	6%	100%
Higher Cultural Level	44%	60%	6%	100%

NOTE: For an analysis of the elements of these two scales, see below p. 182. N = 301.

have higher aspirations, on the other hand, aim higher than their current position and are much more demanding in their relations with the company; it is they who are, in fact, most apt to become interested in the affairs of the company and to discuss them usefully. Lack of self-consciousness is obviously not a necessary condition for participation, but it often seems to go hand in hand with the chances for development of this participation.

The prejudices which have for a long time been kept alive through paternalist myths, and the renewal of these prejudices around the notion of integration are thus, in the case that concerns us here, completely invalidated by the facts. It is not among employees who are well "integrated" that the company can find responsible participants. Integration, in the restricted and passive sense of the term, is not at all a good school for responsibility. If participation is to be active for the employees and fruitful for the company, there must be real involvement and thus freedom of choice.[19] This may explain the paradoxical rapprochement between chances for participation and an off-hand attitude, which can now be interpreted as a sign of freedom rather than as a sign of refusal.

19. This rather unorthodox perspective is, moreover, corroborated when one examines the relationships of the two dimensions of relation to the company with promotional perspectives. When one has prospects for promotion, one becomes more interested in the management, but one is less loyal to the company.

Place of the Union and the Joint-Management Committee

Contrary to current opinion, which an earlier chapter has already shown to be quite unfounded, contrary even to the impression prevalent among employees,[20] unions are relatively powerful in the insurance milieu. Our interviewees are 38 percent unionized, which in present-day France represents a relatively high percentage, one much higher than the average generally found in industry.[21] To be sure, size of membership is only one aspect of union coverage. It nevertheless remains the truest sign of the actual activity of union organizations. Marked differences exist between companies in this regard. In three of them, the percentage unionized fluctuates around 50 percent (56 percent, 48 percent, and 47 percent respectively) while in the fourth and fifth it drops to 30 percent and 29 percent, and in the sixth to 20 percent. Nationalization of companies seems to have no effect since, in the two private companies in our sample, one is 48 percent unionized and the other 30 percent.

What does the union mean to employees? During the course of our exploratory study, we collected many comments which give us a rough idea.

White-collar employees who have never been unionized are sometimes hostile even to the idea of unions, but rarely do they still harbor the traditional stereotype according to which only blue-collar employees—that is persons with no self-respect—would allow themselves to be unionized. More generally they are indifferent or else complain about the politicization of unions. Many of them are repulsed by the esoteric character of union activity; certain organizations look to them like cliques from which they have the feeling of being excluded. Moreover, employees who feel like strangers for whatever reason, whether because of age, social milieu, recent entry into

20. White-collar employees in general think that unions are much more powerful in the blue-collar environment. Those of them who are very union-minded complain of the lack of receptivity in their own environment.

21. Those who were once union members but no longer pay dues amount to 25 percent; only 35 percent never were union members.

the company, or the desire to quit, similarly hesitate to become unionized.

Employees who were once unionized, but then stopped paying dues, are sometimes still in favor of the union idea; they abandoned union membership because of personal reasons, fatigue, old age, personal quarrels, but remain faithful to unionism itself. Most often, however, old union men have more violent grievances to express than nonunionized men. They complain simultaneously and contradictorily about the compromises of unions with political parties and with management, about their lack of activity and about their agitation, and accuse delegates of deception and self-interest.

Those unionized often have enthusiasm and conviction, but little sense of responsibility. Unionism seems to them an important, representative, and necessary institution. But even in their case, it is an institution that remains external to them. There is complaint about its insufficiencies which are attributed to the traditions of the environment, and to the niggardliness of management, but the institution is never seen as an expression and reflection of one's own group; the term *they*, not *we*, is used in speaking of unions. Only a few employees tell us, practically on the sly, that they are unionized "in order to be part of something, to pull together a little bit." In point of fact, it really seems that it is those employees who are most responsible and best integrated with the environment who become unionized; but while the need for participation may appear to be the root motivation for union adherence, this need expresses itself with difficulty and basically seems to be rarely satisfied in the existing context.

In the main study, we attempted to make these initial findings more precise by adding to the question of fact concerning union membership a series of questions designed to determine whether subjects interviewed have any desire to become union delegates, whether they read the reports of the joint-management committee, and whether they took any interest in its work. The responses to these diverse questions are closely related to each other and fall very neatly on one hierarchical scale. Table 20 is a representation of the scale of participation in the joint-management committee. The responses do not, however, have as much of a relationship with belonging to a union as we had thought. Certainly, union members are more interested in the joint-management committee, but the difference is not that considerable.

TABLE 20

Participation in Joint-management Committee

<table>
<tr><td>Category 1</td><td>Category 2</td><td>Category 3</td><td>Category 4</td><td rowspan="4">Errors or Unclassifiable</td></tr>
<tr><td>Are delegates, were delegates, or would like to be</td><td colspan="3">Would not like to be delegates</td></tr>
<tr><td colspan="2">Often read the reports of the joint management committee</td><td colspan="2">Rarely or never read the reports</td></tr>
<tr><td colspan="3">Are very interested or pretty much interested in the activities of the joint-management committee</td><td>Are very little interested or not at all interested in the activities of the joint-management committee</td></tr>
<tr><td>8%</td><td>17%</td><td>35%</td><td>20%</td><td>20%</td></tr>
</table>

More generally, the fact of being unionized or not being unionized is not determined by the same factors and seems to have a somewhat different meaning. Whether one is unionized depends on more contingent factors and more clear-cut elements of one's material situation. Interest in the joint-management committee is more even and regular, and is a function of general intellectual aspirations.

The importance of individual or collective historical factors in explaining adherence to the union is particularly manifest, thanks to the differences that can be found between companies. The particular atmosphere in each company certainly plays a significant role in individual choices. The other determinants of adherence also seem to correspond to the pressure of the past rather than to a projection into the future. More likely to be unionized are those who worked before the age of fifteen, those who are of modest origins, and those who have a lower standing and lower aspirations. On the other hand we must note, in contradiction to this tendency, that employees who have better salaries are definitely more unionized, and that in general those unionized have a higher cultural level than their colleagues. Adherence to a union may thus also signify or express personal promotion, both in the economic and the cultural order.

Interest in the activities of the joint-management committee is much less affected by the influence of the company. Nor does it depend on the modest origin of those involved; at least employees from a higher milieu are just as competent and interested in the matter as those of modest origins, and it is employees of intermediate-level origin who participate the least. Finally, aspirations and standings have no effect. On the other hand, cultural level seems to have a very notable one, even more notable than in the case of union adherence.[22]

Union adherence and interest in the committee also depend on professional category. Differences exist, however, between categories. Policy writers and archivists are highly unionized and very interested in the committee, but keypunchers, though strongly unionized, take no interest at all in the committee.

This contrast recalls to some extent that brought out above in regard to work and to participation. The fact of being unionized seems to reflect more of a search for security, and interest in the committee testifies to a desire for participation and promotion. But this difference is tenuous, and it really seems that the two orientations which we have just distinguished in this way contribute equally to reinforcing interest in the company. It will be noted, for example, that unionized employees are definitely better informed than their nonunionized colleagues

22. Of those interviewees with a not very high cultural level, 64 percent are not greatly interested or not at all interested in the activities of the joint-management committee, compared to 39 percent of those who have a higher cultural level.

(38 percent well informed and 6 percent badly informed among those unionized, compared to 19 percent well informed and 19 percent badly informed among those nonunionized).[23]

Union activity seems in general to operate, if not as a factor for integration, at least as a factor for participation in company life. The thesis of conflictual participation, supported by certain American authors,[24] is thus verified in France, at least in the white-collar milieu. Unions draw their members from among those persons who are best integrated with the environment, and adherence to unionism seems to be accompanied by a greater interest in the activities of the company. Interest of this sort does not signify submission and identification, and may be accompanied by criticism and even hostility. But when all is said and done the distinction between interest and indifference seems to be much more important than the contrast between those who express criticisms and those who are favorable.

This hypothesis, which first appeared during the course of the exploratory study, could not be analyzed in a precise way in the main study; we were, however, able to verify it in an indirect but nevertheless very concrete way for our sample of supervisors. We asked the following questions of all the supervisors we interviewed: "If you were to hear employees criticizing a decision by management, do you think it would be your duty to try to convince them that management surely has valid reasons, or do you think it would be better to be satisfied with pointing out the criticisms to higher authority without taking sides yourself? What about a case where you think the employees are right?"

Of the supervisors we questioned, 24 percent took sides very definitely and positively with the employees and 20 percent sided with management, while 56 percent refused to choose. Yet the two groups that took opposite sides show exactly the

23. Among employees who take a great interest in the activities of the joint-management committee, 66 percent are interested in company management; this percentage drops to 55 percent for those who are moderately interested, 29 percent for those who are little interested, and 15 percent for those who take no interest in it at all.

24. See, for example, Lois R. Dean, "Social Integration Attitudes and Union Activity," *Industrial and Labor Relations Review,* October 1954.

same characteristics; they judge company policy favorably, unreservedly defend the companies when they are attacked, are well informed about and take a great interest in the management of the affairs of their company. Their colleagues who do not take sides are extremely reticent on all these points and are badly integrated into the company. For example, on the question "Does your company make an effort for its personnel?" we obtained the results shown in table 21.

TABLE 21

	Identify with Personnel	Identify with Management	Do not Want to Choose
The company makes a great effort	40%	27%	23%
Some effort	60%	64%	27%
No effort	0%	9%	50%
	100%	100%	100%

N = 57

The Problem of Apathy

Until now we have reflected on the problems of integration and participation, basing ourselves solely on measures relating to the positive feelings of the subjects interviewed. More precisely, we tried to bring to light the differences they show in greater or lesser loyalty to their company, and in the greater or lesser interest they manifest in its activities.

Yet the peculiarities of supervisors' behavior, which we have just analyzed, draw attention to a central phenomenon whose importance had already come out during the course of the exploratory study: the existence of a considerable mass of employees who are completely disinterested in company activities and systematically adopt attitudes of retreat.

It is appropriate, we think, to reflect on this negative aspect of the problem as well, and to attempt to understand the conditions for participation based on an analysis of retreat or apathy.

In the case of supervisors, the consequences of these attitudes of retreat seem clear. Faced with the concrete situation which we described to them and which is perfectly understood by everyone, because it corresponds closely with their experience, a good half of the supervisors in our sample refuse to commit themselves and make every effort to avoid the problem which is presented to them. As one of them said to us, the best thing is to "equivocate and stay uncommitted, let people talk away as much as they like, and ignore the matter." What does this attitude mean? Everything else we already know about supervisors indicates that what is involved here on their part is really a running away from their responsibilities and, more profoundly, a refusal to become involved in their role. This is definitely the classic behavior pattern of anomie, Merton's category of *retreatism.*[25] Unfortunately, we did not present our interviewees with other concrete cases that forced them to take sides. But the indexes we were able to develop, as well as the larger number of "no answer" responses on all the delicate questions, and the much more frequent choice of the laissez-faire style among all the members of this group, lead us to think that the distinction we have established is a basic one. Indecisive or apathetic supervisors do not show, it seems, any marked personal characteristics, either in the matter of origin or in the matter of education. They all seem, on the other hand, to have difficulties with their employees and with management, and generally give the impression of being inferior to their task.

We could not bring to light an equally clear contrast among employees, since they rarely find themselves confronted with such embarrassing choices. No one asks them to become as deeply involved as supervisors, and they can meet the obligations of their role without having to commit themselves.

One uncommon incident, the recent presence of a management consultant in the company where we were carrying out our first study, allowed us, however, to discover the extent of certain retreatist behavior.

25. See Robert K. Merton, *Social Theory and Social Structure* (Glencoe: The Free Press, 1957), p. 187–90.

Thirty percent of those interviewed[26] during the course of this research showed the following characteristics: they had no opinion or refused to express any opinion on the recently accomplished reorganization, said they had no desire whatsoever to be better informed about the activities of the company, did not read the company paper or made ironic comments about its existence, and expressed no opinion in response to a question about the managerial classes which aimed to test their degree of confidence in institutions and in society in general.[27]

Who were the indifferent and apathetic ones? Women in two-thirds of the cases, whether old clerks, or new and badly integrated typists and keypunchers. The men were mostly filers. That is, this group involved persons who, for various reasons, had by and large an inferior status within the company. At the same time, and this is remarkable, they were also persons who, outside the company, manifested just as much apathy with regard to social solidarity. More than half of them, for example, abstained from voting in the elections of 1956, compared to 18 percent in the rest of the sample.

These findings suggest a possible interpretation of apathy as a phenomenon expressing a lack of acculturation, or a rejection by the environment. To develop freely, an individual's chances for participation must have as a starting point a minimum socio-cultural threshold, whose location is determined in each case by general characteristics of the environment for participation. As long as this threshold is not crossed, retreatist attitudes predominate. In the case that interests us, it seems that most of the subjects who have not attained, socially and culturally, the minimum level corresponding to the status of office worker have trouble accepting the conditions necessary for participation. They can become integrated into the environ-

26. The sample comprised one hundred persons, about 30 percent of the total employed.

27. The question was formulated as follows: "Do you think it is true that the managerial classes are not up to snuff?" Contrary to what we expected, it was those who were best educated, best informed, and most integrated into the world of the middle classes who responded most often "no, they were not doing their job" while those with lesser aspirations were more confident. The true test of anomie would prove to be lack of interest and refusal to respond.

ment in a passive way, but cannot take any responsibility there. Though the terms may be different, the same problem seems to present itself outside the company.

The results of the main study only partially confirmed this interpretation. The responses to the questions about management and about information do show that lack of interest in the company life corresponds to inferior status in the company and the absence of promotional perspectives.[28] But, in the absence of concrete events that imposed a choice, the differences are much less meaningful than those we were able to come up with in the exploratory study and those we arrived at for supervisors as well.

The great imprecision of the results of the comparative study on this point prevented us from taking advantage of the particularly favorable research design we had at our disposal to handle the fundamental problem of the influence of company characteristics on the development of the phenomenon of apathy.

Let us note that the company in which the largest number of employees think they have good chances for promotion is also the one where interest in management is strongest, and that both these characteristics seem to be due to the deliberate efforts of management, which is trying to decentralize the functioning of its operations.[29]

The earlier study we conducted in a large Parisian bank allows us to go further, however. The differences between our results in the bank and those we obtained in insurance are remarkable. In the bank, the personnel's level of information is much lower; employees take much less of an interest in management and in the activities of the joint-management committee; they think less often that they have chances for promotion; at the same time, they have fewer friends in the company and outside; generally, they seem to be turned inward more, and their behavior is more apathetic.

28. The interviewees were tested by questions relating to what they foresaw as a possible future in five years, what they thought of their chances for promotion, and the importance they believed they had in the company.

29. A process which ended, it will be remembered, in improving interest in work, but which also provoked the development of more acute interpersonal tensions.

It is usual to attribute the origin of such differences to the policy followed by management, where "policy" refers to its efforts in favor of employees and the quality of its training and its information. Such policy seems to have hardly any effects in the cases that concern us here. It is in the bank that employees are by far most satisfied with management's social policy, and it is in the bank that the largest number of supervisors seem to have had the benefit of training courses.

The fundamental reason for the differences we find does not lie in the immediate decisions by management or in the types of relationships it has directly with its personnel, but in its system of organization and, more precisely, in the arrangement of roles and in the style of relations that such a system entails. That is really what seems to be at issue in the bank-insurance contrast, where three series of factors are at work: first, the large percentage of women, the lower level of education, and the lower social level of the operational employees in the bank; second, the lower chances for promotion, or rather the relatively lower attractiveness of a promotion, due to the length of the hierarchical chain and to the difficult position of first-echelon supervisors; third, and perhaps especially, the absence of stratification between different work posts—a lack of differentiation which seems to lead to greater satisfaction in the matter of position, because of the absence of depressing comparisons, but which also offers no stimulus to participate. Whatever the efforts made by bank management at the top, the weight of its organizational system is such that apathy tends to predominate at the operational level, while in the insurance company conservative "policies" are associated with more active participation, because of a more flexible and more differentiated system of organization.[30]

The White-collar Milieu and Participation

It is difficult to draw some general and clear meaning out of the multiple relations we saw emerge from the problems of participation, which moreover we greatly simplified. One thing

30. Bank employees who have qualifications equal to those of policy men in insurance have, in general, won their stripes a long time ago in the bank.

these analyses do indicate, however, is that the notion of integration, in the narrow sense of the term, does not at all account for the relations between an employee and the organization to which he belongs. On the one hand there is no opposition at all —quite the contrary, there is concordance—between interest in unionism and interest in the problems of the company; involvement in the company does not seem to be tied to faithfulness to it, but rather more to the possibility of safeguarding one's independence in relation to it. Apathetic and retreatist behavior patterns correspond to difficult positions, where those involved have a hard time assuming their roles, whether because they do not have the requisite qualities or because they feel rejected by the environment.

These conclusions could also be applied, it seems, to companies that employ mostly manual workers. Actually, the hypothesis we have developed in the course of this chapter is easy to generalize: the freer a man is in relation to the organization on which he depends, the less vulnerable he is and the greater his chances to become involved and to participate consciously and voluntarily, and therefore more effectively, in its activities. But what are the chances for participation that are peculiar to the white-collar milieu itself? If our hypothesis is correct, we can deduce from it two general consequences. The first concerns the present-day evolution of techniques and the parallel evolution of methods of organization. The transformations we find in this area are not as prejudicial to white-collar employees' participation as is generally thought, because while these transformations may sometimes devalue the employees' qualifications, they almost always tend at the same time to make the employee freer and more independent of the company, and to relieve him of the paralyzing pressure of traditional paternalism. The second consequence relates to the position of white-collar employees in relation to blue-collar employees. In the general progress of human organizations toward complexity, differentiation, and intellectualization, white-collar employees are, despite certain appearances, definitely ahead of manual workers. The norms they submit to are often less constraining, but they are more numerous, more complex, and involve the individual more. The white-collar employees are more socialized, and at the same time there is greater need for their participation. In general they necessarily find themselves pushed to take an interest in the activities of their company.

We were able to make a beginning toward verification of this hypothesis by doing an analysis of a certain number of company studies relating to both white-collar and blue-collar employees, and also by analyzing a certain number of opinion polls. In all these studies we were able to show that white-collar employees had a higher level of aspiration than blue-collar employees, were more preoccupied with the future, thought more about promotion, and above all *were much more sensitized to the morale of the company;* they were, in effect, always either more enthusiastic or else more critical than blue-collar employees, who in turn remained constantly the most indifferent.[31] The same contrasts are manifest in the results of the opinion studies. Throughout a whole series of polls for the years 1947–53 which we were able to examine thanks to the courtesy of the IFOP it appears very definitely that white-collar employees were better informed, more cultivated, more sensitive to style and to opinion, in a word, more involved in the great game of modern life than blue-collar employees and peasants.

Though white-collar employees are generally more involved in the company, it should nevertheless not be forgotten that their chances for participation are often limited by the development of the vicious circle of passivity and indifference which we found to be present both in insurance and in the bank. Apathy is the employee's response to the control procedures and the formalism engendered by the weight and the complexity of the bureaucratic chain; the existence of this apathy makes reinforcement of the controls which give rise to it more necessary. Such a tendency is generally denounced as the consequence of concentration and bureaucratization of human activities. But personally we are inclined to think that it is

31. The reports of these studies, whose results were not published, were generously made available to us for reading by the specialized institutes that conducted them, and in particular by the Institut Français d'Opinion Publique. We published an analysis of these reports in an earlier article: "L'ambiguïté de la conscience de classe chez les employés et les petits fonctionnaires," *Cahiers internationaux de Sociologie* 28 (1955): 78.

much more the consequence of a crystallization of the traditional relationship of faithfulness and paternalism. Loyalty to the company does not engender apathy, but the traditional equilibrium, by reinforcing the need for dependence and for security, makes the development of more active and more conscious forms of participation impossible, and naturally forces a resort to control and formalism in order to obtain indispensable results.

A second obstacle to the development of participation in the white-collar milieu originates in the system of stratification. One cannot participate in the activities of a milieu unless social distances within that milieu are not too large, and unless there is no risk of being rejected. From this point of view, the social stratification of a company, that is, its division into groups that are relatively homogeneous and distinct from each other, has two mutually contradictory consequences. On the one hand, it favors participation by providing sufficiently homogeneous units for participation; on the other hand, it reduces participation to the extent that, by accentuating differences, it contributes to the rejection of certain groups which are considered inferior. In the white-collar milieu, one thoroughly concerned with promotion and differentiation, one can ask whether stratification might not constitute an important means for stimulating interest. One cannot succeed in participating unless one rejects certain individuals and certain groups. The study of the bank seems to suggest that, when differences disappear, participation decreases.

In a general way, however, it seems evident that notable progress has been made and that the resources of the environment are more considerable than those who lead it think. In any case, this is what came out every time from the contacts we had in the process of communicating our results to management and to supervisors. It seems to us that the most significant index of this progress is furnished by the constant convergence of interest in unions and in the joint-management committee with interest in the functioning and the objectives of the company itself. This convergence implies, in effect, that criticism and reasonable opposition can find a place in the social system that is the company, and that the company, in consequence, already has available employees who are sufficiently free and conscious to make their involvement effective. The absence of hostility and of the traditional dichotomy, the minimal pressure on supervisors, who can declare that they take the side of employees without having the psychological conflict thus created become too difficult to overcome—both are signs of a more tolerant atmosphere, where the intensity of participation is certainly higher in the same measure as integration, in the old sense, is lower.

PART THREE
The Social and Cultural World

8 Social Status

Social Status and Status in the Company

Our purpose so far has been to analyze attitudes and the human relations in the company, in an attempt to achieve a better understanding of how the manner in which work life is experienced might determine the development of the personality, or of the various possible personalities, of the office worker in social life.

But, in studying the work environment, we have shown to what extent the behavior patterns which are manifest there, and the mechanisms of equilibrium and autoregulation which shape them, are influenced by the external social environment. For each individual, the expectations aroused by his family environment and his social aspirations profoundly shape his criteria for evaluation and the quality of his reactions on the job. Social status outside the company and status in the company, or through the company, echo and influence each other in a complementary and contradictory way. In order thoroughly to understand their respective dynamics, and the sort of influence they can have as principles of action, these factors must be constantly compared and contrasted.

It would be vain, based on an analysis of work and of status at work, to attempt to draw direct conclusions relating to major social forces. A few very general determinants are at work, but it is extremely difficult to isolate them in practice. We have already been practically forced to determine that, for the individual, it is not status in the company or through the company that determines social status; this is determined through a continual exchange and interplay between one definition of his role and another.

After having analyzed the reactions of employees to the company and its problems, it is appropriate that we now attack the problem from the other end and explore their representations of society and of the place they occupy in it outside the company. We cannot go very far in this direction, since we have only limited information at our disposal. But thanks to the change of perspective that will be imposed upon us by this new study—one we will follow up in the next chapter by analyzing the characteristics of the cultural worlds of white-collar employees—we think it will be possible for us to go beyond the constraint of a kind of reasoning centered too exclusively on work, and to put in greater relief a discussion that has until now remained a little too linear.

Two major problems arise in relation to social status: the collective problem of class differences and class membership, and the more individual problem of aspirations and rank. The place occupied by white-collar employees in French society today depends, above all, as we shall see, on the interplay between these two factors.

Class Differences

The problem of class relations is a difficult one, and our familiarity with it is generally no more than intellectual. We infer the existence of certain feelings based on the logic of the economic and social systems, but we hardly study these feelings. Even though the origins and the consequences of class differences have been passionately discussed by successive generations of social thinkers, it seems that we still have no more than an a priori conception of the way in which these differences are experienced by those involved, of the affective resonances they can have for them, and of the deep motivations which determine conduct in this domain.

We first tried to deal with this problem in depth within the framework of our exploratory study.[1] To this end, we used open-ended questions and drew our inspiration from the spirit, if not the technique, of nondirective conversation.[2] But because we were worried—too much perhaps—about effectiveness and prudence, we decided to focus on only one aspect of the problem, whose decisive importance for the sociological theory of classes we have already indicated, namely, the problem of the relations between white-collar and blue-collar employees. By doing this we restricted—a little prematurely—our field of action; but on the other hand we were able to go further in an analysis which seemed to us essential.[3]

The opening question was as follows.

"They say that class differences, for example the differences between white-collar and blue-collar workers, are disappearing. In your opinion, is this progress. What real differences are there between white-collar and blue-collar employees. What do the real differences between people depend on?"

The comments we collected were abundant but often contradictory. Nor will we content ourselves this time, as in preceding chapters, with giving just the conclusions of our content analysis. A detailed presentation of the diverse attitudes expressed, and of the vocabulary which expresses and colors them, will give us a deeper and more realistic knowledge of the reactions of our interviewees than could be provided by the statistical results; the latter, as we shall see, are still, despite our efforts, far too superficial. We shall structure this analysis around two closely interrelated themes, which we shall distinguish for convenience of presentation: what white-collar employees think of blue-collar employees as a social group, and what white-collar employees think of themselves as a group in contrast to blue-collar employees and to the rest of society.

Blue-collar workers as seen by white-collar employees

The variety in the social origins of our interviewees—which

1. This study, it will be remembered, involved one hundred interviews; this is sufficient to give it a relatively certain indicative value.

2. We did not have enough time to conduct true nondirective conversation.

3. Several preliminary totally free-form interviews allowed us to formulate our opinion on this matter.

makes them quite representative of the world of white-collar employees in general—is nowhere as strikingly translated as in the variety of their evaluations and, most of all, their information about the blue-collar world. While a notable proportion of the subjects questioned are directly in touch with the working class by virtue of filial or marital ties, a certain number of them are radically isolated, emotionally as well as intellectually; these are men who have never seen blue-collar workers anywhere except on a movie screen, have never known any except in novels. This segregation is as complete as that which exists between rural folk and city-dwellers.

One female clerk, for example, declared to us in a tone that evoked the image of an unbridgeable social abyss: "The level of blue-collar workers is rising; you see laborers who do not drink any more."

Numerous interviewees—most of all women, however, whose universe is in general more restricted than that of men—made comments to us that testified to an equal estrangement. This state of estrangement from the blue-collar world, we should nonetheless specify, is not present among the majority of white-collar employees. It is found mostly among the children of businessmen or artisans, that is, among bourgeois or petits bourgeois. There it is often accompanied by an even more widespread state of mind wherein the respect due to the eminent dignity of work is coupled with a mild disgust for the monstrous creations of social life, and also with an indulgence toward being tainted by this original defect; praise is even given to the laudable efforts of these creatures to redeem themselves.

Here is how one typist pleads their case: "It's not the blue-collar workers' fault; they are decent folk, but less well brought up, there is something about them that shocks you . . . you see the difference in everything."

Another typist is magnanimous: "There are those who are blue-collar workers because they had to be, but who are perhaps worth as much as white-collar employees."

The researcher is referred away from the disagreeable superficial appearance of the blue-collar worker (which is imposed upon him by fortuitous circumstances, bad fate) and asked to focus instead on "his fundamental nature [*son fond*]."

But at the same time there is occasionally discerned in him a deliberate will, somewhat diabolical, to be a bad sort. A policy man said to us, for example: "The laborer acts against his own interest. He does not handle himself well; he lacks dignity: yet, he could have as much as anyone else, there is no reason why not."

One of his colleagues echoes him:

"The laborer gives himself a laborer's manner, though it is so easy to stay within the norm."

Whether through congenital defect or perversity of character, the "laborer's manner" is something that sticks to the individual, something that neither education nor fortune can erase. Two interviewees do speak of "birth" in a mildly critical tone.

"It's difficult to get away from an unfavorable family milieu." "Being 'well-born'—it's idiotic but true everywhere—just talking about it stirs up a great deal in me."

Elsewhere: "The white-collar employee believes himself to be superior from the point of view of birth." In most of the interviews that are disfavorable to manual workers, it is always specified that the real differences between people do not come from training or from fortune, which are both things that can be acquired, but from education, which is what puts an individual in a special class.

What does this "laborer's manner," which so estranges him from the norm, consist of? What are the traits which white-collar employees see as working to the disadvantage of manual workers? The following themes appeared in the interviews; we cite them in order of frequency of appearance, coupling them with the most characteristic quotations.

They do not have good manners: "Some of them are vulgar." "Manual workers are prone to slovenly habits." "I would not like to marry a manual worker."

They do not speak the same language. This working class language is sometimes highly valued as more direct and less ceremonious, sometimes condemned as gross, and sometimes simply noted objectively.

Their dress is reputed to be more untidy, less well-groomed.

They are less educated, less capable, their work is less competent: "It's a terrible thing to say, but I find that here, in the company, there are many people who would make acceptable laborers but poor employees." (The same policy man elsewhere requests that, in the company, the difference be made between "the complete moron and others.") "The semiskilled worker is a man who has no personal will, who cannot do anything much, so that nothing is left for him but the factory."

They have different political ideas. Quite often manual workers are noted as being Communists or extreme leftists. This fact is sometimes presented as a natural attribute of the manual worker's situation. It is explained by their intellectual or moral indigence; or, on occasion, by their generosity.

"The extreme left is above all working class; the anti-Communist is in general from a more developed class. The guy with the red-wine bottle in his lunchbox, that's the extreme left."

They are contemptuous or jealous of white-collar employees. "I think that manual workers are jealous of white-collar employees." "A white-collar man, manual workers say, does nothing."

They have no dignity, they do not try to improve themselves. This type of reproach is coupled with others concerning manners, language, and dress. "His social horizons are more limited, he squabbles more with his boss. Manual workers do not try to improve themselves. Out of the factory, into the bar. The white-collar employee does the same, perhaps, but in secret; he handles himself better."

The manual worker earns more money, but in doing so sacrifices his life style. From this point of view, drink always seems to be considered an important attribute of the manual worker.

It should be noted, however, that a certain number of subjects introduce distinctions within the working class, distinctions which they express confusedly, but which always tend to contrast "the manual laborer" or "the manual worker" or "the ordinary laborer" with "the good laborer" or "the skilled worker" or "the specialized worker" or "the specialist." The former one is contemptible, the second respectable and of a social status comparable to that of a white-collar employee.

In contrast to these scornful or condescending attitudes towards manual workers, one also finds a whole gradation of favorable attitudes, running from simple profession of humanist and democratic faith all the way to identification with the working class and violent condemnation of the "white-collar mentality." The following gradations can be distinguished:

1. *Moderate self-criticism of the haughtiness of white-collar employees.* What is needed is more understanding between the two groups; we are getting there little by little.

"Animosity exists, and it is not new, but it has dwindled despite everything." "As soon as he has an education, a good manual worker is worth as much as a white-collar employee." "Perhaps the white-collar employee is disdainful, while the manual worker imagines that the white-collar employee never works up a sweat . . . but we are all on salary: the manual worker is my equal."

The theme of "misunderstanding," for which we have several illustrations, appears frequently. Those who develop this theme are men who feel very deeply they are "white-collar" and who, at the same time, cast themselves as liberal, open-minded, well informed about world developments, not at all clannish. Theirs is a reflective, "good-natured," sage attitude.

2. *Impassioned affirmation of the equality of man.* "Progress must be made, value is what should count." "As far as I'm concerned, there should be no difference. It's just plain nonsense." "I belong to no class . . . in the mind of the average Frenchman we are all the same. To my mind, what matters is what kind of person you are."

Here, status differences are recognized as part of reality; at the same time, they are forcefully denied any moral or metaphysical validity and any claim in the area of rights. What this represents is an ideological position, a more or less explicit doctrine, a conscious or not so conscious adherence to certain values: socialism in the wider sense of the term, Christianity, humanitarianism, or others. This is what makes this position different from the next one.

3. *Direct consciousness of the sameness of the condition of blue-collar and white-collar employees.*[4] "No difference at all;

4. An analogous distinction can be made among attitudes unfavorable to manual workers; that is, between the experience of feeling a social barrier ("I wouldn't know how to explain it, but there is a difference") and the presentation of an elaborated doctrine of segregation ("Classes correspond to a process of selection, a social hierarchy; to the extent that they are based on value and on competence, they are inevitable and beneficial").

when you go to the butcher, you pay the same price." "It's of no concern to me; three-quarters of my buddies are laborers." "I make no distinction: there is none. I am married to a manual worker . . . I've never thought that much about it."

This type of response comes most often from white-collar employees who have close ties with the blue-collar world, through parents, spouses, or by virtue of their own recent past history in a factory. Asked to compare the situation of manual workers to that of white-collar employees, they generally resort to objective criteria, to common sense. They talk about hours, salaries, advantages and inconveniences, retirement—all matters which are rarely dealt with by their colleagues who, in turn, focus their discussions on the virtues and the vices of the blue-collar "mentality."

Curiously, in all the attitudes which we have just described, whether or not they are favorable to blue-collar workers, one always finds, obviously in differing degrees, a sort of glorification of the working class condition. Even those who make a point of noting a distance which is readily exaggerated, always tend to exalt the manual worker's good "fundamental nature" (*fond*), which is made up of courage and generosity, and sometimes disguised by a rough and crude covering whose virtue is exalted.

What are the elements of the manual worker's prestige? First of all there is the arduous work, an index of courage and of character: "The work is harder, often in the cold, not always in good conditions . . . the lunch pail instead of the employee cafeteria, that's what hardens character."

They feel somewhat guilty about enjoying central heating and more free time. The laborer is both pitied and admired: "The manual worker should earn more; the better things go, the less brave the Frenchman; he prefers not to work with his hands."

This hard work is at the same time more technical, more effective, and more down-to-earth. There is ready agreement that there are too many graduates and not enough technicians. The distinction is then made between the skilled laborer, knowledgeable and precise, and the common manual worker: "To be a tool and die maker, you must have certain capacities, education." "You must be intelligent to become a skilled laborer."

The trying nature of his work, coupled with his technical effectiveness, show that the manual worker "is made of solider stuff," while the white-collar employee has "nothing but polish." "They know more about life." "They handle difficulties better."

Besides, their work is more useful to society. This idea is sometimes affirmed directly: "In time, the white-collar employee came to think of himself as someone special, though the services he renders society are no greater, if not less."

But what you see most often is a projection onto the manual worker of a vague feeling of guilt: this is what happens when the idea that office jobs are the work of lazy people or parasites is attributed to laborers.

The moral qualities discerned in the laborer revolve around the theme of the simple man, all of a piece, devoid of pettiness, the noble savage, uncorrupted by either hypocrisy or ambition. This is one of the aspects of the "good prole" character that Jean Gabin created in his prewar films.[5]

"More substance to the manual worker, from all points of view." "The factory mentality is quite a bit better." "The atmosphere is quite a bit better." Manual workers are "frank," "easy-going," "sincere," "more open in relation to others." They are "good-hearted." "You can find a true friend among workers, and good-for-nothings in high society."

White-collar employees as they see themselves

The range of opinions white-collar employees express about their own group is almost as wide as their range of judgments on manual workers. At one end there are those who loudly proclaim the dignity of the white-collar employee, while at the other end we find those who categorically deny that they are in any way distinguished. The tone of the response is, however, completely different. It is generally impersonal, objective,

5. By proposing a choice between Jean Gabin and Pierre Fresnay as preferred actor (1955), we were effectively able to show that subjects favorable to manual workers chose Gabin more often (the probability of independence is less than .01 percent, N = 100).

and sometimes ironic. One's position is viewed from a certain distance. There is a persistent attempt to deny one's ties with it. This false objectivity is obviously a sign of malaise. Yet it should at the same time be noted that our interviewees always evaluate, exalt, or denigrate themselves *in relation to manual workers.*

Four major types of attitudes seem particularly noteworthy, and allow us to specify—by forcing them a little, of course—four ideal models.

1. *The great dignity of the white-collar employee is affirmed in a serious way.* This is a minority position which is never encountered among typists or among filers. It consists principally of loyalty to the idea of hierarchy. Each state has its own proper dignity, like a burden which must be assumed. The essential thing is not to lose the dignity, to hold on to one's rank, not to *debase* oneself, as certain colleagues do. As one clerk put it: "Classless society is a utopia." "I am for hierarchy, every man in his place." "It is better that each man stay in his niche."

Within this hierarchy, the white-collar employee enjoys a particularly high status, which he deserves not only by virtue of his good education, but because of the intellectual character of his work, his moderating and intermediary position, and, related to this, the objectivity of his viewpoints.

"The differences do not disappear. Some say so, but it's not true. The white-collar employee is superior because he is not a manual worker." "The white-collar employee is in a better position to understand the life of the whole nation. He understands better." "The middle class has always been the source of France's strength."

2. *The dignity of the white-collar employee is affirmed in an ironic or critical way.* This is a much more widespread attitude. Even when it is not directly expressed, it more or less colors most of the interviews. The virtues of the white-collar employee are exposed, but no responsibility is taken for them. Nobility is emphasized at the same time that its vanity is shown. One talks about it while making clear that one does not put much stock in it. Pro alternates with con, self-criticism is carefully measured out.

If all of these types of comments are collated, you come out with the paradox that most white-collar employees declare that their colleagues believe themselves to be superior to manual workers, but that they are wrong. The citations that follow are characteristic of this ambiguity.

"The paper-shuffler has a tendency to take himself to be an intellectual. There is nevertheless a difference of origin: the fallen aristocrat will come to work in an office, but he will not become a stonemason."

"The white-collar employee is a bit of a dude: he has his little way of living, a little more elegant. He considers himself superior. On certain points, he is wrong, but he has intellectual superiority."

"The white-collar employee has a small bourgeois character."

"I am a petit bourgeois."[6]

The principal traits which give rise to this balancing of pro and con are work qualification, greater research into manners and bearing, sense of thrift, and desire for upward social mobility. The white-collar employee's work is called "intellectual," but immediately the phrase "so to speak" is tacked on. He is recognized for his good grooming and his good manners, but mildly faulted for being "distant," "foppish," "bragging," "carping," "pretentious." He is complimented for aiming high, for having a sense of thrift, "for having a plan," but is it really worth it? "He bleeds himself white, he earns less and shows off more; it is misery in disguise."

3. *The dignity of the white-collar employee is endangered.* This theme is evoked very frequently. For some, what is most likely to endanger the status of the white-collar worker is improvement of the conditions of blue-collar life; for others, it is internal decomposition, decadence on the part of white-collar employees. The reaction to the menace may be resignation and passivity, or indignation.

"Now, everything is mixed up: blue-collar workers marry typists." "There are less differences from the point of view of salary; I don't know whether that's progress." "Education is losing its value." "There is leveling going on." "In the sub-

6. Note the use of the word "little" (*petit*) in the last three quotations, highly characteristic of this "measuring out."

urban trains, everyone plays cards or knits." "Impossible to find the least difference." "The white-collar employee has a tendency to debase himself."

4. *The dignity of the white-collar employee is attacked and denied.* In this case, men are not content to break their solidarity with the white-collar group, but pass over to the other side of the barrier. The different elements of the status of the white-collar employee are violently criticized:

"Everyone should be educated, blue-collar and white-collar alike, and that's still a long way off." "An archivist is nothing but a manual worker." "The tide will necessarily turn the day that offices have had it and when the guys in overalls begin to have high regard for themselves." "Insurance company employees are definitely spoiled . . . always you hear the complaint, 'in my time things were different.' "

This is very much a minority attitude, at least in its categorical form, but we have seen that it lightly colors the majority evaluations.

The two dimensions of class prejudice

In an attempt to unravel these contradictory sentiments and to specify the types of attitudes and individual choices somewhat better, we carefully formulated a series of closed-ended questions which we presented to the subjects interviewed during the main study. They involved six current stereotypes relating to white-collar and blue-collar employees which we simply asked them to approve or reject.

Three of these stereotypes focused on blue-collar characteristics.

1. Manual workers are more candid, more direct, friendlier than white-collar employees.
2. Manual workers are less egotistical.
3. Manual workers are more useful to society.

The other three related more to white-collar characteristics.

1. White-collar employees have better manners; they handle themselves better than manual workers.
2. Manual workers are proletarians, but white-collar employees belong to the middle classes.
3. White-collar employees are more concerned with education.

The answers we collected fell into separate groups for each series, and allowed us to put together two scales, one of which measures idealization of blue-collar employees and the other affirmation of the dignity of white-collar employees. These two scales, curiously enough, have no relation to each other at all. The fact that someone idealizes blue-collar employees does not mean that that person is any less likely to affirm the dignity of white-collar employees, and vice versa.

A third of the subjects questioned idealize blue-collar employees a great deal, that is they accept the three favorable stereotypes we presented to them. The one that is least often accepted (by only the most "laborite" third of the total) is the stereotype about the greater usefulness of manual workers. Idealization of the manual worker seems to be equally widespread among the professional categories and among the companies; it absolutely does not depend on sex, and seems to correspond more than most other attitudes to unstable individual motivations, or to motivations that are difficult to fathom. Let us note, however, that the impression we obtained in reading the free-form interviews, that idealization of manual workers does not exist among white-collar employees who are closest to them is verified. Generally, white-collar employees with the lowest social origin and at the lowest social level are the ones who idealize manual workers the least, and those whose social aspirations and cultural level are higher idealize them the most. But these tendencies are not very strong.[7] Only their convergence allows us to think that our hypothesis has at least some basis to it.

Affirmation of the dignity of white-collar employees is, on the other hand, a somewhat more firmly-rooted attitude, though the amount of relative uncertainty about it can be surprising. One-third of our interviewees, highly conscious of the dignity of white-collar employees, approve of at least the stereotype concerning the middle classes and the stereotype concerning education. Another third deny all of them. This distribution is greatly affected by the company to which subjects belong; in the most bourgeois company, 49 percent of the employees interviewed accept the stereotypes favorable to

7. The probability of the null hypothesis is greater than 0.10.

white-collar employees, and 14 percent deny them, while in the most "laborite" company, the proportions are reversed—only 15 percent accepted them and 56 percent deny them.[8] The distribution is also affected by sex and by social origin. Males and persons of higher social origin give greater support to the idea of the dignity of white-collar employees. But other variables, social and cultural ones particularly, have relatively less influence. Those whose social aspirations and cultural level are higher, those who are conscious of their rank and their social position, those who think they have chances for promotion have a slight tendency to affirm that white-collar employees have better manners and are more concerned with education. But the differences are not very significant.

This whole collection of relationships is characterized above all by its lack of coherence. Not only are the most contrary sentiments expressed simultaneously, even by the same persons, but when the subjects questioned are forced to choose an opinion, their choices are relatively haphazard. Basically, two contradictory tendencies appear to be constantly present in their minds: desire for advancement and affirmation on the one hand, remorse and malaise in relation to the inferior group on the other.[9] The white-collar employees studied would very much like to make open affirmations about themselves, but they find it hard to take such a psychological risk; as a result they experience that much more discomfort in relation to those from whom they most need to distinguish themselves, that is manual workers. This state of uncertainty is what makes opinions and coherence of those opinions impossible.

Class membership

In addition to these questions which tested class relations, we asked a more classic question about class membership. We

8. This latter company is the one where the number of white-collar employees with blue-collar origin is largest; it is also the one where union members are most numerous and where, as we shall see later, we find the highest percentage who choose "workers' class."

9. The interpretation in terms of remorse and malaise seems to us to be suggested also by the much greater idealization of manual workers among supervisors (65 percent of the latter say, for example, that manual workers are less egotistical, compared to 45 percent of employees who say so).

asked our subjects which of the following expressions they considered most appropriate to their position and to their feelings: *middle class, bourgeois class,* or *working class.* This form of presentation has already been used many times. All we did was add to the first three classic terms the term *intellectual class,* which appeared to us to have considerable resonance during the exploratory study.

We found the distribution shown in table 22, which is quite close to the one obtained several years ago by the INED on a national sample, for the "white-collar employees—civil servants" category.

TABLE 22

Class Membership

	Middle Class	Intellectual Class	Bourgeois Class	Working Class	No Answer
Study of six insurance companies	45%	7%	2%	50%	6%
INED study of white-collar-civil servant category	52.2%		9.4%	32.8%	5.6%

Curiously, however, we find that this average covering six organizations hides some quite perceptible differences between each of them. In the most "laborite" company, 60 percent of the subjects questioned choose the working class, and in the most "bourgeois" company, only 30 percent choose it.

Contrary to what we found in attitudes toward manual workers, choices of class are governed more by social influences than by individual motives. They seem to be determined above all by education and by professional category. The less education one has, the greater the tendency to place oneself in the working class. In the higher categories (those whose members have two years of college or more) the answer is more often intellectual class (24 percent) and bourgeois class (8 percent). Here again "errors" are very numerous. The differences between professional categories are pretty much of the the same order. Clerks and typists have the highest percentage who consider themselves middle class (56 percent and 53 percent). Archivists and keypunchers are highest in saying working class (53 percent and 54 percent). Claims adjusters are the only ones who say intellectual class (15 precent) and bourgeois class (5 percent) in rather large number. Finally, among supervisors, we get a distribution that is closer to that of clerks than to that of claims adjusters. Table 23 is the comparative table of responses.

TABLE 23

Class Membership by Position

	Middle Class	Intellectual Class	Bourgeois Class	Working Class
Supervisors N = 57	56%	5%	9%	16%
Clerks N = 82	56%	7%	1%	28%
Claims adjusters N = 39	31%	15%	5%	33%

Choice of class is also related, in a limited way, to intellectual level. Choice of "intellectual class" correlates with reading of literary journals, and choice of "working class" correlates with reading of leftist political weeklies. But even at this level coherence is very weak and what should be particularly noted, it seems to us, is that these choices do not jibe at all with the deep preoccupation with personal standing and social advancement. Though these choices are a little more coherent than attitudes toward manual workers, they also seem more superficial. Anyway, they do not seem to have—any more than do attitudes toward manual workers—even the least effect on adaptation to work, adaptation to the human environment, and participation in the company.

Individual Aspirations

Contrasting with this incoherence of attitudes and class prejudices are a much greater deep-rootedness and stability in individual aspirations in the matter of social advancement.

We tried to analyze these aspirations on the basis of a series of questions relating to children, friends, marriage, and the future. Our results were only partially positive, because this domain, which we had not explored in advance, proved in the end to be difficult to understand. Nevertheless, a certain number of substantial facts appeared, which will allow us to sketch a first interpretation.

First of all two groupings of the responses imposed themselves, which we were able to concretize by establishing two hierarchical scales of the Guttman type. These two scales are closely related and also point in similar directions, but it was impossible to merge them. The first, which includes one question on choice of spouse and two questions on family situation, expresses mostly the perception our interviewees have of their standing and its corresponding demands;[10] meanwhile, the second, which includes one question on friends' professions, one on tastes in theater, and one on children's future, is more a description of aspirations about the future.[11]

Choices in the matter of marriage, some of which fall on the scale which measures standing and social demands, are also interesting in themselves. Our question[12] provoked a very def-

10. The topmost level of this scale comprises subjects who consider only the professions of pharmacist and teacher as suitable in choosing a spouse, declare that their family was well-off or at least average, and that their position is not as good as their father's; at the other end of the scale, in the lowest level, we find subjects who say that their position is better than their father's, that their family was of modest circumstances or poor, and who would accept professions other than pharmacist and teacher in choosing a spouse.

11. Subjects placed at the top of this scale have at least one friend in a liberal profession or equivalent, go to the theater to see plays with recognized cultural content, and want to orient their children toward professions with higher prestige.

12. We presented our interviewees with a list of professions (for the women, pharmacist, teacher, electrician, ditchdigger; for the men, pharmacist, teacher, salesgirl, cleaning woman), and asked them which ones would be acceptable to them in an eventual mate.

inite malaise among subjects of not very high social level,[13] who very often refused to answer or gave us contradictory answers. On the other hand, it showed, at the same time, to what extent aspirations increase not only with original social standing but also with social level attained so far. In table 24, for example, is a comparison of the choices made by employees and by supervisors (it will be remembered that there is no difference at all in social origin or in education between the two groups).

TABLE 24

Choice of Occupation by Position

	Male or Female Pharmacist	Male or Female Teacher	Electrician or Salesgirl	Cleaning Woman or Ditch-digger	No Answer
Supervisors N = 58	68%	87%	52%	0%	25%
Employees N = 301	48%	74%	66%	15%	35%

NOTE: The subjects questioned were allowed to make several choices, and as a result the totals exceed 100%.

The scores on the two scales, like the choices in the matter of marriage, seem to be closely determined by the social position of each person involved. There is a very definite tie between the reality of this position, which we measured objectively by a third scale,[14] and the perception that white-collar employees have of their standing, their social aspirations, and the frame of reference they use to pick an eventual mate. The better an interviewee's social position, the higher his demands and his aspirations. Within this general determinism of position, we should, however, note that the most important factor is, in the end, level of education.

13. In particular among subjects who had only primary education or who went to work before they were fifteen.

14. This scale distinguished between white-collar employees who began working before the age of fifteen, those who had primary education or higher, and those where neither parent was in a high-status profession.

Demands and aspirations seem in turn to have a very clear-cut influence on cultural level. This is almost the same dimension, since the question on theater used in the scale of aspirations is already a cultural question.

But the most significant relationships are those which we have already noted in part in the preceding chapters, and which concern satisfaction with position, evaluation of atmosphere, choice of "good managers" as an advantage of the situation, and loyalty to the company. Employees who have higher demands and aspirations have a tendency to be more discontent with the situation, to complain more about atmosphere, to not choose "good managers" as an advantage, to be less loyal to the company, and to have less of a desire for information.

Two supplementary characteristics are worth noting. Employees who have higher demands and aspirations declare themselves happy less often than their colleagues.[15] Moreover, they think much more often about quitting. For example, 52 percent of the interviewees who have higher aspirations are interested in a different position, while 38 percent say they do not want to leave the company; these percentages are almost inverted, 32 percent and 53 percent, for the interviewees with modest aspirations.

As will have been perceived from this brief summary, individual aspirations and demands are at the center of all attitudes toward work and toward the organization. It seems to us that they express, in part at least, the individual's relationship to society, in the same way as the scale of satisfaction with position measured his relationship with the organization. They correspond, in any case, to the reasonable choices made by the subjects interviewed in the matter of social advancement, and express their intimate point of view about the world —their satisfaction or dissatisfaction, their activity or passivity—much better than the social stereotypes they make use of to explain that world. The same phenomenon we found in the interplay between the individual and the organization seems to be found here as well. The more one rises in the social hier-

15. The same relationship, just as clear-cut, exists not only with the scale relating to demands and standing, but also and above all with the scale measuring social reality.

archy, the more demanding and dissatisfied one becomes, but at the same time the more one becomes capable of openness, restlessness, and activity.

Insurance Company Employees in French Society Today

Can we draw any lesson at all from such partial and barely structured results, in order to understand the place of white-collar employees in French society today? It is difficult, to be sure, to generalize from a limited experiment, but we can, by reflecting on the case of the subjects we interviewed, throw some light on more general phenomena.

A series of remarks are worth making, or recalling anew, in such a perspective.

In the first place, it is very important to emphasize that, in the milieu under discussion, attitudes and class prejudices absolutely do not coincide with individual aspirations and social destinies. Attitudes and prejudices appear to be more or less contradictory rationalizations, which may eventually have important repercussions in the political area, but seem to have no influence in the personal game played by each individual with his milieu and with society in general. There is no coincidence at all between individual destiny and social choice. Ideas put forth on the matter are of the common stock, they express and betray difficulties and misgivings, but in no way inspire action. One might think that such a distinction would have less truth to it in a blue-collar milieu, where the social factor would carry more weight. It is in any case the rule in the white-collar milieu, where their is no parallel between the world of discussion and social reflection, and the real world of the struggle for life.

The second characteristic concerns the persistence—more marked than is sometimes suspected—of traditions in social matters. For a good number of subjects who seem to us quite representative of their milieu[16] the world has hardly evolved since 1914, social distances appear to be considerable, and social relations must be governed by a protective formalism.

This traditionalism is rarely expressed in an open way. We

16. We think, for example, that in the provinces such attitudes must be even more marked.

noted the importance of evasive attitudes and ironic reactions. One cannot fully assume one's position; one holds on to white-collar prerogatives, but one dare not affirm them. The malaise provoked by the question on marital choices is particularly significant. Personally we would tend to think that the white-collar milieu is deeply marked by problems of social rank, and that its members try to mask the difficulties imposed upon them by the thankless game they play—many hopes but few real chances for success—by resorting to reassuring generalization and relying on a protective stratification.

A third important characteristic emerges from the results of the study: a deep conflict—which we apprehend poorly, but which is constantly rediscovered—between, on the one hand, the need for protection and supervision which underlies all collective choices, from the point of view of faithfulness to the company as well as from the point of view of respect for traditions, distance, or even "laborite" protests, and, on the other hand, individual desire for advancement. The more the employees we studied rise on the social scale, within or outside the company, the more they seem to be capable of doing without protection and supervision, of openly assuming the risks of their individual adventure. We then see them avoiding the faithful submission of the paternalistic model, as well as the various class ideologies.

The fourth and last characteristic, the relative incoherence of the responses we obtained, seems to us to require analysis not only from a methodological point of view, but as a distinctive characteristic of the white-collar milieu.[17] Modern urban social life is characterized by the multiplicity of choices offered to individuals. White-collar employees are particularly affected by this phenomenon. We placed great emphasis, during our theoretical analysis of the facts of the problem, on the profound ambiguity of their position. The relative incoherence which we find can be considered its consequence.

Certainly all the arrangements white-collar employees give themselves up to are artificial; through them they are no less

17. We think that researchers attach too little importance to the incoherences and anomalies they discover; these are sometimes of greater interest than the coherent relations those researchers always bring to light.

able to escape a summary determinism and to innovate, even though with stereotyped elements. Coherence might make the sociologist's work easier; in return it would express an oppressive determinism. Certain contradictions and the uncertainties we bring out are, it is true, deceptive; a truly rational attitude would consist of consciously assuming the ambiguity of the situation. But when rationalizing their situation in an arbitrary intellectual arrangement, the employees we interviewed communicated to us the contradictions in their behavior more honestly than if they had adopted a more logical and rigid system. This freedom on a superficial level is not simply an avoidance of coming to grips with reality more profoundly; it can also be considered an effort to avoid traditional rigidity, and a step forward toward greater consciousness and a more authentic freedom.

9 The Cultural World

White-collar Employees and "Mass Culture"

The relative incoherence we have just found in the matter of social status is even more profound for the cultural world. If it is difficult to make any predictions about the social aspirations of the subjects interviewed, their demands, and the illusions they take advantage of to mask the way they interrelate with society, the risks of error are even more numerous when it comes to predicting their behavior patterns, their aspirations, and their "rationalizations" in cultural matters.

This should not be surprising. The two phenomena are closely related. Cultural life attracts and molds the citizens of a modern society by acting both as social sanction and as a means for participation. When insurance company employees keep up with the times by going to the theater and by reading magazines, they are looking for a form of participation which integrates them into society and at the same time confirms their quality and even their superiority. The relationship is not at all one-sided, however, and the development of "mass culture" certainly seems to have immediate and profound consequences for social relations. Cultural changes, which continue to accelerate, tend more and more to break down the traditional hierarchies. To the incoherence in social status there corresponds an incoherence in the cultural world which, in part at least, precedes and determines the former.

This interpenetration of the cultural and the social, which is so characteristic of the urban milieu in industrial, or rather postindustrial, society, is perhaps nowhere so manifest as in a milieu like the Parisian white-collar and civil service milieu. Working in the center of the city, at the very heart of the social and cultural activities of their society, the benefits of which they reap only to a minor degree; effectively dependent on the managerial strata with which they are continuously in contact and the prestige of which overwhelms them, it is natural that white-collar employees and civil servants should yield easily to the attraction of commercialized culture. This culture gives them the illusion of immediate assimilation into the values of a bourgeois society which they cannot oppose, but from which they feel, on the other hand, constantly excluded.

Small businessmen, artisans, technicians, and middle-level managers on the one hand, and manual workers on the other, are all victims of the same mirage. It is only a question of degree, not of substance. But it can be said that, in general, white-collar employees and civil servants do not have the traditions of revolt and the virtues of independence of the blue-collar milieus, which were subject to a greater isolation and to a more total rejection. Nor do they have the conservatism and the obstinate resistance of the old middle classes, nor the greater chances for more active participation accorded to executives and members of liberal professions. If we consider only the broad outlines, we can readily allow that these employees form the core of the mass public that is the main concern of all the entrepreneurs of the mass media. To such employees best applies the currently stylish image of the modern man, victimized by mass civilization and manipulated by forces whose existence he does not even suspect.

The data we collected in this area is naturally once more very limited. It will nevertheless allow us to clarify a little better the meaning of the cultural activities of Parisian insurance company employees, and to pose in new terms the problem of their participation and membership in bourgeois or postindustrial society.

This effort will aid, we hope, in dispelling the cultural pessimism which we have just evoked. Despite all its faults, "mass culture" is in the process of allowing an enormous advancement of the lower strata in the cultural order, and it can be maintained that, in the end, it will have contributed more than recent political and social struggles to the reduction of social distances and the softening of hierarchical relations.

Participation and Nonparticipation in Cultural Activities

The first problem that arises in the study of cultural activities is that of participation or nonparticipation. Who participates and who does not participate? Why? Are there factors that determine the importance of the activities in which each individual engages?

The questions we asked related to movie-going (frequency, type, films preferred), theatre-going (the same), actors preferred (in the case of the preparatory study only), reading of books, magazines, and newspapers (titles and frequencies). Finally, a few comments were collected on radio-listening and other types of leisure-time activities.[1]

As far as the quantity and the sum of activities are concerned, the following series of findings are worth emphasizing.

1. Generally, there does not seem to be as much competition as one might have thought between different types of leisure-time activities; great activity in one area often seems to be accompanied by great activity in other areas.
2. The sum of activities is related tc type of work and attitude towards work, but the relationship is more complex than is generally supposed, and is in any case only rarely in the order of compensation.
3. Nonparticipation and inactivity are characteristic of persons badly adapted to their social position.

Competition between Different Types of Activities

We have data only on mass leisure-time activities (movies, theater, magazines, newspapers), and on only one leisure-time activity of a more traditional nature, the reading of books. But even within this restricted domain, one can raise the problem

1. The study was done before TV had any substantive impact in France.

of the relations between different activities. Is there competition between them, or do the diverse activities stimulate each other?

Such a question cannot be answered in a categorical way. Competition and stimulation each act within different borders. But it clearly appears that, in the roughest sense, the answer is stimulation rather than competition. First of all, subjects who go to the theater from time to time all go to the movies at least once a month. Those who very rarely go to the movies practically never go to the theater. In the second place, subjects who never go to the theater or to the movies read books and magazines much less. Subjects who read magazines of higher standing such as *Paris-Match* and especially *Elle* and *Marie-Claire* are characterized by definitely greater cultural activity.[2]
On the other hand, those who read magazines of lesser standing, such as *l'Echo de la mode* or *Femmes d'aujourd'hui*, are much less active.

It seems that inactivity in the area of commercial leisure-time activities corresponds to a turning inward to a quite delimited family group, and to a diminution or even an absence of social interchanges. Subjects who very rarely go to the theater or to the movies declare, for example, a much smaller number of friends than their colleagues.

Cultural Activities and Responsibilities at Work

Among the factors which may condition cultural activities, type of work seems a particularly interesting one to study. Do the generalization of meaningless work and the depersonalization of tasks affect, as is claimed, the propensity toward commercial leisure-time activities? Does the worker who is divested of all initiative at work try to compensate for this

2. Readers (females) of *Elle* and *Marie-Claire* are divided as follows:
—culturally quite active—30 percent (go to the movies at least once a month, to the theater at least once a year);
—moderately active—48 percent;
—not very active—27 percent (very rarely go to the movies or to the theater).
Nonreaders:
—very active—13 percent;
—moderately active—46 percent;
—not very active—41 percent.

powerlessness by greater activity outside work? In general the results of the study provide nuanced responses. The differences found seem to result more from differences in cultural level than from the direct influence of type of work.

"Policy men," for example, are definitely more active culturally than typists, but the differences are not significant, and in any case they are weaker than those caused by age and family situation.

It is worth noting, however, that, in a Parisian civil service milieu hardly different from the insurance company milieu in professional and social status, the extreme standardization of work posts allowed us to make a very fruitful comparison[3] from which we can at least, for the sake of a hypothesis, generalize results. With environment, working conditions, education, origin, and professional status remaining exactly the same, the influence of responsibility at work appears altogether striking (see table 25).

TABLE 25

Cultural Activity and Work Responsibility

	Low Activity	Average Activity	Intense Activity
Posts involving pure routine	24%	45%	31%
Posts involving a certain amount of responsibility	5%	80%	15%

NOTE: See Crozier, *Petits fonctionnaires,* p. 115.

Employees who have a certain amount of responsibility at work have an average level of participation in leisure-time activities. Employees who have no responsibility at all behave in contradictory ways; some seem to intensify their activities, other tend to withdraw within themselves. The same situation can lead to totally different reactions, to overactivity or to underactivity. A case-by-case analysis shows that overactivity

3. This similarity, it is true, applies only to the middle and lower categories in insurance; we do not have the equivalent in this administration of the "policy men" categories.

is found among persons of a higher cultural level, or among those trying to attain it; apathy, on the contrary, develops among employees of a modest social and cultural level. No difference is found between involvement in commercial and noncommercial leisure-time activities. All we are able to determine is that, to the extent that the employee does not find it possible to express himself at work, the greatest risk is that of apathy and nonparticipation rather than that of commercial leisure-time activities. Movies, the theater, reading of magazines and books constitute a means for evasion, to be sure, but at the same time and, in many cases, for the common people they are a means for social advancement which allows them to find a better equilibrium.[4]

To What Does Inactivity Correspond?

Let us now raise the fundamental problem. What is the origin of nonparticipation?

The quantitative importance of leisure-time activities is naturally a function of age, sex, and family situation. Young people, women, and bachelors are more active than old people, men, and those with family responsibilities. But the nonparticipant group is very much a group unto itself, whose makeup is extremely significant.

We find the following.

1. Inactive subjects are badly integrated into the social milieu of their company. There is a certain relationship between inactivity in the area of leisure and inactivity within the company (persons who are uninformed, little interested in what goes on, nonunionized, less loyal to their company, are less active).

2. Inactive subjects are, in general, badly integrated into the "white-collar" social milieu. They call themselves workers more often, they admit less often to the stereotypes which testify to adherence to norms of respectability (white-collar employees think more about the education of their children, white-collar employees have better manners, and the like).

3. Inactive subjects are also, in general, from an inferior

4. Among the common people (*milieu populaire*), intense leisure-time activities correspond to better adaptation to work, while inactivity corresponds to greater disgust.

social milieu; we find among them the white-collar employees of rural origin, and a portion of those whose parents are both manual workers. At the same time, they have a lower level of education.

More generally one can say that inactivity in the area of leisure is a sign of withdrawal into self, and that it is a characteristic of employees who find it difficult to adapt themselves to their environment, in part at least because of their social origin.

This paralyzing effect of a "common" social milieu allows us to explain the findings we made which may have appeared to some as paradoxical. Low social origin does not at all coincide, in the white-collar milieu, with a leftist orientation, at least in the area of political opinions. The apathetic ones do not read newspapers or read *le Parisien libéré*. They vote much less than their colleagues. It is among subjects of higher cultural and social level that readers of leftist weeklies are recruited, as well as readers of all political weeklies.

The Problem of Cultural Level

The quantity of cultural activities constitutes only a first approximation of the cultural universe. Our analysis so far has brought out only the significance of absence of activity, of non-participation. If we wish to go further and understand participation itself, we must get into the details of the various activities and try to interpret them.

A Few Descriptive Elements

Insurance company employees do not go to the theater very often; in fact more than a third never go.[5] Among those who go, 55 percent mention musicals, 27 percent mention the Comédie-Française or the Opera, 19 percent mention light revues, and only 9 percent mention more intellectual shows (avant-garde plays, classical drama, and the like). Among the

5. This constitutes an altogether normal percentage for those who live in the area of Paris; but the employees in the clerical agency we studied in an earlier inquiry go to the theater much more often (nearly a third of them go at least once a month, and only one out of ten never go). Cf. Crozier, *Petits fonctionnaires*, p. 57.

supervisors we again find the same number of abstentions, but the choices are of a relatively higher level. Musicals fall to 40 percent, while the Comédie-Française and the Opera rise to 43 percent, and intellectual plays to 18 percent.

Similarly, employees go to the movies much less, and the films they mention are widely diverse. The news has a lesser place in this milieu, where the proportion of young people is relatively small. On the other hand, radio is listened to regularly.[6]

As for reading, in a general way we have one-quarter non-readers, and among the readers an analysis made on the basis of the exploratory study gives 17 percent as readers of detective novels, science fiction, and adventure; 12 percent as readers of nineteenth-century novels like *Notre Dame de Paris* or *Eugénie Grandet;*[7] 44 percent as readers of best sellers, whether these be modern translations from the English (*Bromfield, du Maurier, Cronin*), or medical novels (*Men in White*), or conventional best sellers; "highbrow" literature (Gide, Camus, Sartre, Aragon, Hemingway) is patronized by only 7 percent of the sample.

Magazines are read much more assiduously. At the top of the list are *Sélection* and *Constellation,* chosen by 55 percent, and *Paris-Match* with 53 percent.[8] There is no difference between men and women in readership of these magazines. On the other hand, *Elle* and *Marie-Claire,* chosen by 35 percent of the total, are at the top of the list for women (51 percent), but are also read by 18 percent of the men. *L'Echo de la mode* and *Femmes d'aujourd'hui* have a more exclusively female audience (45 percent of the women, but only 8 percent of the men, read them). Still in a good position are weeklies of the *Ici Paris* kind, with 35 percent of the total, literary weeklies such as *les Nouvelles littéraires* and *le Figaro littéraire* (21 percent). Left-wing political weeklies (*l'Express, France-Observa-*

6. At the time we did the study (1957) television was not enough of a mainstay to make it possible to include it in our questionnaire. Only 25 percent of the interviewees say they listen rarely.

7. What we are dealing with here are not true readers, but those who, searching their memory for titles of books, are able to recall only classics.

8. What we are dealing with here are not really faithful readers, but subjects who say they read these publications at least from time to time.

teur) are read at least occasionally by 19 percent of the subjects, right-wing weeklies (*Carrefour, Rivarol, Aspects de la France*) by only 10 percent.[9] Finally, "true-love" magazines are chosen by only 12 percent, but this is distributed equally among both sexes.[10]

Finally, as far as newspapers are concerned, the predominance of *le Parisien libéré* is very great; it is read by 41 percent of white-collar employees. *Le Figaro, Paris-Presse,* or *Le Monde* are read by 15 percent, 9 percent read *l'Aurore,* 4 percent read *l'Équipe,* 4 percent read *Franc-Tireur* or *Combat,* 3 percent read *l'Humanité* or *Libération,* and 20 percent do not read any newspaper.

Cultural Norms: An Attempt at Classification

The juxtaposition of these percentages relating to cultural choices gives a kaleidoscopic view which is not useless, at least in a first attempt to organize our thinking, but which very quickly proves to be deceiving. All the scattered signs we have brought out inform us imperfectly about the matter that is of greatest import to us: the type of cultural behavior characteristic of individuals and of the social group. To get further, two methods are possible: a gross empirical method which consists of establishing, as a function of a normative—and therefore arbitrary—classification, cultural behavior patterns and a scale of models of behavior. This method is attractive, but it is open to criticism because it depends on a priori and therefore contestable judgments by the analyst. To avoid criticism, another method can be used. Instead of prejudging cultural levels as a function of the researcher's own personal scale of values—not withstanding the researcher's attempts at impartiality—an objective classification can be elaborated based on the statistical relationships which exist between the different cultural choices.

9. Let us recall that the study was done in 1957.

10. Here again it is possible that this type of reading is not as readily admitted by subjects who are trying to assume a respectable air. In any case, in a general way, polls show that employees read such magazines much less than manual workers, and we find this same difference again between employees who are children of manual workers and those whose parents were white-collar employees, businessmen, or executives.

The second method is the one we wanted to follow; but we were able to get only summary results, because to be successful such a method assumes relatively considerable means. These results are nevertheless interesting to the extent that they echo quite well the conclusions we had reached, based on a normative and arbitrary classification, in the study of the Parisian accounting firm.[11]

What comes out of this analysis is that theater attendance is the best criterion for classification. Literary tastes appear to be a second discriminatory criterion for groups at a higher cultural level, while at lower levels type of magazine read seems to be most significant. As might have been expected, the social environment subjects interviewed belong to constitutes the dominant factor in determining cultural level. But exceptions are numerous, which implies the existence, in this young milieu, of a rather large number of instances of individual advancement in the cultural order.[12]

This highly important phenomenon of development and advancement in the cultural order is closely associated with a greater interest in the union and in company policy. In the area of attitudes and activities within the company, it corresponds to greater interest in work and in the department, while in a bourgeois or petit bourgeois milieu the same cultural activities have a totally different meaning, since they are always associated with an estrangement from and a distaste for the working environment. In higher social milieus, cultural tastes seem to correspond to a need for compensation or evasion, while in lower-level milieus they appear on the contrary to be means for advancement.

The attempts we made to arrive at an objective classification were not able to give us results which were intellectually as satisfying as the hierarchy we established earlier. We do rediscover relationships of the same order as those we found before, but in this case they are only partial relationships be-

11. Crozier, *Petits fonctionnaires,* pp. 113–14.

12. It is altogether remarkable to find that leisure-time activities provide better indicators of social advancement than style of dress, though dress appeared at first glance to be the key area for social climbing in a young and female milieu. It seems that these young women deviate more readily from the norms of their milieu in the matter of culture than in the matter of style of dress.

tween two or three criteria, and we cannot manage to integrate all the activities into one classification.

A few characteristic traits, however, confirm our first assessments. First of all, theater attendance constitutes by far the most discriminative criterion in the matter of cultural level. Four levels are clearly marked out: nonattendance, attendance of musicals only, attendance of popular first-run theater but mostly of a light type, attendance of plays at a higher cultural level. (This hierarchy does not constitute a universally valid scale; depending on which activity you are talking about, it is this or that level which discriminates best; in any case each of the activities has some importance.)

By comparison, movie attendance appears to be a much less coherent domain, where it is impossible to distinguish a hierarchy of audiences. All that is worth noting is that below a certain cultural level fashionable films are not known.

Analysis of book-reading brings out two levels. Not being able to indicate even one title constitutes a significant low-level criterion, while, at the highest level, knowing highbrow authors distinguishes a small fringe-group of more cultivated employees.

On the other hand, newspaper reading, which was neglected in our first attempt, proved to be particularly interesting. Reading *le Figaro*, *Paris Presse*, or *le Monde* (the audiences are just about the same) is, in our universe of employees, a very clear distinguishing characteristic of the highest stratum.

In the end, the most solid scale of classification which we were able to establish statistically was the following.[13]

Group 1, high cultural level: 15 percent of the total
- —read *le Figaro*, *le Monde*, or *Paris Presse*
- —go to see popular intellectual first-run plays or classics
- —read books

Group 2, average cultural level: 20 percent of the total
- —go to see first-run plays or classics

13. Given the method used (the hierarchical analysis systematized by Guttman) the groups constituted are, in their internal structure, simple statistical arrangements. The normative characterizations we attached to them (high, average, or low-level) are naturally not justified statistically, but we think they can hardly be subject to dispute.

—read books
—do not read *le Figaro, le Monde*, or *Paris Presse*

Group 3, low cultural level: 40 percent of the total
—go to see musicals or light revues or do not go to the theater
—read *le Parisien, France-Soir*, or *l'Aurore*, or do not read newspapers
—still mention books they have read

Group 4, very low cultural level: 25 percent of the total
—go to see musicals or revues or do not go to the theater
—read *le Parisien, France-Soir*, or *l'Aurore*, or do not read newspapers
—do not read or are unable to mention even one book

Magazine reading is highly stratified, but we were not able to mark out levels that were as clear-cut because, among too many interviewees, readership is inconsistent. It is, however, significant that on our basic scale the choices of magazines fall in a regular way. Table 26 shows this very well.

Stratification in Culture

Cultural level, as we have characterized it, is naturally very closely related to social origin. Seventy-nine percent of the employees whose parents were both blue-collar workers fall in the two lower groups on the scale; 67 percent of those with one blue-collar and one white-collar parent fall in those two groups; for those who had one parent who was a businessman or in a liberal profession the figure is 19 percent.

The curve is just about the same for education: 77 percent of employees with only primary education are in groups 3 and 4, compared to 55 percent for those with junior high school, 39 percent for those with high school, and 14 percent for those who had higher education.[14] As we see, social determinism is strong, but we could not fail to note, nevertheless, that 14 percent of employees who had higher education have an extremely low cultural level, while on the other hand nearly a quarter of the employees with primary education go to see plays and read books, which makes them participants in the bourgeois cultural world.

14. The complete breakdown for the four groups shows even more precise correspondences.

TABLE 26

Readership of Magazines According to Cultural Level

	Group 1 15%	Group 2 20%	Group 3 40%	Group 4 25%
Literary Weeklies	more than two-thirds	15% to 30%	15% to 30%	less than 10%
Paris-Match	more than two-thirds	40% to 60%	40% to 60%	30% to 40%
Left-wing Weeklies	40% to 60%	15% to 30%	15% to 30%	less than 10%
Right-wing Weeklies	15% to 30%	15% to 30%	less than 10%	less than 10%
Scientific Magazines	40% to 60%	40% to 60%	30% to 40%	15% to 30%
Elle and *Marie-Claire*	30% to 40%	30% to 40%	30% to 40%	15% to 30%
L'Écho de la Mode and *Femmes d'Aujourd'hui*	15% to 30%	15% to 30%	15% to 30%	15% to 30%
Magazines of the *Ici Paris* Type	15% to 30%	15% to 30%	40% to 60%	30% to 40%
"Heart-throb" Press . .	less than 10%	less than 10%	15% to 30%	15% to 30%

(solid) more than two-thirds of the members of the group
(vertical lines) from 40% to 60% readers
(dense dots) from 30% to 40% readers
(diagonal lines) from 15% to 30% readers
(sparse dots) less than 10% readers

The question asked was the following: "Do you ever read any of the following magazines?" (The list was presented to the respondent on a card.) Only "Yes" or "No" responses were used.

Another finding which is just as natural is that networks of friendship are directly related to cultural level; having at least one friend in a liberal or intellectual profession automatically classes subjects in the upper part of the scale. Finally, in a more general sense, it will be remembered that the scale of social aspirations (profession of friends, profession one would like to see one's children enter) and the scale of demands (perception of one's personal social position, profession acceptable in a mate) are closely related to cultural level. The higher one's cultural level, the more one has important aspirations and demands. One gets the impression of a sort of general timidity of employees at a lower cultural level, which paralyzes their drive to participate in the values of society; this timidity expresses itself especially in the responses to the question on spouses, when subjects either refuse to choose or else choose only professions at a lower level.

Even such an imprecise measure of cultural level provides us with a useful instrument for locating our subjects in the social hierarchy. We readily conclude that, for them as well, it constitutes a means for classification, and at the same time a means for participation. By going to see a particular show or by reading a particular book one affirms that one is a member of society at a certain level as much as one participates in the values of that society.

But cultural level expresses not only stratification outside the company; it also determines, at least in part, the demands and the chances for adaptation within the company. Even if interest in work is not affected by cultural behavior patterns, the satisfaction one finds in one's position is, it will be remembered, closely related to it. Employees at a higher cultural level are much more discontent with the place they occupy; they find that being an insurance company employee does not carry much prestige, and in general they declare that their position is worse or, in any case, no better than that of their parents. Employees at a lower cultural level are, on the contrary, much more satisfied; they think they have a good position, and that their situation is better than that of their parents.[15] In the same way, as we have noted, activities in the company express something relatively close to cultural level. The lower one's cultural level, the less one participates in activities which imply personal affirmation or expression. Employees at a lower cultural level participate less than their colleagues at a higher level in the activities of the joint-management committee and

15. Cf. above, pp. 181–84.

of unions; on the other hand, they are more satisfied and more loyal—though in a passive way—to their company.

The importance of these behavioral traits for the individual is attested to by a quite unexpected relationship between cultural level and the feeling of well-being. It will be remembered that for the sake of control we asked a direct question on the feeling of well-being experienced by the individual. The responses, which distributed in an extremely regular way in relation to most of our variables, seem to be clearly influenced by cultural level. But this time it is the members of intermediate groups who are the most satisfied; 70 percent of them declare themselves to be mostly happy, while among employees of higher cultural level this percentage drops to 44 percent, and among those with lower cultural level to 53 percent. We can relate this finding to the analysis we did of the conditions for equilibrium in the environment; subjects of a higher socio-cultural milieu (the detached ones) feel that they are déclassés, and those of a lower socio-cultural milieu (the apathetic ones) suffer from difficulties with adaptation.

Culture as a Means for Stratification and Participation

Many fine minds distrust the "false culture" of the mass media. According to them the development of "mass culture" brings with it the negation or at least the dulling of true culture. Our results do not seem to be oriented in this direction at all. Certainly we can say that many of the employees we studied content themselves with the superficial participation afforded them by magazines and movies. But participation in a stunted culture is better than absence of participation. From this point of view, the only danger of the mass media would be to turn people aside from true culture by facilitating introversion and abandonment to the manipulations which lie hidden in this new version of *panem et circenses* in postindustrial society. Yet, on this point, our results seem to show clearly that we cannot hold the mass media responsible for much of the turning inward and abandonment to the easy way. Individuals who are truly maladapted, those who, feeling rejected, give up making the effort to break through the barrier erected by bourgeois society and its values, also abandon the mass media. As for those who give themselves over to the easy stunted culture criticized by the really cultivated, it would seem that they do so much more in an attempt to get closer to the sources of "true culture" than in order to run away from it. And this approach, as imperfect as it may be, is nonetheless effectively quite useful. In the white-collar world, or at least in its lower strata, one might say that crutches are indispensable. The more one consumes of the mass media, the more one seems able to become interested in somethnig else. All the relationships which we have been able to establish point in the direction of stimulation, not in the direction of deadening.

In addition to their significance as a means for advancement, cultural activities also showed themselves to be a means for social stratification. Every culture wants to be universal, and each individual in effect seeks to participate, through his culture, in the universal values of his society. But every culture is, at the same time, exclusive. And each one of us makes use of this exclusivity to affirm his status in society. Insurance company employees also want to participate in *culture*, and are profoundly humiliated each time they feel excluded; but at the same time all their cultural choices constitute an affirmation of the level which they think they have reached, and express a desire for closure and exclusion vis à vis inferior categories. They are in easy and immediate, but superficial, contact with the cultural activities of the managerial classes, and are particularly sensitized to the hierarchy implied by these activities. For them, the different forms of culture are domains into which one must make the effort to lift oneself, despite the great resistance presented, and the first criterion of their success is to be able, in turn, to exclude others. A few activities which are easier at first allow for more rapid assimilation; these are the ones that first attract attention, but they do not retain it very long. The most difficult forms of culture acquire only greater prestige, while within the easier forms new barriers are created.

The rivalry and even the stratification in the media are one consequence of this phenomenon and at the same time reinforce it. We were unable to push the analysis choices in the matter of movies and radio any further. But, as for magazines, newspapers, and books, the succession of degrees which correspond, for the consumer, to cultural advancement is striking. The readers of the "heart-throb" press (*presse du coeur*), those of *l'Echo de la mode* and *Femmes d'aujourd'hui*, and those of *Elle*, make no attempt to cover up. For each of them, their favorite weekly represents a window on the world, more and more obscured to be sure, as one descends the scale, but which helps them to discover and to assimilate a new universe. What is shocking in this participation, what makes it so narrow and superficial, is that it also expresses the desire to affirm superiority and to put behind oneself the barrier one thinks one has broken through. In this, the "mass culture" in which insurance company employees are immersed is no more than a caricature of the deep-rooted tendencies of the whole aristocratic culture of European societies, which is based above all on a mechanism of privileges and exclusions.[16]

The social stratification which manifests itself through cultural behavior patterns does not assume its full meaning, however, unless one takes into account that it also corresponds to the stratification introduced within the company by job and by responsibility, and that by virtue of this fact it constitutes a lever and a means for action which each individual can utilize. We have made much of this interdependence, but we have until now focused only on the mechanical and deterministic aspect of it. It remains for us to examine the other possible side of the relationship, and to investigate in particular how "cultural advancement" can be a means for transformation of status.

Our results give us hardly any sure information on this point. They show us that individuals in whom there is no coincidence between the various elements of status are much more dissatisfied than their colleagues. This finding confirms in part the remarks of numerous American authors who insisted, following George Homans, on the importance of the phenomenon of "congruence" in the elements of status.[17] According to these

16. We are not saying that a different mechanism would be easy to establish. We are quite ready to admit that man cannot yet live without privileges and exclusions, but it seems to us that considerable progress could be made from this point on, and that, though it be slow and insufficient, current evolution is pushing in this direction.

17. Homans, "Status among Clerical Workers," *Human Organization*, pp. 5–19.

authors, there would be a natural tendency in all individuals to make all the elements of status coincide, and this universal will for reduction of tensions caused by "noncongruence" would constitute one of the driving forces of social relations. The theories elaborated on this subject still remain conjectural, and our study did not give us the means to assess their validity. But we would like to propose the following hypothesis. The employees we studied, like all members of postindustrial society, are not only trying to reduce tensions, they are also trying to use the existence of these tensions as a means to demand advancement; they are constantly making an effort to reduce their personal incoherences, but do so by trying to align all their behavior patterns around those they consider superior, so much so that objectively one would say that the elements of "noncongruence" are for them an essential lever in their effort for advancement. The essential role of "mass culture," from this point of view, lies in the fact that by introducing multiple instances of incoherence it stimulates the drive for improvement and advancement.

From this point of view, the complexity and the relative incoherence of the activities and cultural behavior patterns of the subjects we questioned take on great importance. We are well aware of different cultural levels, and we could elaborate an acceptable typology of these different levels which would verify a sufficient number of relationships. But it would be impossible for us to put together truly rigorous scales, because the most extraordinary "errors" would constantly emerge. We think that this absence of coherence is one of the essential characteristics of the postindustrial urban environment, and that the development of "mass culture" tends to increase it more and more. In a recent article, Vito Ahtik presented an elaborate analysis of the cultural behavior patterns of Yugoslavian workers.[18] The most striking element in his analysis was the coherence and relative stability of the different categories of behavior. The contrast between the milieu he described and the Parisian white-collar milieu is considerable. Actually we cannot prove that this contrast is not due in part to the instruments utilized and to the very conditions of the

18. "Participation socio-politique des ouvriers d'industrie yougoslaves," *Sociologie du Travail* 5, no. 1 (1963): 1–23.

study. But we readily perceive in it a profound cultural fact. The society to which the white-collar employees we studied have access is a society in which social determinism has greatly declined. There is no common measure between their freedom of choice and that of the subjects of the Yugoslavian study. Our subjects' freedom of choice introduces much incoherence in their behavior. It is a source of tensions, but at the same time constitutes a permanent stimulus for advancement and for more active participation.

This sort of interpretation allows us to retain a more optimistic view of the new developments in cultural life. It is not a question of denying the existence of the unfavorable effects brought about by the appearance of mass culture, but of properly assessing them. One should not dread the dehumanization of culture; better a mediocre culture that favors personal advancement than the persistence of the chasm which cuts off all participation by the masses and imprisons an advanced culture in its own forms. The real problem lies more in the psychological difficulties imposed upon modern man by the incoherence of the elements of his status and the intellectual chaos which can result from the shock of contradictory values, as long as the constraint of traditional hierarchical norms remains.

It is because of these psychological difficulties that man subject to mass culture desperately searches, through all his cultural behavior patterns, for opportunities to class himself and to exclude others as a means of reassuring himself. In the social context that remains his, he succeeds in participating and in raising himself only if he feels sufficiently well protected. Stratification is, for him, an obligatory means for protection, and also the very condition for his participation. The remedy is inextricably intermingled with the ill itself, which it contains and attenuates, but at the same time reinforces. When modern man finally renounces his hierarchical demands, when he no longer feels at a loss when confronted with the high level and the esoteric character of a culture that rebuffs and humiliates him, he will be able to bear more easily the considerable tensions imposed upon him by participation in the infinite complexity of the cultural world of tomorrow. He will then be able to avoid that terrified anguish in the face of uncertainty about social status which has frightened so many observers. Progress in this area necessarily happens through an increase in the flexibility of cultural norms, a lowering of barriers to communication, and a raising of tolerance for the approximations necessary to any learning and, in particular, for the immense collective approximations that the most "vulgar" mass media constitute.

10 Class without Consciousness: Prefiguration of the Classless Society

At the beginning of this work, we asked ourselves a certain number of questions about the class membership of white-collar employees, about the existence and the very coherence of a "white-collar" social category, and about its strategy.

The data we collected does not yet allow us to provide satisfactory answers to such general questions. On the one hand, our research touches upon only one sector, significant to be sure, but which constitutes no more than one small part of the white-collar world, and can absolutely not be considered as representative of the whole.[1] On the other hand, and above all, the results we obtained, both in regard to attitudes and behavior patterns at work and outside work, do not organize in any rigorous

1. We are well-aware, for example, of how notable are the differences between a Parisian white-collar employee and one in the provinces, and also of how different a white-collar employee working in a small company can be from an employee working in a large or very large organization; whether or not one works in a company whose personnel is composed primarily of manual workers introduces another very important source of variation which we could not take into account. A sector like the Parisian insurance company sector is significant, on the other hand, insofar as it seems to accentuate—much more than would a provincial sector or a small business sector, or even an industrial white-collar sector—the problems that will be raised for the white-collar stratum by the society of tomorrow.

way, and seem to reflect all too imperfectly the influence of those large macro-sociological factors we would most like to treat.

Must we declare bankruptcy, and acknowledge that it is hardly possible to shed light on the sociology of class relations through empirical studies such as the one we have just presented? We do not think so. All through this presentation, we have been able to bring out a number of complex relationships, sometimes unexpected, each of which suggested a correction or a more thorough elaboration of generally-accepted ideas in the area of class relations. We are still far from being able to understand the complex ties that must exist between the findings we are able to produce by analyzing the situations experienced, and the interplay of variables which has traditionally been the focus of attention in looking at society as a whole. But, based on all the convergent approximations we have been able to treat, we can nonetheless already suggest other ways of approaching the macro-sociological problems, and propose a few more general hypotheses for understanding them.

In this perspective, one preliminary remark is necessary concerning the relations between attitudes at work and attitudes outside work. Very often these two series of attitudes appeared to us to be related, but their relationship was always very loose, and in any case much less clear-cut than the relationship of each attitude to other more immediately determinant factors. If we put aside the effects of individual personalities, attitudes at work are always a reflection of position and role in the system of organization made up by the company, while attitudes outside work are a reflection of position and role within an environment that can also be conceived, though more vaguely, as a system of relationships and roles.

The fact that there is correspondence between these two systems, that the hierarchy within the company is related to the hierarchy of roles within society as a whole, allows us to explain the relationships which we find, but does not imply that these relationships are a result of classical determinism and that, for example, class position as defined by the mechanism of relations of production can in turn determine attitudes at work and outside work. It is not really attitudes that can be determined, but rather the rules of the game and the possible strategies of the actors. The attitudes we have been able to study express the positions taken by individuals in their struggle, or in their negotiation, with the environment, rather than the direct pressure of an environment that would mold them. This explains why these attitudes turn out to be much more contingent than a simplistic determinism would prefer. Such a determinism would apply only at the limit, to the extent that those involved would have absolutely no freedom of choice and no alternative solution. But the white-collar situation—the study confirms very well our initial hypothesis on this point—is a complex situation. The possibilities it affords are varied, and the attitudes of those subject to it can be understood only through the more and more nuanced strategies they accompany and mask.

We have not devoted ourselves here to analyzing those strategies, because to do so we would have had to study, much more systematically than we did, the frameworks in which they are integrated, which was moreover not immediately possible except in the matter of strategy within the work organization; strategy in the social and cultural system remained much more difficult to define operationally.

But nothing prevents us from investigating, through the reflections of these strategies provided by the attitudes expressed, what the essential elements are that govern them. This empirical and inductive method, as uncertain as it may appear, is an indispensable step in the elaboration of a new approach to the problem. The sociologist cannot, as the Marxists thought, interpret life-experience exclusively as the expression of an abstract schema, given once and for all, as though each actor had only one possible strategy, and as though the incoherences that are necessarily found could only result from a lack of understanding. But neither can he interpret it based only on the attitudes expressed by actors, since attitudinal determinism is just as ineffective in understanding reality as situational determinism; the incoherences discovered by the sociologist at this level can be of just as great, if not greater, importance as the correlations. Only through the confrontation of many systems of attitudes, with each other and with the situations that correspond to them, can he infer the existence of underlying strategies. He cannot postulate the determinism he is looking for by basing himself on situations, nor can he find it by taking things at face value; he must patiently reconstruct it by making the effort to understand the subtle interplay between different aspects of social behavior, as well as between the image a person involved may have of it, and the image of it he wants to project.

Let us look somewhat more closely at the results obtained during the course of this study. In the end what comes out most, in the different areas explored, is that beyond the linear correspondence between attitudes, we can find comparable contrasts and oppositions, and that each of these contrasts and each of these oppositions can be analyzed in a relatively similar way in terms of strategy.

This analysis seems particularly clear as far as adaptation to work is concerned. The deep opposition between feelings in the matter of position and in the matter of work led us, it will be remembered, to propose an interpretation of the following sort: The more one rises in the hierarchy, the more job, qualification, and mastery of work become trump cards, and the more one is able, as far as one's position is concerned, to protest, to demand, and to hope. The weakest and most defenseless employees are satisfied; those who appear to be stronger and more assured are discontent. Those in the low echelons make themselves even smaller than they are, while adventure attracts those who feel sufficiently well protected.

The same process reappears as far as involvement in the company and faithfulness to the organization are concerned. The weaker a person is, the more he is faithful. The better he is armed for the struggle, the less he is loyal to the company; but at the same time the more he is disposed to participate in its activities. At the bottom of the scale, whether in the matter of work or in cultural matters, individuals are easily alienated within the organization. At the top of the scale, on the contrary, participants become more independent and more critical. And it would seem that participation in an active way does not occur unless one is independent and critical. Involvement in the organization thus appears also to be a sort of adventure into which only those who feel sufficiently well-armed can succeed in deciding to take the plunge.

In the area of social status and culture, the contrast is not as clear. We were not able to find marked differences in individual behavior according to differences in rank in the two areas. But we were nevertheless able to determine that higher social status and cultural level are accompanied by more demands, more desire to participate, and more involvement in one's position and in the organization. As one rises in this hierarchy, and therefore stops being vulnerable, one becomes more demanding, more discontent, and even more unhappy, but at the same time one finds oneself more able to participate.

In all these strategic systems, which do not repeat each other totally but which converge in a surprising way, we find a profound opposition between a defensive approach, which entails a sort of retreat and alienation in the present situation, and an approach that aims at advancement and social climbing; in everyday life the latter approach becomes a constant tendency to depreciate the present situation in anticipation of the possible forthcoming situation. The defensive approach is always a collective approach; it is more of an expression of the determinism of situations. The offensive approach is a much more individual one, and becomes more and more fruitful exactly to the extent that the advance achieved authorizes a greater freedom of choice.

The two approaches are, however, profoundly intermingled, and reversals can frequently be noted. Switching over to the offensive mode signifies, in some measure, the success of the defensive approach. The role of unionism seems to be particularly significant from this point of view. It attracts the weak more, but by constituting a reinforcement for them it helps them in their advancement; this is so much the case that, paradoxically, unionists seem to be more involved than their colleagues at any given level in the individual process of cultural and social advancement.

Finally, all these convergent elements confirm the initial hypothesis we presented concerning the ambiguity of the white-collar situation. On the one hand, the white-collar employee participates in the game of individual advancement; on the other, he plays the game of collective defense. He cannot truly participate in the system of human relations, because he still finds himself stopped by social and cultural barriers. But at the same time he does not want to alienate himself completely by a posture of traditional bourgeois faithfulness, nor does he want to freeze into an attitude of collective defense, because he does not want to give up his chance for promotion. He therefore uses two strategies at the same time, pushing one or the other more heavily depending on which is his strong suit at the moment.

These strategies, it is true, do not show up directly; we discover them only after they have been mediated and transformed by the system of organization through which they must express themselves. Involvement and participation cannot develop in an abstract way; they must find their place in the entire chain of human relations made up by a company and by a social environment. These chains of human relations can be considered as both a crystallization of those strategies and as their organization and manipulation by the collectivity, with the aim of achieving the goals of collective efficiency that each member accepts. To go further, or even simply to test our present hypotheses, they would have to be relocated in these systems, since the strategies we have glimpsed cannot be separated from them.

Neither these results, nor the interpretation we have just attempted, invite us to engage in any extrapolation. But the facts to which they draw attention should allow us to reflect somewhat better on the consequences that the general evolution we find can have for the white-collar group.

All the developments in industrial society or, to adopt Daniel Bell's expression, in postindustrial society, are in the direction of de-hierarchization and greater flexibility, and functionalization of human relations at work, on the one hand, and an attenuation or confusion of models and of class differences in consumer society on the other. From this point of view, we are well on the way to the middle-class society that C. Wright Mills seemed to dread so much. But such a society is very different from the model imagined by Mills, which we criticized at the beginning of this work. Certainly, alienation in that society still remains considerable, but we are not at all witnessing its extension. On the contrary, it really seems that this alienation in the mass media, or in the bureaucratic relations denounced by those who despise modern society, is in the end no more than the necessary counterpart of the accelerated increase in participation. The multiplicity of alienations possible, and the incoherence which naturally emerges as a result, tend to liberate the individual. The more the choices offered allow him a diversity of combinations, the more easily he can escape the determinism of his group, of his condition, and even of his society.

Some will object that social and cultural life tends to come apart in a dehumanizing collectivity that is subject to all sorts of manipulations. Certainly the traditional oppositions—and in particular the class oppositions—through which we interpret human relations are being attenuated and seem to be due for disappearance. But this does not make modern citizens any more likely to blend into a single group. They seem, quite the contrary, to need to differentiate themselves more and more by a multitude of nuanced and ambiguous roles, which they often occupy successively if not at the same time. The only thing new is that those roles are now less constraining, that they allow more room for individual invention, and that a good number of them are no longer imposed, but rather are chosen.

The traditional white-collar role was one of these first socially ambiguous and contradictory roles that appeared in lower milieus and, in some measure, it prefigured current evolution. This role is now losing its singularity, to the extent that all social roles in the lower strata are also acquiring a little of this complexity. At the same time, the white-collar role is itself becoming differentiated and more liberalized. Formerly, the white-collar employee found himself both deeply alienated in his faithfulness to the company and in his assiduous imitation of the bourgeois model; he was deeply tried by the opposition between aspirations, which he could see no other way to realize, and the desire for defense, which he generally was able to express only in an indirect way. Today, the promotion game is easier; as soon as he has achieved a sufficiently strong position in his job, in his culture, and in his status, the white-collar employee begins to escape traditional alienation; unionism facilitates the acculturation of the most deprived, and alienation in the mass media and bureaucratic habits is much less deep-rooted than respect for the agreements, the rites, and the symbols proper to the traditional bourgeois world.

The social game played by the white-collar employee of today is—at least when qualifications are held equal—much richer and more subtle than that of yesterday.

In a certain way, the world of classes without consciousness seems really to herald a classless society. But what we are talking about is a society dominated by an extremely complex interplay of material and affective interests, that express themselves in more and more numerous roles, that bears no resemblance at all to the undifferentiated and egalitarian mass whose coming has for so long been passionately feared or desired.

This pattern of evolution which we are sketching is just now in the process of developing, and accounts only imperfectly for present attitudes and behavior patterns. We are still able to detect the survival of old models. Like many other groups in a period of great transformation, the white-collar employee of today often seems to march toward the future while obstinately keeping one eye on the past. He regrets the prerogatives he used to enjoy, without seeing that he in fact owed his relative superiority to the existence of the deep separation between social categories to which he himself was subject. Yet his progress, his new freedom of choice, as well as his chance to attain more directly and without alienation a place in a higher world, depend very directly on the loss of such prerogatives. By freezing into a defensive position, he paralyzes himself.

This resistance afforded by the past does not, however, seem that unshakable, at least in a milieu like that of insurance company employees. It seems to us reasonable to predict that the social category of white-collar employees, which owes its individuality and its importance only to the position it occupied in a world deeply marked by class separation, will increasingly lose its originality, its coherence, and will even go out of existence, much sooner than could until now be foreseen.

Name Index

Ahtik, Vito, 204
Argyris, Chris, 38

Bahrdt, Hans-Paul, 18, 27–30, 106
Bayer, R., 31
Bell, Daniel, 212
Bernstein, Edouard, 22, 23, 25
Blauner, Robert, 100
Bodin, L., 48
Burns, Robert K., 13, 14, 88

Capwell, 94
Christensen, C. R., 142
Clark, Colin, 10
Coch, Lester, 121
Collinet, Michel, 31
Corey, Lewis, 27
Croner, Fritz, 7, 9, 31, 32
Crozier, Michel, 34, 71, 74, 90, 95, 102, 118, 130, 132, 191, 193, 196

Danos, Jacques, 48
Dean, Lois R., 152
Dolléans, Edouard, 44
Dreyfuss, Carl, 25, 26, 27

Edwards, Hugh, 35
Ehrmann, H., 48

Fallada, Hans, 25
Fisher, Lloyd, 136
Fourastié, Jean, 10
French, John R. P., 121
Friedmann, Georges, 10

Galenson, Walter, 100
Geiger, Theodore, 26
Gibelin, Marcel, 48
Girod, Roger, 8, 31, 33
Guérin, Daniel, 26
Guetta, Pierre, 74, 90, 95

Halbwachs, Maurice, 30
Hartfiel, G., 31
Herzberg, Frederick, 94
Heuyer, Dr., 34
Homans, George, 38, 142, 203

Kahn, Robert, 89
Kassalow, Everett, 8, 11
Katz, Daniel, 89, 121
Kautsky, Karl, 22, 23, 24, 25
Kerr, Clark, 136
Kinsey, Alfred C., 34
Klingender, Francis D., 28
Kracauer, Simon, 25, 26, 27
Kulpinska, Jolanta, 62

Laurent, B., 44

Lautman, Jacques, 130
Lederer, Emile, 25, 31
Lenin, Nikolai, 24
Lewin, Kurt, 121
Liebermann, Seymour, 35
Lippit, 121
Lipset, Seymour M., 58, 100, 128
Lockwood, David, 13, 27–29, 62
Lorwin, Val, 48

Maccoby, N., 121
Mann, Floyd, 38
Mann, Heinrich, 25
Marx, Karl, 21, 23
Mausner, J. P., 94
Mayer, J. P., 23
Mayo, Elton, 136
Mercillon, Henri, 14
Merton, Robert K., 154
Mills, C. Wright, 27, 28, 212
Morse, Nancy, 38, 95, 100, 121

Neundoerfer, L., 31
Nikisch, A., 31

Palmer, Gladys, 100
Peterson, 94
Piat, R. P. Stephane, 45
Pirker, Th., 31
Pradier, Bernard, 130

Remitz, Uno, 101
Roethlisberger, F. J., 142

Schmoller, Gustav, 22, 25
Siegfried, André, 10
Smigel, Erwin O., 38
Sturmthal, Adolf, 11, 41
Super, Donald, 100
Szepansky, Pr., 62

Thomas, Lawrence G., 100
Touchard, J., 48

Verdin, Paul, 45

Weber, Max, 23
Weiss, Robert, 100
White, William Foote, 121
Wilensky, Harold L., 35
Williams, L. K., 38
Worthy, James, 38

Zaleznik, Abraham, 142

Subject Index

Adaptation to work, 101–2, 210
Administration, increase in, 10–12
Advancement. *See* Aspirations; Promotion
Age, conflict over, 110–11
Alienation: economic, 26; in middle-class society, 212–13; and participation, 137; spiritual, 25–26, 27–28
Ambiguity: 32, 33, 37, 40, 41, 133, 185–86, 211–13; toward class differences, 174–75, 178; of participation, 137
America, white-collar employees in, 10–11, 13, 62–63
Anomie. *See* Alienation; Apathy
Anticipatory socialization, 34
Anti-Marxists, 22
Apathy: cultural, 190–92; of employees, 155–61; of supervisors, 153–54
Archivists, 80–81, 113, 114, 144, 151, 180
Aspirations: and class attitudes, 180, 184-85; and class differences, 166, 177–78; and company loyalty, 144–47; and cultural level, 187, 200; and education, 182; and friendships, 181; intellectual, 150–51; level of, 159; and marriage, 181–82; and satisfaction, 100; and work attitudes, 183–84
Atmosphere, office, 110–13, 124–25
Attitudes: class, 178, 184–85; political, 34, 63, 155, 193; toward work, 88–104, 122, 183–84, 208
Authoritarianism, 121–23, 126-32
Automation, 12, 16, 17–18, 30, 87
Autonomy, 80, 81, 86; and satisfaction, 99, 105

Banks: apathy of employees, 156–57; contrasted with insurance companies, 156–57; hierarchy in, 128–29, 132; satisfaction of employees, 101, 104, 105; and unionism, 46, 50, 51, 55–56
Bernstein-Kautsky polemic, 22–24
Blue-collar employees: embourgeoisement of, 38;

homogeneity of, 39; hostility toward, 24, 52, 56n, 168–71; idealization of, 172–73, 177; participation of, 158–59; proportion of, 1–2, 10–11; salaries of, 12–15; status of, 2; and unionism, 50; white-collar view of, 167–73, 176–77
Books, choice of, 189–90, 192, 197, 202–3
Bourgeois. *See* Middle class
Brothers of the Christian Schools, 45
Bureaucracy. *See* Hierarchy

Camaraderie, lack of, 110
Catholic church, 45, 46
Census: American, 10; French, 8–9
Centralization, of unions, 57–58
CFDT, 45, 53, 54, 56
CFTC, 48, 49, 50, 52, 55, 57
CGT, 42–45, 46–47, 48, 49–50, 52–54, 55, 56
CGT-FO, 52–53, 55
CGTU, 46, 47
Chambre syndicale des employés de la région parisienne, 48
Chambre syndicale fédérale des employés, 42–43
Chautemps memorandum, 47
Children, intellectual level of, 34
Christian employees, and unionism, 46, 49
Civil servants: classification of, 9; class membership of, 179; contrasted with white-collar employees, 56, 58, 59–60, 61, 64–65, 71; political attitudes of, 63; salaries of, 60; status of, 39, 60; unionism among, 39, 43–45, 47–48, 49, 52–54, 58, 61
Claims adjusters, 85–87, 96, 139–40, 144, 180. *See also* Policy writers
Class attitudes: and social aspirations, 184–85; and social position, 178; of white-collar employees, 2–3, 167–80
Class differences: disappearance of, 3, 213–14; and social status, 166, 177–78; white-collar attitude toward, 167–78
Classification: of employees, 7–9, 79–87; of executives, 8–9, 15. *See also* Hierarchy; Professional category
Class membership: of research subjects, 72; white-collar attitude toward, 2–3, 178–80
Class struggle, Marxist theory of, 21–22, 37
Clerks, 83–85, 144, 180
Colleagues, relations between, 109–16, 131
Collectivity. *See* Organization
Commercial employees, and unionism, 43, 45, 47–48, 49
Commercialism, cultural, 188–90, 192
Communication: with research subjects, 78; between social groups, 62, 63, 64
Communists, 46, 49, 50, 51
Companies: employees' assessment of, 138–39, 141–47, 152–53; interest in, 139–41, 147, 151, 155–56; knowledge about, 139–40, 151–52; loyalty to, 141–47; participation in, 135–47
Company policy: and apathy, 157; employee knowledge of, 140; influence on subordinates, 131; and leadership style, 125–28, 131
Competition: professional, 111; between activities, 189–90; among unions, 57
Complaints: about atmosphere,

113; about supervisors, 117–18; about unions, 148–49
Compliments, by supervisors, 122
Conflict: between colleagues, 110–11; as participation, 136, 138, 152
Conflict thesis, 19
Conformity, pressure for, 64–65
Conscientiousness. *See* Loyalty
Contentment. *See* Satisfaction
Contradictions. *See* Ambiguity; Incoherence
Contribution-retribution equivalence, 142–43
Cooperative organization, 30
Correspondents, 86
Criticism: of companies, 152–53; of unions, 149
Croix de Feu, 48–49
Cultural activities: participation in, 188, 189–93; quality of, 193–206; and social stratification, 201–6; and work responsibility, 190–92
Cultural level: and advancement, 203–5; and aspirations, 183, 200; determination of, 193–98; and education, 198; and friendship, 199; and participation, 200; and satisfaction, 100, 200, 201; and social origin, 198; and status, 210–11; and unionism, 151, 201. *See also* Origin, social
Cultural norms, 195–201
Culture , mass, 187–89, 201–6

Data processing, of research material, 75 n
Defensive approach, 211–12, 213, 214
Delegates, union, 149–50
Demands, social. *See* Aspirations
Demonstrations, union, 56, 59
Department, as social unit, 109
Department stores, 42–43, 46, 47–48, 49, 54–55
Depression (1929), 13–14
Design, research, 69–76, 108
Determinism, social, 198, 205, 208–13
Devotion. *See* Loyalty
Dictatorship of the proletariat, 25
Dignity, 174–76, 177–78
Discontent, with office atmosphere, 112–13. *See also* Satisfaction
Dispositions, psychological, 101–2, 145–46
Dress, style of, 196 n

Education: and aspirations, 182; and class differences, 169; and class membership, 179; and company loyalty, 144, 146–47; and cultural level, 198; and knowledge of company, 140; of research subjects, 72; and satisfaction, 100; of supervisors, 72
England, white-collar employees in, 13–14, 62–63
Equality, white-collar attitude toward, 171–72
Estrangement, from blue-collar employees, 24, 168–71
Executives: classification of, 9, 15; junior, 22; role of, 22, 56; salaries of, 15; status of, 19. *See also* Supervisors
Expenses, reduction of, 143

Facism, 48
Factor analysis, 88
Fatigue, 80, 87
Favortism, fear of, 111
Fédération générale des fonctionnaires, 47
Fédération nationale, 48
Fédération postale, 47

Females. *See* Sex; Women
Feminization of office jobs, 15–17
FEN (Fédération de l'Education nationale), 54, 57
File clerks, 80–81
Finances, of unions, 58
First World War, 13
FO, 52–54, 55, 56
Foremen. *See* Supervisors
Formality, 113–14, 131, 133
Freedom of choice. *See* Determinism, social
Freemasons, 42, 44
Fresnay, Pierre, 173
Friendships: and aspirations, 181; and cultural level, 199; of supervisors, 72

Gabin, Jean, 173
Generational conflicts, 110–11
Generosity, of company, 141–42
Germany: class debate in, 21–26, 27–28; white-collar employees in, 62–63
Grievances. *See* Complaints
Groups: influence of, 2–3, 108–9; social, 77

Happiness. *See* Satisfaction
Hierarchy, 37; and apathy, 159; and cultural change, 187–89; and cultural level, 201–6; importance of rank in, 128–30; involvement in, 131; occupational, 80–87; and participation, 138, 140; personal relations in, 116–33; and satisfaction, 103–4; social, 30, 31, 38; white-collar attitude toward, 174
Hostility: toward blue-collar employees, 24, 52, 56 n, 168–71; toward supervisors, 120, 122
Human environment. *See* Interpersonal relations
Hungarian revolt, 57

Idealization of blue-collar employees, 172–73, 177
IFOP (Institut Français d'Opinion Publique), 34, 179
Inactivity. *See* Cultural activities; Participation, lack of
Incoherence: cultural, 187; of responses, 184, 185–86. *See also* Ambiguity
Indemnities, for dismissal, 50
Indifference, of supervisors, 118. *See also* Apathy
Individual: disposition, 101–2, 145; and organization, 135–47
Industrial sector, 11
INED, 179
Information. *See* Knowledge
Insurance companies: choice of study sample, 74–75; contrasted with banks, 156–57; milieu, 69–73; number of employees, 69–70; unionism in, 47–48, 50–51, 55–56, 148. *See also* Subjects, research
Integration: and activity, 192; and apathy, 158; of individual and organization, 135–38; and participation, 147; and unionism, 152–53
Intellectual class, 179–80
Intellectual level, 180. *See also* Education
Intellectuals, role of, 24
Interest in company, 139–41, 147, 151, 155–56. *See also* Apathy
Interest in work: measurement of, 90–92, 94, 95, 97–101; and satisfaction, 95–101, 104
Interpersonal relations: between colleagues, 109–16, 131; methods of evaluating, 108; and work attitudes, 107–16
Interviews. *See* Questionnaires

Joint-management committees, 149–52, 160, 200

Keypunchers, 18, 81–82, 96, 114, 143–44, 151, 180
Knowledge: about blue-collar employees, 168; of company, 139–40, 151–52, 155–56

Laborers. *See* Blue-collar employees
"Laborer's manner," 169
Laissez-faire supervisors, 113 n, 121, 123–25, 127, 132, 154
Lateness, 122
Leadership styles, 120–28, 131–32
Leisure-time activities, 189–93, 196 n
Liberalism, 121, 122–23, 127
Liberation period, 50
Literacy, 36
Loyalty, company, 141–47, 160, 183, 210

Magazines, choice of, 187, 189–90, 192, 193, 194–95, 196–98, 202–3
Mailmen, 43–44, 45
Malaise, 174, 178, 183
Malcontents, 113
Management: identification with, 33–35, 152–53, 154; interest in, 139–41, 147. *See also* Joint-management committee
Managers. *See* Supervisors
Manual workers. *See* Blue-collar employees
Marriage, and social aspirations, 181–82, 185. *See also* Wives
Marxism, 2, 21–24, 32, 209
"Mass culture," 187–89, 201–6
Mass media, 201–6, 212, 213
Mechanization. *See* Automation
Middle class: growth of, 22–23, 35; new, 22–23. *See also* Class differences; Class membership
Militants, 47, 48, 50–51, 55, 59
Misunderstanding, between classes, 171
Modernization, 11. *See also* Automation
Morale, 88–101, 135–36, 159. *See also* Interest in company; Participation; Satisfaction
Movie attendance, 189–90, 192, 194, 197

Nationalization, 50–51, 55, 61, 148
Nazism, 21, 22, 26
Neo-Marxism, 27
Newspapers, choice of, 193, 197, 202–3
1936, crisis of, 47–50
1920s, crisis of, 25, 46–47
Nonmanual workers. *See* White-collar employees
Nonparticipation. *See* Participation

Objectivity, in self-evaluation, 173–74
Occupational categories, 7–9, 79-87. *See also* Professional category
Office: atmosphere, 110–13, 124–25; size of, 111; as social unit, 109
Office workers. *See* White-collar employees
Old people, 110–11, 113, 115, 144
Organization, individual and, 135–47. *See also* Companies
Organizational system. *See* Company policy
Origin, social: and class attitudes, 167–68, 178; and company loyalty, 144–47; and cultural level, 198; of research subjects, 71–72; and satisfaction, 100, 102–4; of supervisors, 72; and unionism, 151

Overseers. *See* Supervisors

Parents. *See* Origin, social
Paris, and union movement, 57–58, 61
Participation: conflictual, 136, 138, 152; in cultural activities, 188, 189–93; and cultural level, 200; in decision making, 137; forced, 137; lack of, 192–93; in organizations, 135–47; and status, 210–11; and unionism, 149, 151–52; in white-collar milieu, 158–61
Parti social français, 49
Paternalism, 160, 185
Patronage system, 64
Pay. *See* Salaries
Petit-bourgeois, 24, 32
Pluralism, of unions, 57
Policy. *See* Company policy
Policy writers, 85–87, 139–40, 144, 151. *See also* Claims adjusters
Political attitudes, 34, 63, 155, 193
Position: and class attitudes, 178; and company loyalty, 144–47; satisfaction with, 91, 93, 95–101, 104; struggle for, 51
Postal workers, 43–44, 45
Prestige. *See* Status
Pride, office, 115–16
Private sector, 56, 58, 59–60, 61, 64–65
Privilege, social, 33–34, 37, 62
Productivity, demand for, 81, 86–87
Professional category: and choice of mate, 145; and class membership, 179–80; and company loyalty, 144, 145; and satisfaction, 95–98; and unionism, 150. *See also* Occupational categories
"Proletarians in false collars," 25–26
Proletariat. *See* Blue-collar employees
Proletarization, 13–15, 16, 19, 22–24, 25–26, 27, 32, 38
Promotion: criteria for, 33–34, 55, 64–65; desire for, 151, 203–6; and interest in company, 147; prospects for, 156, 157. *See also* Aspirations
Public sector, 11–12, 56, 58, 59–60, 61, 64–65. *See also* Civil servants

Questionnaires, 74, 75, 138–39, 141–42, 145, 149, 152, 154–55, 167, 176–77, 178–79, 181–82, 189. *See also* Research design

Radio, 194
Rationalization of operations, 85, 87
Reading materials, 180, 187, 189–90, 192, 193, 194, 196, 197, 199, 202–3
Redactors, *See* Policy writers
Rejection, social, 155–56, 160
Remorse, 178. *See also* Malaise
Reputation, of companies, 140
Research design, 69–76, 108. *See also* Questionnaires
Respectability: desire for, 192; pressure for, 64–65
Responsibility: and cultural activity, 190–92; and integration, 147; and unionism, 149
Results, analysis of, 210–14
Retreatism, 154–55, 158. *See also* Apathy
Revolution: administrative, 1; economic, 42; industrial, 10; socialist, 23–24
Rivalry, 111
Ruling classes, 34–35

Salaries, 25, 55–56, 60; of blue-collar employees, 12–15; of

civil servants, 60; and company loyalty, 144; differences in, 12–15; of men, 15–16; of research subjects, 73; satisfaction with, 90; of supervisors, 73; and unionism, 60, 151; of women, 15–16, 50
Satisfaction: and cultural level, 200, 201; dimensions of, 90; and education, 100; lack of, 113; measurement of, 88–101; and social origin, 100; and status, 210–11
Scales. *See* Questionnaires
"Scientific socialism," 21
SECI (Syndicat des employés de Commerce et de l'Industrie), 45
Second World War, 13–14
Security, desire for, 146, 151
Self-consciousness, 147
Seniority, 99, 144
Sex: and apathy, 155; and class attitudes, 168, 178; conflicts of, 110; and loyalty, 143; and satisfaction, 99. *See also* Women
SGEN, 54
Skilled laborers, 13–14, 170, 172–73
SNI (Syndicat national des instituteurs), 47, 54
Social climbing, 34–38. *See also* Aspirations
Social distance, 62–63
Socialism, 49, 50
Socialization, anticipatory, 34–35
Social origins. *See* Origins, social
Social privilege, 33–34, 37, 62
Status, 165–66; and apathy, 155–56, 159; and attitudes, 165–66, 177–78; consciousness of, 90; and cultural level, 203–6, 210–11; and loyalty, 210; and participation, 210; and satisfaction, 102–4, 210–11
Stenographers, 83
Stereotypes, 108, 176–77, 192
Stimulation, of activities, 190
Stockholders, 23
Stores, and unionism, 42–43, 46, 47–48, 49, 54–55
Strategies, social, 2, 4, 209–12
Stratification: and cultural level, 198–206; need for, 183; and participation, 160–61; and satisfaction, 105–6. *See also* Hierarchy
Strikes, 46, 48–49, 51, 56
Subjects, research, 70–75, 79
Supervisors: and atmosphere, 113; authoritarian, 121–23, 126–27; class membership of, 180; cultural level of, 194; evaluation of, by employees, 118–19, 124–25; evaluation of employees by, 119–20, 124; grievances against, 117–18; identification with management, 152–53, 154; indifference of, 117–18; laissez-faire, 113 n, 121, 123–25, 127, 132, 154; leadership style of, 120–28, 131–32; liberal, 121, 122–23, 127; and office pride, 115; participation of, 140; personality of, 113–14, 119; place in hierarchy, 116–20; and retreatism, 154; role of, 22, 56, 116; satisfaction of, 97; social characteristics of, 72. *See also* Executives

Tasks, transformation of, 17–19
Teachers, 45, 54, 64
Technicians, 9, 12, 19
Technology, and social organization, 40
Theater attendance, 187, 189–90, 192, 193–94, 196, 197
Theories of white-collar group, 21–24

Traditions, social, 184–85
Training, 17, 157. *See also* Education
Turnover, rate of, 136
Typists, 82–83, 96, 112, 143–44, 180, 191

Unions: activities of, 59; bank, 46, 50, 51, 55–56; Catholic, 45, 46; civil service, 39, 43–45, 47–48, 49, 52–54, 58, 61; commercial, 43, 45, 46, 47–48, 49; Communists and, 46, 49, 50, 51; competition among, 57; complaints about, 148–49; and cultural level, 201; current status of, 52–65; diversity of, 57; finances of, 58; former members of, 149; history of, 41–65; in insurance companies, 55–56, 148; and integration, 152–53; interest in, 160; leaders of, 51; membership of, 52–56, 148; modes of action of, 59–60; and national differences, 60–63; and participation, 136, 152; political influence of, 64; power of, 51, 60, 61; relations with management, 58; and salaries, 60, 151; and social advancement, 211, 213; staff members, 58; in stores, 42–43, 46, 47–48, 49, 54–55; white-collar, 22, 29, 36, 39–65; white-collar attitude toward, 148–52
University of Michigan, 90, 91, 95
Upper management. *See* Company policy

Voting behavior, 155
Vulnerability, 146, 158

Well-being. *See* Satisfaction
White-collar employees: alliance with blue-collar employees, 46, 47, 49, 50, 61; attitude toward blue-collar employees, 167–73, 176–77; characteristics of (*see* Subjects, research); class status of, 2–3, 34, 39, 62, 178–80; compared with blue-collar employees, 33, 34–39, 62, 158–59; compared with civil servants, 56, 58, 59–60, 61, 64–65; definition of, 7–9; devaluation of, 18–19; development of group, 9–12, 26, 38; evaluation of, by supervisors, 119–20; national differences, 60–63; number of, 1, 9–12, 19, 22; place in society, 184–86; relations with blue-collar employees, 35–36, 38; self-evaluation, 173–78
Wives, of supervisors, 72
Women: apathy of, 155; attitude toward blue-collar employees, 168; and company loyalty, 143; discontent among, 113; formality of, 114; increase in office jobs for, 15–17, 18; and interest in company, 140; recruitment of, 16; salaries of, 15–16, 50; satisfaction of, 99; status of, 18; and unions, 53–54
Working class. *See* Blue-collar employees
Work load, 122

Young people, 110–11